CW01642456

Designing Memo

This innovative study of memorial architecture investigates how design can translate memories of human loss into tangible structures, creating spaces for remembering. Using approaches from history, psychology, anthropology and sociology, Sabina Tanović explores the purposes behind creating contemporary memorials in a given location, their translation into architectural concepts, their materialization in the face of social and political challenges, and their influence on the transmission of memory. Covering the period from the First World War to the present, she looks at memorials such as the Holocaust museums in Mechelen and Drancy, as well as memorials for the victims of terrorist attacks, to unravel the private and public role of memorial architecture and the possibilities of architecture as a form of agency in remembering and dealing with a difficult past. The result is a distinctive contribution to the literature on history and memory, and on architecture as a link to the past.

SABINA TANOVIĆ is an award-winning architect and a postdoctoral researcher at Delft University of Technology. In 2017 she won an international architectural competition to design a Memorial Museum and a Research Center for Sarajevo's 'Tunnel of Hope'.

STUDIES IN THE SOCIAL AND CULTURAL HISTORY OF MODERN WARFARE

General Editor
Jay Winter, *Yale University*

Advisory Editors
David Blight, *Yale University*
Richard Bosworth, *University of Western Australia*
Peter Fritzsche, *University of Illinois, Urbana-Champaign*
Carol Gluck, *Columbia University*
Benedict Kiernan, *Yale University*
Antoine Prost, *Université de Paris-Sorbonne*
Robert Wohl, *University of California, Los Angeles*

In recent years the field of modern history has been enriched by the exploration of two parallel histories. These are the social and cultural history of armed conflict, and the impact of military events on social and cultural history.

Studies in the Social and Cultural History of Modern Warfare presents the fruits of this growing area of research, reflecting both the colonization of military history by cultural historians and the reciprocal interest of military historians in social and cultural history, to the benefit of both. The series offers the latest scholarship in European and non-European events from the 1850s to the present day.

A full list of titles in the series can be found at: www.cambridge.org/modernwarfare

Designing Memory

The Architecture of Commemoration in Europe, 1914 to the Present

SABINA TANOVIĆ
Delft University of Technology

CAMBRIDGE
UNIVERSITY PRESS

CAMBRIDGE
UNIVERSITY PRESS

University Printing House, Cambridge CB2 8BS, United Kingdom

One Liberty Plaza, 20th Floor, New York, NY 10006, USA

477 Williamstown Road, Port Melbourne, VIC 3207, Australia

314-321, 3rd Floor, Plot 3, Splendor Forum, Jasola District Centre, New Delhi - 110025, India

103 Penang Road, #05-06/07, Visioncrest Commercial, Singapore 238467

Cambridge University Press is part of the University of Cambridge.

It furthers the University's mission by disseminating knowledge in the pursuit of education, learning and research at the highest international levels of excellence.

www.cambridge.org
Information on this title: www.cambridge.org/9781108707824
DOI: 10.1017/9781108760577

© Sabina Tanović 2019

This publication is in copyright. Subject to statutory exception and to the provisions of relevant collective licensing agreements, no reproduction of any part may take place without the written permission of Cambridge University Press.

First published 2019
First paperback edition 2022

A catalogue record for this publication is available from the British Library

ISBN 978-1-108-48652-1 Hardback
ISBN 978-1-108-70782-4 Paperback

Cambridge University Press has no responsibility for the persistence or accuracy of URLs for external or third-party internet websites referred to in this publication, and does not guarantee that any content on such websites is, or will remain, accurate or appropriate.

For my family

The life of a man is driven
between extremes,
between dim and vast regions of
imaginative thought and the more narrow
bright and lucid ones of wisdom,
at one moment elevated by heroic vision,
at yet another
turned upside down
mockingly self-conscious,
now finding harmony and light,
now dissonance, decay and darkness,
until the cycle of a life is woven
wholly into immortal ones of the world.

Lebbeus Woods,
'Einstein Tomb', 1980.[1]

[1] Lebbeus Woods, *Einstein Tomb*, Pamphlet Architecture 6 (New York: Princeton Architectural Press, 1980). © Estate of Lebbeus Woods.

Contents

Figures

Acknowledgements

This book is a product of more than a decade-long engagement with memory and spaces of remembrance. Fittingly, it has developed out of work both in practice and research. This means there is a host of people who have contributed in different ways. It is impossible to thank them all individually, but I will mention those who had the greatest impact.

I am deeply grateful that I had the opportunity to carry out a four-year research post at the Delft University of Technology which would not be possible without the support of the Netherlands Fellowship Programmes (NFP), the Memorial Museum Westerbork's chairman Dirk Mulder and Mersed Smajović from the Memorial Center Srebrenica. These years were essential for shaping this project, with helpful insights coming from Tom Avermaete, Adnan Pašić, Carola Hein, Ornella Selvafolta, and especially Jay Winter and James Young who helped me sharpen my approach. I had a close relationship with my brilliant mentor, Franziska Bollerey, who was influential in the formative years of my research and remained so throughout. Both she and her partner, Axel Föhl, were generous and inspirational in a unique way.

My horizons expanded through connections and work with scholars, activists and practitioners in different fields, and they receive a special thank-you note. At the very beginning of my research I met Joost van Bodegom whose incredible past and memory-activism encouraged me to go further. On a few occasions, I have benefited from working with gifted colleagues from the Leiden University Centre for the Arts in Society (LUCAS) and the Amsterdam School for Heritage, Memory and Material Culture and their interdisciplinary approach. In particular, discussions with Rob van der Laarse helped me write about sociological aspects of commemorative processes. The interdisciplinary focus was certainly reinforced by Jos de Keijser who assisted me in navigating through the complex field of trauma research and the process of bereavement. Understanding commemoration of the Great War in Belgium would certainly be more daunting without the knowledge of Pieter Uyttenhove and his valuable input. Meeting Karen Remmler was delightful, and her views on memory transmission had a profound impact. I am also indebted to Susan

Nial and her highly motivating passion for preserving architectural heritage. Recently, I was fortunate to collaborate with Sanja Horvatinčić and Beti Žerovc, who opened a whole new field of interest for me.

Furthermore, I am grateful to employees of several memorial sites who provided deeper insights into particularities of their work, such as memorial museums in Drancy and Mechelen, Jasenovac memorial site, 11-M memorial, Mittelbau-Dora memorial site, Varanger museum in Vardø, Westerbork and the list continues. It was always a great pleasure to have fruitful conversations with many designers and think together with them about how memory can be translated into space. They have contributed to this book in many ways. To name just a few: Buj+Cólon architects, Christoph Hinterreiter, Adnan Omerović, Jeroen Geurst, Lodewijk Baljon, and Jonas Dahlberg. Special thanks to Jo Noero, Blakstad Haffner Architects, Diener & Diener Architects, Museum of Modern Art in Warsaw, Museum '21 October' in Kragujevac, Risiera di San Sabba, Bas Smets, 3RW Architects, Michael Arad and Aleksandra Wagner.

It was delightful to work with Linda Bleijenberg and Jon Wilcox who, in different stages of writing this book, helped me with their edits, insights and a pinch of madness when it was needed. I am deeply grateful for this.

Sarajevo had impact, as always: having the honour to design the Memorial Museum and Research Center for Sarajevo's 'Tunnel of Hope' memorial site allowed me to test in practice my theoretical knowledge with the great assistance and collaboration of the museum's managerial team. They demonstrated exemplary openness, and I am grateful for that. Particularly inspiring were the initiators of the War Childhood Museum, Jasminko Halilović and Selma Tanović, with their incredibly creative, responsible and professional approach. It was a constructive merging that, once again, convinced me how significant it is to work in practice. I also had the privilege of meeting Elma Hašimbegović, a director of the History Museum of Bosnia and Herzegovina, and Amra Čusto from the Institute for Monument Protection – activists and intellectual authorities on topics of remembering through art and architecture. Satko Mujagić showed me how memorials can be instrumental in fighting political indifference. Lejla Kreševljakovic enriched my work with her own research on memory and heritage. Dario Kristić influenced this book through our design projects and many thoughtful suggestions. Ena Kukić provided fresh and, at times, provocative ideas that made me re-examine some of the conclusions I made. Documentary filmmaker Kenan Kulenović was equally inspiring in envisioning augmented reality as a way to remember. Also, the

Association of Architects was of great assistance on several occasions and in that way contributed to steering this book to its finish line.

I am certainly most indebted to Jay Winter, who with intellectual rigour, charisma and patience offered guidance whenever it was needed. He had the most profound influence on refining my work, and I was incredibly lucky to have his trust.

Two of the valuable influences outside the professional context will sadly never read this book, my father Murat Tanović and my father-in-law Hans R. de Vries. And then there are those I want to thank for their patience, companionship and practical help, to name but a few: Dina, Ardin, Samra, Samija, Willemien, Berend, Laura, Marijn, and Nqoc and friends Sogol, Stephan, Orçun, Ary, Swarna, Ambar, Aida, Mirela, Narcisa, Almir, Šahin, Naida, Dinka, Hajra, Amra, Azadeh, Negar, Wendy, Alma and Yann. And, of course, Jasna and Tarkan, for their hospitality at the wonderful seaside retreat and their encouraging support.

Finally, all this would not have been possible without my dear Paul, his love and his understanding.

Introduction

Emptiness is not nothing
But something that is there
That which indicates something is missing.[1]

Nick Hullegie

Like most architecture, designed memorial spaces can be perceived as collective efforts that rely on resources provided by political and financial powers. At the same time, memorial architecture, being an act of representation, touches upon the essence of architectural creation and the question of how space mediates some of the most intricate social and cultural processes. Both the predicament and the allure of the task of designing a memorial space became clear to me in a very personal quest to commemorate through architecture the Siege of Sarajevo (1992–95).[2] In 1992, when American architect Lebbeus Woods was working on his book *War and Architecture*, the destruction of Sarajevo and its citizens by heavy artillery and sniper fire was in full swing.[3] While one of the many targets was being destroyed – the city's twin towers, 'Momo & Uzeir' – Woods made the pessimistic statement that the burning towers of Sarajevo were 'markers of the end of an age of reason, if not reason itself, beyond which lies a domain of almost incomprehensible darkness'.[4] As a compassionate observer who entered the besieged city in the midst of the ongoing carnage, he preoccupied himself with Sarajevo's architectural wounds. Intuitively recognizing a need for order and some sense of control that was lingering

1 Author's translation of the words that accompany Nick Hullegie's 2011 sculpture, *Not There*, which combines plexiglass and tree stump. The original text reads 'Leegte is niet niets, maar iets dat er is wat aangeeft dat er iets mist.'

2 The Siege of Sarajevo by the combined forces of the Yugoslav People's Army and the Army of Republic of Srpska, often referred to as the longest siege of a capital city in the history of modern warfare, started on 5 April 1992 and officially lasted until 1 November 1995 when the Dayton Agreement was signed. However, it was only in March 1996 that the occupying forces left the city.

3 Lebbeus Woods, *War and Architecture*, Pamphlet Architecture 15 (New York: Princeton Architectural Press, 1993).

4 Ibid., p. 3.

among its citizens, Woods focused on the city's wounded tissue and looked at the smallest details, for example a damaged window, in an effort to preserve traces of war.

To understand destructed space, Woods aimed to make a distinction between architecture as a weapon of destruction, or part of the problem in war, and architecture as a system of protection. Along this typically Janus-faced characterization of architecture, he proposed architectural solutions for establishing the order needed for the continuation of life in peace. He termed them as 'the scab' and 'the scar', arguing that 'the natural stages of healing might not be pretty, judged by conventional aesthetic standards, but they are beautiful in the existential sense.'[5] In this view, architecture can act as a symbol of the resilience of the human spirit and the will to live of those targeted for destruction.

My interest in the role of architects as creators of order in devastated environments started in the post-war atmosphere of Sarajevo, when making sense of things was a priority. After having been continuously exposed to severe urbicide for almost four years, in 1996 the city and its citizens faced the prospect of peace in a place defined by overwhelming architectural and psychological debris which now had to be confronted in its real scale and meaning. An eagerness to tell the story of survival was widely present among citizens, and it seemed to be getting stronger as life continued to be normalized and the eternal fire of the Second World War memorial in the centre of the city was lit again, exactly 50 years after 'justice had vanquished two tyrannies, bringing forth a new paradigm of world history'.[6] At the same time, the 'other' side – the participants in the war who, actively or inactively, supported the destruction of the city – had and still have a different memory of events. As the issues surrounding possible ways of memorializing the war started to become more prominent, the complexities of the memorializing process began to unfold, demonstrating the contemporaneity of memory and the presence of counter-memory. In his contemplation on negative memory in the German collective consciousness, German historian Reinhart Koselleck touched upon three interlinked questions: who and what should be remembered, and how should it be done?[7] Observing through a lens of a designer whose experience was shaped

[5] Ibid., p. 24.

[6] Jeffrey K. Olick, *The Politics of Regret: On Collective Memory and Historical Responsibility* (New York and London: Routledge, 2007), p. 175.

[7] Reinhart Koselleck, *Sediments of Time: On Possible Histories*, trans. Sean Franzel and Stefan-Ludwig Hoffmann (Stanford, CA: Stanford University Press, 2018), p. 243.

by a post-conflict environment, my focus was inherently inclined to the 'how' conundrum, or more precisely the official (and to a lesser extent unofficial) memorials, because these are usually the most challenging and controversial assignments architects can receive. This is a daunting topic in the electric age where information is abounding and available to everyone, creating 'memory of the multitude' that 'softens history, changing the parameters of the who, what and why of remembering'.[8]

Monument versus Memorial?

While I was contemplating what a memorial for Sarajevo should be, on the other side of the Atlantic similar issues were raised in a difficult discussion about how to commemorate the events of 9/11 in New York. What was instantly clear, amid the arguments between those who fought for reconstruction and those who pleaded to leave the newly created void as a signifier, was that whatever form it took, the memorial had to carefully communicate the emotional tension and stay objective, informative and truthful. It seemed an impossible balancing act. If we understand representation of memory, both individual and collective, as 'the function by which symbols, or simulacra, or surrogates, come to stand for some absent referent', it is inviting to comprehend how this might manifest and what it means for memorial architecture in particular.[9] What are the symbols, simulacra or surrogates used in contemporary memorial projects? Now that the memorial for 9/11 is built, the question of how to design a structure as a signifier of something that is missing due to violent destruction remains relevant and equally as challenging.

The distinction between monument and memorial remains ambiguous. The two notions are continuously interchangeably used both in academia and practice. The general process of creating is similar for both typologies in that they are (almost always) directly faced with strong emotions and sentiments. And like in all design projects, there are restrictions of funding and resources. However, building a memorial is further complicated by the involvement of additional tasks such as preservation and questions of education and tourism. As a rule, all these aspects are the subject of multilayered views on a particular memory or set of memories and are

[8] Andrew Hoskins (ed.), 'Memory of the multitude. The end of collective memory', in *Digital Memory Studies: Media Pasts in Transition* (London and New York: Routledge, 2017), pp. 85–109, p. 88.

[9] Richard Terdiman, *Present Past: Modernity and Memory Crisis* (Ithaca, NY: Cornell University Press, 1933), p. 8.

deeply embedded in the political and social context. As well as these defining tasks, a memorial is normally the focal architectural edifice within its built context and is therefore perceived as a representation of that particular context (even if this is not necessarily the case), often becoming a frequented visiting attraction and mental signifier for that physical location in the collective imagination.

The extensively quoted remark by Robert Musil that 'there is nothing in this world as invisible as a monument' perhaps best describes the process of disregarding a monument's power as an *aide memoire*.[10] In his 1927 essay, Musil was of course referring to the traditional notion of a public monument, an edifice dedicated to the memory of a person or an event, usually taking the form of a sculptural work installed on a pedestal.[11] The discussion about the invisibility of monuments implies that there is an expiry date for the monument's performance of memory, related to the intricate set of circumstances that produced the monument in the first place. Referring to Musil's observation, the scholar James E. Young argued that the reason for this invisibility is 'the essential stiffness monuments share with all other images: as a likeness necessarily vitrifies its otherwise dynamic referent, a monument turns pliant memory to stone'.[12] In this sense, monuments imply an act of termination since monuments are seldom erected for the living, but the affective nature of a monument keeps memory alive for posterity.[13] The affective nature of a monument is what is often neglected, a tendency also recognized by Young, who argued that 'too often, a community's monuments assume the polished, finished veneer of a death mask, unreflective of a current memory, unresponsive to contemporary issues.'[14] The supposed short-term familiarity of public monuments, Peter Carrier argued, is

[10] Robert Musil, 'Monuments' (1927), in *Posthumous Papers of a Living Author*, trans. Peter Wortsman (Hygiene, CO: Eridanos Press, 1987), pp. 64–8, p. 61.

[11] According to the *Oxford English Dictionary*, a 'monument' has its origin in Middle English (denoting a burial place), deriving via French from the classical Latin *monumentum*, from *monēre* 'to remind' and stands for: a statue, building or other structure erected to commemorate a notable person or event; a statue or other structure placed over a grave in memory of the dead; a building, structure, or site that is of historical importance or interest; an enduring or memorable example of something. See Angus Stevenson (ed.), *Oxford Dictionary of English*, 3rd edn (Oxford: Oxford University Press, 2010).

[12] James E. Young, *The Texture of Memory: Holocaust Memorials and Meaning* (New Haven, CT: Yale University Press, 1993), p. 13.

[13] David Lowenthal, *The Past Is the Foreign Country* (Cambridge: Cambridge University Press, 1985), p. 323.

[14] James E. Young, 'Memory/Monument', in Robert S. Nelson and Richard Shiff (eds.), *Critical Terms for Art History*, 2nd edn (Chicago, IL and London: University of Chicago Press, 2003), pp. 234–47, esp. p. 245.

> compounded by the long-term familiarity of a form of symbolic communication and cultivation of collective memory whose semantic and political function – urging us to understand and identify with, love or fear historical figures and events – harbours few surprises.[15]

Hence the generic form of monuments fails in the face of dramatic changes of human perceptions and means of communication. Today, however, artists like Christo and Jean-Claude and, more recently, Tatzu Nishi make us rediscover monuments with long-passed expiry-dates by changing their context and literally bringing them closer to us through the use of contemporary architectural space.

The longevity of using the symbolic monument genre for communicating social and political messages has been consistently used throughout history. The French historian Françoise Choay argued that a monument entails the concept of a defence against the traumas of existence and that the affective nature of a monument rests upon its being an 'antidote to entropy, to the dissolving action of time on all things natural and artificial, it seeks to appease our fear of death and annihilation'.[16] Hence, the power of a monument resides in its affective nature and the ability to stir up emotions in people with regards to the monument's story. According to the Viennese art historian Aloïs Riegl, a monument in its oldest and most original sense is 'a human creation, erected for the specific purpose of keeping single human deeds or events (or a combination thereof) alive in the minds of future generations'.[17] According to Riegl, the perception that future generations will have of a monument is dependent on the existing context, norms and values or the *Kunstwollen* or 'artistic will' of that epoch and how a monument responds to these.[18] Riegl recognized three types of monuments: intentional, unintentional and monuments possessing 'age-value'.[19] In preservation, the first category, intentional monuments, is

[15] Peter Carrier, *Holocaust Monuments and National Memory in France and Germany since 1989. The Origins and Political Function of the Vél'd'Hiv' in Paris and the Holocaust Monument in Berlin* (New York and Oxford: Berghahn Books, 2005), p. 16.

[16] Françoise Choay, *The Invention of the Historic Monument* (Cambridge: Cambridge University Press, 2001), p. 7.

[17] Aloïs Riegl, 'The modern cult of monuments: its character and its origin', *Oppositions*, 25 (1982), 25–56, 21.

[18] See Kurt W. Forster, 'Monument/memory and the mortality of architecture', in K. Michael Hays (ed.), *Oppositions Reader: Selected Readings from a Journal for Ideas and Criticism in Architecture, 1973–1984* (New York: Princeton Architectural Press, 1998), pp. 18–35.

[19] Unlike historical value which relates to historical knowledge and is therefore restricted to a few monuments, age value has broader appeal since everyone can perceive it immediately. See Choay, *The Invention*, pp. 111–16.

specific because these had a more or less protected status in the course of history, unlike the historic monument, a term introduced in the nineteenth century with the emergent interest in the preservation of historical heritage and the recognition of 'style'. The intentional monument commemorating a person existed in many cultures, but it was only with the Renaissance, Riegl argues, when the notion of beauty was given a prominent place, did people begin to understand and appreciate monuments for their commemorative value, as part of their heritage and not simply a mere display of patriotic recollections.[20]

An intentional monument in its original sense is not only an informative structure from a specific historical period, but also an engaging edifice invested with living memory. To this category belong only 'those works which recall a specific moment or complex of moments from the past'.[21] Much later, art historian Horst Janson made a distinction between three categories of Western monuments: the funerary monument, the monument to historical ideas and events and the monument commemorating great men.[22] In principle, a commemorative monument is always built with the intention to last. However, this has often proved impossible and led many monuments to end up as mere signs of the failed infrastructure of memory they initially embodied, transforming them into uncanny or unwanted reality.[23] Looking closely to two national memorial sites, the Vél d'Hiv in Paris and the Holocaust Memorial in Berlin, Carrier stressed that the essential significance of commemorative projects is in their 'non-prescriptive heuristic stimuli that enable individuals to encounter and understand both the past and their relation to the past via representations of it'.[24]

In memory studies, the term memorial is used interchangeably with the notion of a monument, and distinctions are rarely made between the two. This is also true in the field of architecture since designers often intertwine the two notions. In the late nineteenth century, there was a significant development in the design of public monuments, what Kirk Savage dubbed 'spatial monument', which moved from 'an object of reverence to a space

[20] Riegl, 'Modern cult of monuments', p. 26. [21] Ibid., 24.

[22] Horst W. Janson, *The Rise and Fall of the Public Monument* (New Orleans, LA: The Graduate School, Tulane University, 1976), p. 1.

[23] Andrew Shanken, 'Towards a cultural geography of modern memorials', in Jill A. Franklin, T. A. Heslop and Christine Stevenson (eds.), *Architecture and Interpretation: Essays for Eric Fernie* (Rochester, NY: Boydell & Brewer, 2012), pp. 357–80.

[24] Carrier, *Holocaust Monuments*, p. 230.

of subjective experience'.[25] In addition, as Sergiusz Michalski signalled in his history of public monuments, the years before the First World War were characterized by a certain zest for experiments in commemorative sculptures.[26] A more psychologically-oriented approach was introduced: the sculptural compositions descended from their high pedestals to stand eye to eye with their audience and enclose beholders into their space, thereby inviting more engagement with the monument.[27]

Erika Doss demonstrated how in the American context the two words are used to depict a variety of commemorative projects, ranging from traditional stone obelisks to other facilities including parks, highways, libraries and so forth. This is the heritage of the post-WWII debate about 'living' memorials.[28] The word 'memorial' appears to be more popular, but there is also a hint that designers seem to perceive monuments as celebratory whereas memorials are commonly understood as spaces of a profoundly contemplative nature that can offer more possibilities.

Some aimed to establish parameters that turn a war monument into a memorial and hence argued for a symbolic repertoire that focuses on the acceptance of violence and recognition of sacrifice that enhances understanding of a debt by the living and thus their will to reciprocate – a memorial as

> A sustenance for memory achieving significance for the past sacrifice in order that future devotion will require further commitment to confirm the social order and establishing the key social relationships that make life worth having or at least worth bearing.[29]

This distinction in purpose and content was also recognized by philosopher and critic Arthur Danto, who explained:

[25] Savage commented on the monument to Abraham Lincoln (1887) in Chicago by sculptor Saint Gaudens and architect Stanford White. The monument, together with other monuments built at the time, was perceived as innovative since it combined sculptural monument with architectural solutions and allowed visitors to penetrate the sculpture. See Quentin Stevens and Karen A. Franck, *Memorials as Spaces of Engagement: Design, Use and Meaning* (New York: Routledge, 2016), p. 14.

[26] Sergiusz Michalski, *Public Monuments: Art in Political Bondage 1870–1997* (London: Reaction Books Ltd, 1998).

[27] Ibid., p. 41.

[28] Erika Doss, *Memorial Mania: Public Feeling in America* (Chicago, IL: University of Chicago Press, 2010), pp. 37–48.

[29] Michael Rowlands, 'Remembering to forget: sublimation as sacrifice in war memorials', in Adrian Forty and Susan Kuchler (eds.), *The Art of Forgetting* (Oxford: Berg, 2001), pp. 129–45, esp. p. 144.

> Monuments make heroes and triumphs, victories and conquests, perpetually present part of life. The memorial is a special precinct extruded from life, a segregated enclave where we honor the dead. With monuments we honor ourselves.[30]

Danto situated his argument in a discussion about the well-known Vietnam Veterans Memorial (VVM), designed by Maya Lin and inaugurated in Washington, DC in 1982, representing a memorial to defeat instead of victory. Danto perceived the memorial as a moral connection between the Washington Monument (1885) as a symbol of triumph and the Lincoln Memorial (1922) as a temple of submission. While this is perhaps true in this specific context, it cannot be taken as a formula since many monuments do invite retrospection, and at the same time memorials are not necessarily non-celebratory quiet precincts. After the VVM was erected, the opposing views in the bitter debates regarding the memorial's appearance and meaning marked its first years. Consisting of two long dark granite walls inscribed with the names of the dead, cutting into the landscape, the memorial constitutes an important development in the conception of an architecture of remembrance. The memorial embodies some of the ideas that changed the perception of what a monument should look like. The VVM invites participation on several levels and manages to remain in a contemplative and emotional realm, demonstrated by its ongoing acceptance and popularity. The memorial's unobtrusive horizontality is also contradictory to its physical setting: the National Mall in Washington, DC. Similarly to the 'counter-monument' (*Gegen-Denkmal*) generation of artists, Lin claimed that she designs memorials and anti-monuments.[31]

In collective memory studies there is a tendency to see memorial spatial expressions primarily as characterized by the 'primacy of the visual'.[32] And so art historian Daniel Sherman writes that 'sight is the only sense powerful enough to bridge the gap between those who hold a memory rooted in bodily experience and those who, lacking such "experience," nonetheless

30 Arthur C. Danto, *The State of the Art* (New York: Prentice Hall Press, 1987), p. 112. Several authors similarly argued that monuments are a means to acknowledge the past, whereas memorials pay tribute to the dead. See for example Marita Sturken and James E. Young, 'Monuments: historical overview', in Michael Kelly (ed.), *Encyclopedia of Aesthetics*, vol. 3 (New York: Oxford University Press, 1998), pp. 272–8, p. 274.

31 Doss, *Memorial Mania*, p. 39.

32 Raphael Samuel, *Theatres of Memory*, vol. 1: *Past and Present in Contemporary Culture* (London: Verso, 1994), p. viii.

seek to share the memory.'[33] For the purposes of this study, the visual is the axes in the definition of a monument as an architectural or sculptural composition, or a combination thereof, dedicated to a person, event or particular act. A monument is intended primarily as a visual marker and a symbolic tool for communicating social and political ideas. This depiction relates to what has been understood as a 'traditional' sculptural monument. Accordingly, as a representation of its political, social and cultural context a memorial has a similar goal and designation, but it differs from a monument in several aspects. Different from a monument, a memorial is an architectural construct that is defined by its employment of space as an architectural tool. A memorial's symbolic function is not necessarily apparent and often requires visitors' engagement to be discovered. In other words, instead of only creating a representation of what is being commemorated, a memorial is a custom-designed experiential space in reference to its topic. In this way, a memorial space is inevitably engaging visitors on several levels, not only on the level of visual perception.

When engaged with the memorial, a visitor is exposed to its designed mnemonic power, participating as audience and performer at the same time. Furthermore, a memorial addresses the facilitation of mourning instead of only representing loss. A useful definition of public memorials is the one used in the field of transitional justice by which public memorials are 'designed to evoke a specific reaction or set of reactions, including public acknowledgment of the event or people represented; personal reflection or mourning; pride, anger, or sadness about something that has happened; or learning or curiosity about periods in the past'.[34] Although this definition is concerned only with the representation of past events, a contemporary memorial is usually involved with present events or, rather, the existence of the past in the present, and in some cases memorials deal with ongoing but also anticipated future events.[35]

33 Daniel J. Sherman, *The Construction of Memory in Interwar France* (Chicago, IL and London: University of Chicago Press, 1999), p. 14.

34 Sebastian Brett, Louis Bickford, Liz Ševčenko and Marcela Rios, *Memorialization and Democracy: State Policy and Civic Action* (New York: International Coalition of Sites of Conscience, 2007). The report is based on the international conference of the report's title held on 20–22 June 2007 in Santiago, Chile.

35 One example of this is a memorial planned for a location in Carlsbad, New Mexico, which is used as a transuranic waste site by New Mexico's Waste Isolation Pilot Plant. In the year 2030, the storage facility will reach its maximum capacity. This provides the rationale for the memorial as a structure that would warn future generations of the lethal toxicity of the site. See Julia Bryan-Wilson, 'Building a marker of nuclear warning', in Robert S. Nelson and Margaret

Scope and Boundaries

Technically, this book is focused on architecture as a space for remembering and is therefore concerned with the memorial genre as a designing process that aims to understand and respond to social currencies. The main questions I ask are concerned with the purpose of creating a memorial in a given location, its translation into an architectural concept and its materialization. To see how memorial form originated and evolved I focus on the following key points: how architectural space supports memory and commemoration, what innovative design solutions are proposed in the face of social and political challenges, and how are these solutions implemented. To a limited extent, the investigation explores what the impact of the design is once the memorial is installed in real time and space.[36] In-depth research on the effects that discussed memorials have on their visitors and built environment will require research of its own. Before addressing these questions, I seek to situate memorialization in a wider context to be able to observe it more critically, and attend to several points which are relevant to the process of creating a memorial.

In an approach that explores different disciplines (namely history, psychology, anthropology and sociology), the aim is to establish a relevant framework for analysing contemporary projects. This framework constitutes the base for the analysis of the case studies that we will discuss. By focusing on contemporary memorial architecture in Europe and a few examples from the United States, I aim to take a closer look into processes of designing memorials today and how these translate memories and experiences of human loss into an architectural space. Memorials were selected to complement each other and to give a diverse range of practices in commemorative topics dedicated to war and contemporary violence. With the selection of projects gathered in this book I do not want to claim to make representative statements that apply for all Europe. Instead the discussion tries to offer a larger perspective

Olin (eds.), *Monuments and Memory, Made and Unmade* (Chicago, IL: Chicago University Press, 2003), pp. 183–205.

[36] I address the spatial influence on the visitor based on several points: my own experience as a visitor (I purposefully conducted visits before pursuing any in-depth exploration, in that way trying to assimilate with a common visitor); information from existing reviews left by visitors; and information gained from interviews with employees about the most utilized routes and reactions of the visitors. Any more comprehensive and data-based observations would require a further research project.

on how spaces of memory are perceived from a viewpoint of a designer who, in the end, solidifies calls for remembrance. Without attempting to make bold statements about how these memorial spaces influence their specific contexts and thereby, arguably, collective consciousness about events commemorated, my goal is to take a closer look into conceptual and aesthetic characteristics of contemporary memorials to try to discern current day perceptions in the production of public memorial spaces dedicated to wars and contemporary violence. The impact memorials of our internet-based time have on the collectives will most likely start to be understood in the future, since we are only now beginning to realize the effects on how media from the beginning of the century influenced processes of collective remembrance.

Before going any further, I need to address the historical literature on the politics of memory – a field that is huge, and growing daily. Much of it focuses on three sets of problems:

(1) How do those in power orchestrate projects focusing on remembering the dead of the two world wars in uniform? Here the works of German historians – in particular Reinhart Koselleck and George Mosse take pride of place.[37]

(2) How, if at all, has remembering the Holocaust transformed patterns of remembrance of the Second World War? Here state projects and those arising from within civil society are significant. In this domain, many historians from different Western countries have made foundational contributions. Among them are Deborah Lipstadt,[38] Saul Friedländer,[39] Peter Novick,[40] Aleida Assmann,[41] Jeffrey Alexander,[42] Omer

[37] Reinhart Koselleck, 'War memorials: identity formations of the survivors', in *The Practice of Conceptual History: Timing, History, Spacing Concepts*, trans. Todd Samuel Presner et al. (Stanford, CA: Stanford University Press, 2002), pp. 285–326; Reinhart Koselleck (ed.), *Zur politischen Ikonographie des gewaltsamen Todes. Ein deutsch-französischer Vergleich* (Basel: Schwabe, 1998); George L. Mosse, *Germans and Jews: The Right, the Left, and the Search for a "Third Force" in Pre-Nazi Germany* (New York: Howard Fertig, 1970).

[38] Deborah E. Lipstadt, *The American Press & the Coming of the Holocaust 1933–1945: Beyond Belief* (New York: The Free Press, 1986).

[39] Saul Friedländer, *Nazi Germany and the Jews: The Years of Persecution, 1933–1939* (Frome and London: Butler & Tanner, Ltd., 1998).

[40] Peter Novick, *The Holocaust in American Life* (Boston, MA and New York: A Mariner Book, Houghton Mifflin Company, 2000).

[41] Aleida Assmann, *Der lange Schatten der Vergangenheit – Erinnerungskultur und Geschichtspolitik* (Munich: C. H. Beck Publishers, 2006).

[42] Jeffrey C. Alexander, 'On the social construction of moral universals. The "Holocaust" from war crime to trauma drama', *European Journal of Social Theory* 5 (2001), 5–85.

Bartov,[43] Alon Confino,[44] Charles Maier,[45] Dominick LaCapra,[46] Kerwin Klein,[47] Dan Diner,[48] Henry Rousso,[49] Annette Wieviorka[50] and Jay Winter.[51] They write from different theoretical standpoints, but in different ways all wrestle with the problem of identifying and exploring the implications of an epistemological break between before and after the Holocaust.

(3) How did the ossification and collapse of the Soviet empire affect patterns of remembrance in what Timothy Snyder has called the 'Bloodlands' of Eastern Europe and Russia, where the majority of the victims of both Hitler and Stalin lost their lives?[52]

This study cannot possibly interpolate the profound insights of all these scholars, but it engages in a dialogue about these three questions, and takes the view that while states try to orchestrate commemoration, they rarely succeed on their own in setting a society's commemorative agenda. In addition, from the late 1970s, remembering the Holocaust has entered into the public history of the Second World War, and necessarily architects and designers have joined others in braiding together war and genocide. This is not the case everywhere, especially in Eastern Europe, but the public disagreements over how to remember the Second World War in, say, Poland or Hungary return time and again to the Holocaust. It is on the commemorative agenda, even when it is minimized or marginalized.

This study starts with the assumption that while politics on the local, national and transnational level is ever-present in commemorative

43 Omer Bartov, *Murder in Our Midst: The Holocaust, Industrial Killing and Representation* (New York and Oxford: Oxford University Press, 1996).

44 Alon Confino, 'From Psychohistory to Memory Studies: or how some Germans became Jews and some Jews became Nazis', in Roger Frie (ed.), *History Flows through Us: Germany, the Holocaust, and the Importance of Empathy* (London and New York: Routledge, 2018), pp. 17–30.

45 Charles S. Maier, *The Unmasterable Past: History, Holocaust, and German National Identity* (Cambridge, MA: Harvard University Press, 1998).

46 Dominick LaCapra, *Writing History, Writing Trauma* (Baltimore, MD: Johns Hopkins University Press, 2001).

47 Kerwin L. Klein, *From History to Theory* (Berkeley, CA: University of California Press, 2011).

48 Dan Diner, *Beyond the Conceivable: Studies on Germany, Nazism, and the Holocaust* (Berkeley, CA: University of California Press, 2000).

49 Henry Rousso, *The Vichy Syndrome: History and Memory in France since 1944* (Cambridge, MA: Harvard University Press, 1991).

50 Annette Wieviorka, *The Era of the Witness*, trans. from the French by Jared Stark (Ithaca, NY: Cornell University Press, 2011).

51 Jay Winter, *War beyond Words: Languages of Remembrance from the Great War to the Present* (Cambridge: Cambridge University Press, 2017).

52 Timothy Snyder, *Bloodlands: Europe between Hitler and Stalin* (New York: Basic Books, 2011).

projects, so is the question of the organization of space and the visualization of memory. What an architect can offer modestly is a spatial counterpoint, a sight and senses-driven approach to the question as to how do monuments and memorials emerge in space and time? This always involves material issues of funding as well as the inevitable tendency of those who have survived violence to claim privileged knowledge not only about their experiences but also about how to represent them to posterity.

In a sense, for a designer to enter this domain is to move into a minefield. And yet designers have a viewpoint which has not been central to much of the vast literature cited above. Some historians, in particular Reinhart Koselleck and James E. Young, have a deep sense of what Young has termed the *texture of memory*. This book follows their lead by serving as a commentary and an examination of the ways artists and architects have designed the texture of a number of important commemorative projects over the past century. It has been, of necessity, selective, but it is my hope that the book will add a relevant and until now neglected viewpoint to the vital and vibrant debate about commemoration of the victims of violence in today's world.

Having dealt with violence and representing violence throughout most of my life and career, I am well aware that to focus on visual forms of remembrance is to invite a descent into the nightmares of our times. I see engagement with this task not as a matter of choice, but as a moral obligation. Each of us - architects included - brings to that task what we can.

*

To address these questions, I carefully consider both theoretical approaches and how mourning and memorial practices unfolded over time. I undertook fieldwork to study many projects in situ. Accordingly, the structure of this book is divided into two parts. The first and largest part of this book is dedicated to addressing several issues such as the notion of memory and the process of mourning, funeral architecture, the limits of architectural representation, and a historical overview of significant architectural developments following the First World War up until the present day. In an interdisciplinary approach that takes cues from psychology, philosophy, anthropology, political and social history, together with art and architectural history, the purpose of this part is to establish a framework in which contemporary examples can be analysed. The second part, chapters three, four and five, is focused on a detailed analysis of contemporary memorial projects commemorating wars and more recent atrocities, including their design, construction and performance.

The first chapter presents a brief historical overview of significant architectural developments with regards to memorial projects, as shaped by different political climates. The overview is primarily concerned with architectural projects and concepts in Western Europe. There are a few examples from the United States and fewer still from Eastern Europe, as well as countries from other continents. My aim is to show the development of commemorative architecture in Europe and in the United States at a time when transcultural exchanges of information have been frequent and fruitful. I also discuss examples from Eastern Europe and the former Soviet Union where architects and designers have historically been seen as more resistant to 'Western' influences and are more directly the product of state policies. Certainly, there are many stories to be told of commemoration in Southern Europe, in Scandinavia, in Asia Minor, but the mountain of material available on Western Europe, Central Europe, and the United States is daunting enough to climb. I recognize that more needs to be done, and hope I have shown some ways in which a more complete history of the architecture of commemoration in the twentieth century and after can be written.

The first chapter follows the development of commemorative architecture after each of the world wars – the interwar period and the late 1940s and 1950s – as well as the upsurge in commemorative efforts during the 1960s and after 1980. Throughout, the politics of memory is the resultant of many different vectors, but among them is the shifting perspectives of artists and architects on the legacies of the two world wars and in particular on the legacy of the Holocaust. Others matter, but this book focuses on the group of architects and designers, men and women, who have sketched out and realized commemorative projects.

The second chapter, 'The Dual Role of Memorial Architecture', is focused on the intricate relationship between architecture and representations concerning death, psychological aspects of mourning, particularly mourning related to the experience of trauma, and the facilitation of its ritual. By trauma, I follow the general usage that the experience of mass death in the twentieth century shattered the sense of self of many survivors and made it difficult, and at times impossible, for them to resume their *ante bellum* lives.

Other issues relevant to the contemporary context and the production of memorial spaces are also tackled here, namely the private and public role of memorial architecture and the possibilities of architecture as a form of agency in remembering and dealing with a difficult past. The overarching question in the creation of a memorial space is how the design can add meaning to the memory-work that naturally involves many participants, with a variety of expectations and demands. Moreover, memorials can possibly provide a significant locus to future generations for processing the legacies of trauma, since studies have shown that an attuned physical environment is beneficial to psycho-emotional health.[53] Various proposals and designs for both memorial and funerary architecture by different architects in different historical periods are observed. In this framework, attention is also given to cemeteries as commemorative landscapes containing features relevant for memorial architecture, such as transitional spaces. Since funerary architecture strongly influenced the evolution of the architectural memorial, this chapter will trace how the topic of death inspired some of the most influential designers of monuments and memorials in the nineteenth and twentieth centuries.

In the third chapter, I examine several memorials dedicated to the victims of contemporary terrorist attacks. These include the 11-M memorial in Madrid, the 9/11 memorial in New York, the July 22 memorial in Utøya, and the recently dedicated European memorial to victims of a war incident – the MH17 memorial in Haarlemmermeer municipality in the Netherlands. The Madrid memorial, now over a decade old, is analysed in depth with the intention to create a framework through which to observe current efforts in designing memorials that have a similar purpose. By looking at the process of creating the 11-M memorial and whether and how it has fulfilled its purpose during the last decade, a reference point is introduced for contemporary developments that still need to perform in practice and create the much-needed time distance to observe them critically.

The fourth chapter is a comparative analysis of two Holocaust memorial museums: the Kazerne Dossin in Mechelen, Belgium and the Cité de la Muette in Drancy, France. In these two case studies, architects were faced with a similar task, namely to design new museums adjacent to or on sites that were used as internment transit camps during the Second World War. Several scholars have argued that the commemoration of the Holocaust has set the precedent for memorials dealing with violence in recent decades.[54] Memorial museums as a relatively young form of

[53] See Bessel van der Kolk, *The Body Keeps the Score: Brain, Mind, and Body in the Healing of Trauma* (New York: Viking Penguin Group, 2014). In addition, recent research indicates that psychophysiological trauma can have intergenerational effects. See, for example, Rachel Yehuda et al., 'Holocaust exposure induced intergenerational effects on FKBP5 methylation', *Biological Psychiatry: A Journal of Psychiatric Neuroscience and Therapeutics* 80.5 (1 September 2016), 372–80. This is the first demonstration of an association of pre-conception parental trauma with epigenetic alterations evident in both the exposed parent and his or her offspring.

[54] Michael Rothberg, *Multidirectional Memory: Remembering the Holocaust in the Age of Decolonization* (Paolo Alto, CA: Stanford University Press, 2009).

commemoration emerged from the predicament of finding ways to commemorate the Holocaust in physical spaces associated with genocide. As museums are becoming more popular and technologically advanced, it is inviting to understand how these projects address the task of dealing with Holocaust sites in their spatial, material and operational logic, and how these projects set agendas for other forms of commemorative architecture dealing with other crimes and other victims.

The fifth chapter examines two projects dedicated to the centenary of the First World War: the 'Ring of Memory' at Notre Dame de Lorette near Arras in northern France and the project entitled 'Remembrance Park 14–18' in Flemish Belgium. The centenary has so far produced numerous commemorative activities and architectural projects across Europe. The two projects analysed here are inviting as examples of different design efforts undertaken during the centenary of the war. The chapter will look closely at the architectural, spatial and semantic qualities of the two projects to gain a better understanding of their significance in the societal and political environment of the twenty-first century in Western Europe.

In these later chapters, the discussion focuses less on theoretical and formal descriptions and more on problems of practice. Hence, architecture's emphasis on operating time and space as a medium of communication with visitors is the primary focus of the analysis of case studies. The architectural examples were selected based on the following questions: who is the commissioner and what is the context? What were the demands and expectations of the commissioners? What was the design solution to a particular problem and how did the design process develop? How does the realized building operate in practice and how does it affect the visitor?

The scope of this book is wide. But its remit is neither to be a summary of memorial architecture nor to develop a singular optic for understanding all contemporary memorials. Rather, the aim is to distinguish a set of issues, demonstrated by means of case studies, which are commonly addressed by commissioners and designers of contemporary memorials and, in this way, provide a framework for future projects. I argue that this way of approaching the topic can contribute to a better understanding of the design process and can increase the options that can be applied in practice. My aim is both to understand the history of the dialectical relationship between people and spaces of memory, and to add to it in the hope of recognizing meaningful ways to commemorate victims of war and violence.

PART I

Scaffolding Memory

1 | Commemorative Architecture since 1914

The notion of a modern monument is virtually a contradiction in terms; If it is a monument it is not modern, and if it is modern, it cannot be a monument.

Lewis Mumford[1]

Architecture's role is not to create strong foreground figures or feelings, but to establish frames of perception and horizons of understanding.

Juhani Pallasmaa[2]

Most nineteenth-century official monuments are figurative depictions of historical personages and narratives that reinforced the political agendas of nation-states. Monumentality was a constituent part of public commemorative projects that normally recalled victories and triumphs. Even though it was French revolutionaries who called for memorialization of each fallen individual, only occasionally did memorials mournfully commemorate dead soldiers.[3] Consequently, the public perceived monumental commemorative projects as conventional and state-oriented. After 1914, the relationship became problematic and continued to be incongruent after 1945, when the very existence of war commemoration was questioned. Lewis Mumford's statement, made in the late 1930s, captures this distinction between nineteenth-century and twentieth-century memorial architecture.

The commemorative memorial, as defined for the purposes of the present study, is a relatively novel and distinctly modern phenomenon. As explained in the introduction, this particular type of commemorative architecture developed in reaction to the unprecedented carnage of the

1 Lewis Mumford, *The Culture of Cities* (New York: Harcourt, Brace, and Company, 1938), p. 438.

2 Juhani Pallasmaa, *Encounters*, vol. 1: *Architectural Essays*, ed. Peter MacKeith (Helsinki: Rakkenustieto, 2012), p. 31.

3 For instance, King Ludwig I commemorated 30,000 dead soldiers killed during Napoleon's infamous 1812 Russian campaign with a large dark-coloured obelisk, designed by Leo van Klenze and installed at Karolinenplatz in Munich. See Adrian von Buttlar, *Leo van Klenze: Leben, Werk, Vision* (Munich: C. H. Beck, 1999), p. 70.

First World War, which occasioned the search for a kind of symbolic structure that religion and existing rituals were unable to provide. In many participating countries, the need for a new framework of mediation was expressed in new forms, such as the motif of the Tomb of the Unknown Soldier, alongside certain older motifs. Although the death toll and destruction of the First World War had no precedent, in the decades preceding it several particularly bloody conflicts challenged conventional forms of ascribing meaning to war, such as the American Civil War (1861–5). The North claimed it as a victory, and the defence of the Union was accomplished at an enormous price; but what about the dead of the South? Did they die for nothing or for a noble lost cause? Many chose the latter, and expressed this sentiment in a host of ways. Nationalist and imperialist sentiment framed German understandings of their victory in the Franco–Prussian War of 1870–1, although the erection of triumphal arches seemed to be problematic. A number of large ossuaries and battlefield monuments were established instead.[4]

Similarly, after the First World War, attempts at building monuments to victory were problematic, when millions of families focused on suffering and loss rather than on victory alone. This difficulty led to a fundamental shift in the purpose and form of war monuments, of great significance for later commemorative projects. The bloodbath of the First World War required attention not to us but to them – the endless armies of the dead. They were owed a debt that could never be repaid. In that simple statement we can find the key to the commemorative revolution that followed the First World War. As with most revolutions, a counter-revolution swiftly followed. We shall trace in this chapter some iconoclastic projects that move away from monumentality to a kind of universal – rather than national or imperial – form of commemoration. Then we shall turn to the resurrection of the older forms of monumentality in fascist Germany and Italy, which bluntly bypassed the innovative forms of war memorials developed in particular in the Imperial War Graves Commission cemeteries and in the sculptural work of Sir Edwin Lutyens.

Like monuments, memorials are highly political. As Sergiusz Michalski has demonstrated in his work on public monuments[5] – a term including the late nineteenth-century Parisian 'statuomania', the Bismarck cult and *Nationaldenkmäler* in Germany, as well as the 1990s upsurge in Holocaust

[4] See John Carman and Patricia Carman, *Bloody Meadows: Investigating Landscapes of Battle* (Stroud: Sutton Publishing Limited, 2006).

[5] Michalski, *Public Monuments*.

memorials – they have been used for various political purposes, and their aesthetics have routinely followed changes in the political climate. This chapter offers a succinct overview of the successive stages in the development of the architectural memorial, starting in the period of the two world wars and concluding with a discussion of the practices and debates of the early twenty-first century. In addition to sketching broad trends and important points of dispute and discussion, it will zoom in on a few influential projects that shaped subsequent practice, such as Jochen and Esther Shalev-Gerz's Monument Against Fascism (1986) and Maya Lin's Vietnam Veterans Memorial (1982).

1.1 Commemorating the First World War

Disruption, Universality and Non-Figuration

The term *Totenlandschaft*, originally associated with early nineteenth-century paintings by Caspar David Friedrich,[6] was also the term the Austrian soldier and writer Robert Musil used to describe the landscape of the Italian front after the First World War.[7] The overall horror of the war was documented by a number of other artists, many of whom experienced life in the trenches, for example Otto Dix, Fernand Léger, Egon Schiele, Otto Nussbaum and Paul Nash. Profound war experiences caused each of these artists to search for a different mode of representation.[8] Meanwhile, poignant artworks such as Käthe Kollwitz's sculpture *The Grieving Parents* (1932) and George Clausen's painting *Youth Mourning* (1916) depicted the omnipresent grief of survivors, embodied in human figures placed in sombre and featureless landscapes. Such private scenes of grief have been referred to as 'the invisible foundations of mourning upon which public commemorative activity, be it local, national, or imperial, was overlaid'.[9] In these works of art, individual identity was replaced by a symbolic representation of 'every mother's son'.

6 In 1813 the German poet Karl Theodor Körner referred to Friedrich's painting *Abbey Under Oak Trees* as a 'landscape of the dead'. Theodor Körner, 'Friedrichs Totenlandschaft', in Kurt Eberlein (ed.), *Caspar David Friedrich: Bekenntnisse* (Bremen: Europäischer Hochschulverlag GmbH&Co KG, 2010), pp. 260–1.

7 Geoff Dyer, *The Missing of the Somme* (London: Phoenix Press, 2001), p. 117.

8 Uwe M. Schneede, 'The avant-garde and the war: the visual arts between 1914 and 1918', in *1914/18 Retrospektiven, Paradoxien, Perspektiven 2014/18*, Goethe-Institut, November 2013, available at www.goethe.de/ges/prj/nzv/par/en12354686.htm, last accessed 26 October 2017.

9 Catherine Moriarty, '"Remnants of patriotism": the commemorative representation of the greatcoat after the first world war', *Oxford Art Journal*, 27.3 (2004), 291–309, 293.

The same universalist tendency was also present in the various efforts at commemorating those who perished, as illustrated by the development after the war of the Tomb of the Unknown Soldier and the 'Greatcoat' motifs in representing not the soldier but his discarded clothing. The public commemoration of the dead of the First World War was approached in an urgent manner, since countless bereaved men and women needed their losses to be acknowledged. Indeed, building war memorials and staging commemorative events in their presence served as official recognition of these losses. In addition to this task, public commemorations had a strongly defined long-term goal: 'to locate the war as an event of great significance within a historical continuum and to create an exemplar of collective service and duty for future generations'.[10] As a consequence, thousands of memorials were built on the territories of the countries most affected by the war.[11]

An intriguing development in most of these commemorative efforts was the disappearance of figural expression in official memorials. A good example is the so-called Greatcoat monuments, whose form departed from the monumental, with the overproportioned bodies of soldiers proudly wearing the well-known military coats worn in the war, to the intimate and tragic, in which the coat became a barrier between the living and the dead.[12] Eventually, the body itself disappeared altogether from the memorials and they became empty coats, symbolizing the absence of the body.[13] In many official commemorations there was a similar penchant for non-figuration in memorials, famously displayed in Lutyens' Cenotaph in London – a monument stripped of any national symbolism that was unexpectedly embraced among veterans and grieving surviving relatives. Numerous municipal and private monuments and memorials that thematized mourning by venerating the dead, however, incorporated figural representations. Depending on the country, depictions on these can arguably indicate changes in national consciousness about the war.

[10] Moriarty, 'Remnants of patriotism', 293.

[11] See Michel Ragon, *The Space of Death: A Study of Funerary Architecture, Decoration, and Urbanism*, trans. Alan Sheridan (Charlottesville, VA: University of Virginia Press, 1983), p. 107.

[12] See Moriarty, 'Remnants of patriotism'.

[13] Ibid. The symbolism of an empty coat was employed in funerary monuments in the nineteenth century, together with the motive of the *cheval d'honneur*. Some monuments represented a pile of things, among them a coat, typically discovered with the dead body of a soldier on the battlefield.

Not surprisingly in this atmosphere of bereavement, commemorative efforts to celebrate 'triumph' were overshadowed by a new type of memorial to fallen soldiers, the Tomb of the Unknown Soldier. In France, for example, monuments initially conceived to glorify the French victory and to honour military leaders soon became memorials to the suffering of millions of families of soldiers who never returned. Together with the transition from monumental sculptural representation to mournful lament, in which the heroic soldier became an abstract form, the representation of death in public architecture took a new turn. Numerous battlefield memorials, usually consisting of cemeteries with uniform gravestones and a few memorial sculptures, powerfully translated the mechanized destruction of men into a palpable reality.

War Cemeteries

Post-war governments also faced the task of organizing military burial places for the innumerable war casualties. It was common to have graves for soldiers whose names can be identified, a practice guaranteed by peace treaty since 1871. Those who cannot be found are commemorated in the memorials for the missing – a number that often exceeds the soldiers memorialized. In this way, the political role of the soldier cemeteries and memorials for the missing 'fuse every fallen citizen with the identity of the nation, for which the death of these individuals serves as a pledge'.[14] Already during the war, the British Army had created a Graves Registration Commission to document and mark the location of graves for those killed in battle. After the war, the Imperial War Graves Commission took on the responsibility to lay out cemeteries for the fallen British soldiers of the First World War, for which it employed the architect Edwin Lutyens. Having to represent death on such a large scale, and often of complete anonymity, Lutyens opted for abstraction of forms in his work for the Commission. Hence, he designed the *Stone of Remembrance*, a 'non-normative, universal architectural expression of an imperishable mass, which perpetuates commemoration in all eternity'.[15] The massive horizontal white stone, a recurring feature of large British First World War cemeteries, is reminiscent of an altar. However, its non-figurative, universal symbolism had to be accompanied with some more explicit forms in

[14] Koselleck, *Sediments of Time*, p. 218.

[15] Jeroen Geurst, *Cemeteries of the Great War by Sir Edwin Lutyens* (Rotterdam: 010 Publishers, 2010), p. 22.

order to emphasize the scale of commemoration. As a result, Lutyens' abstract design was accompanied by other symbolic forms, adapted to the varying conditions and specificities of particular cemeteries.[16] These memorials, in their form and inclusivity, recast the older triumphal character of monumental designs into a memorial to the ubiquity of disappearance and death, as was the case with the Thiepval Memorial in northern France, where Lutyens designed a 43 m-high arch resting on 16 brick piers inscribed with the names of missing soldiers. Unlike the Arc de Triomphe, or other memorials to the First World War inspired by classical architecture,[17] Thiepval's arches create an interplay of hallways around the central edifice – the *Stone of Remembrance* installed on the main east–west axis of the memorial. In this position the stone adds to the overall atmosphere, reminiscent of a Hall of Honour, but stripped of every trace of triumphalism.[18] Located in the area of the Battle of the Somme, Thiepval's staggering scale accentuates the *genius loci* and its importance. The memorial is visible from afar and rises prominently over the fields of the Somme. At the same time, its interior provides spaces for personal encounters with the individual names inscribed on the walls. The memorial demonstrates simplicity and austerity as key aesthetic features for First World War commemoration. This was the premise for all British battlefield memorials and cemeteries. Their highly recognizable uniformity was essential for two reasons: the equality of death and the 'intention of ignoring national differences among soldiers who fought for an imperial identity'.[19] These cemeteries remain limited to the long rows of white unified tombstones, in the manner of the *artificial infinite*, underlining the enormous waste of life but also enhancing the unity and equality of the 'glorious dead'. Only by approaching each individual tomb at these cemeteries is the identity of a single death revealed, except for the unknown whose lost identities are immortalized with inscriptions on the tombstones, powerful mnemonic codes to represent the reality of a death that was so harrowing as to strip men of their identity.

16 Ibid.

17 For instance, the Asiago War Memorial on Leiten Hill (1938) by Venetian architect Orfeo Rossato and Çanakkale Martyrs' Memorial (1958), the Dardanelles monument to the Turkish victory against England in 1916 and the Turkish soldiers who fell in the Battle of Gallipoli (for which Feridun Kip, Ismail Utklar and Dogan Erginbas were awarded first prize at a competition in 1944).

18 See Geurst, *Cemeteries*, pp. 414–15.

19 Ahenk Yilmaz, 'Memorialization on war-broken ground: Gallipoli war cemeteries and memorials designed by Sir John James Burnet', *Journal of the Society of Architectural Historians*, 73.3 (September 2014), 328–46, 335.

Simultaneously, the American Battle Monuments Commission erected 11 monuments and memorials on European soil. These memorials were conceived with the intention to be 'both sufficiently attractive to induce Americans not to repatriate their own kin and sufficiently impressive to hold their own against the larger and more numerous cemeteries of other nations'.[20] American architects like John Russell Pope and Paul Philippe Cret, who also served as a consulting architect for the Commission, designed a large number of commemorative projects in a style influenced by antiquity, and in some instances ancient Egypt – a well-travelled form for the contemplation of death. Pope's funerary designs displayed his ability to manipulate the emotional effect of elemental forms.[21] The victorious Allied forces indeed relied on the classical style, which was perceived to be the most appropriate language to communicate order, as opposed to the chaos of the First World War.[22] 'Stripped Classicism' was an established style for the architecture of commemoration, which employed basic elements of classical architecture in order to augment austerity and solemnity. Perhaps the most inspiring reference in this tradition was the Roman Pantheon.[23] The motif of the oculus already appeared in Reginald Blomfield's design for the Menin Gate in Ypres (1927). One embittered reading of this memorial, by soldier poet Siegfried Sassoon, termed it 'a sepulchre of crime'.[24] Blomfield's vision was entirely different. His aim was to commemorate thousands of dead soldiers without a known grave, in an unusually deep neoclassical arched structure, reminiscent of visionary architectures from the eighteenth century.[25]

[20] Elizabeth G. Grossman, 'Architecture for a public client: the monuments and chapels of the American Battle Monuments Commission', *Journal of the Society of Architectural Historians*, 42.3 (May 1984), 119–44, 120.

[21] Pope's design for a tomb for Peter Fenelon Colier in 1910 at Wickatunk, New Jersey, was described as 'an admirable exercise in the use of architectural form to create a hauntingly contemplative locus'. Steven McLeod Bedford, *John Russell Pope: Architect of Empire*, 1st edn (New York: Rizzoli, 1998), pp. 122–3.

[22] See Franco Borsi, *The Monumental Era: European Architecture and Design 1929–1939* (London: Lund Humphries, 1987).

[23] The fascination with the Pantheon can be traced to the years preceding the First World War, for instance in Heman Sörgel's design for a 'Predigerkirsche auf Kreisgrundriss mit Pantheon-Kuppel' (1912). An earlier example is Henri Labrouste's competition entry from 1841 for the tomb of Napoleon Bonaparte.

[24] Siegfried Sassoon, 'On passing the new Menin Gate', in Tim Kendall (ed.), *The Oxford Handbook of British and Irish War Poetry* (New York: Oxford University Press, 2007), p. 551.

[25] See Helen Rosenau (ed.), *Boullée & Visionary Architecture*, trans. Sheila de Vallée (London: Academy Editions; New York: Harmony Books, 1974), p. 23.

From Social Democracy to Fascism in Germany and Italy

Meanwhile, German war cemeteries were attuned to older German pastoral traditions, in which the spirit of the dead would inhabit 'Heroes' groves' of trees. Käthe Kollwitz felt that they had to be sombre and melancholic, unpleasant and without any of the trappings of heroism – just like the war was.[26] In 1919 the German War Graves Commission (Volksbund Deutsche Kriegsgräberfürsorge) was formed out of necessity since the Weimar Republic was neither politically nor economically in a position to take care of the graves of the soldiers killed in action during the First World War.[27] Robert Tischler, the chief architect of the institution, designed these cemeteries to blend in with the landscape and predominantly used rugged masonry and dark sandstone to achieve this. Following strict design guidelines, all German war cemeteries were demonstrations of the everlasting German spirit and art expressed through natural materials and trees. For this purpose, mostly dolmen structures were used, as well as large trees such as oaks and beeches to reinforce the reference to the mythic symbolism of the Teutonic forests and their endurance through the ages.[28] By combining landscape architecture and uniform design solutions, the Volksbund believed that after a century or two the cemeteries would become a part of 'eternal nature', while the former enemy's cemeteries 'would have fallen into despair'.[29] The Volksbund praised its own modesty and peaceful approach in communing with the dead, and criticized the megalomaniac size of the cemetery projects that were taking shape in France. American cemeteries did not appeal to them, appearing repetitive in their composition.

It is important here to note two distinctive features of German commemorative design. The first is that the German dead lay on enemy territory, and former enemies were loath to grant German organizations more than minimal terrain to bury their dead. That is why so many

26 Käthe Kollwitz, 'June 23, 1932. In Belgium', in Hans Kollwitz (ed.), *The Diary and Letters of Kaethe Kollwitz*, trans. Richard and Clara Winston (Evanston, IL: Northwestern University Press, 1955), p. 122.

27 See Volksbund Deutsche Kriegsgräberfürsorge, 'Reconciliation above the graves – Work for Peace'. See 'A Brief Introduction', Volksbund Deutsche Kriegsgräberfürsorge, available at www.volksbund.de/en/volksbund.html, last accessed 2 November 2017.

28 Gunnar Brands, 'From WWI cemeteries to the Nazi "fortresses of the dead"', in Joachim Wolschke-Bulmahn (ed.), *Places of Commemoration: Search for Identity and Landscape Design* (Washington, DC: Dumbarton Oaks Research Library and Collection, 2001), pp. 215–56.

29 Ibid., p. 231. While in Allied cemeteries tombstones were engraved with individual names and inscriptions containing epigrams or religious affiliation, the German war cemeteries only recorded names and regiments so as to emphasize 'the unity of the nation'.

German cemeteries have mass graves in them. Secondly, the Volksbund was a private institution, not a state agency or an imperial association like the Imperial (later Commonwealth) War Graves Commission. The Volksbund was a representative not of the German state, but of the Protestant voluntary tradition. To this day, student volunteers maintain these cemeteries.

On German soil, the story of commemorative practices was different. The National Socialists destroyed memorials and monuments that were too defeatist or pacifist and instead preserved designs with heroic pathos. This was the case with Ludwig Mies van der Rohe's Liebknecht-Luxemburg Memorial in Berlin-Friedrichsfelde (1926) – a valuable example of modernist memorial that used materiality as a reference to terror – in this case a symbolic brick wall as the usual background against which executions of revolutionaries were performed, composed from the remains of buildings destroyed during the Spartacist uprising. Another notable example that shared the same destiny with other 'degenerate art' was Walter Gropius' Monument to the March Dead (Märzgefallenen-Denkmal, 1922), placed on Weimar's central cemetery to commemorate the dead of the reactionary Kapp Putsch in Weimar. Perceived as 'light from the bottom of the grave' and recognized as an important work in the architect's career, the memorial was later rebuilt.[30]

Many First World War memorials were repurposed for the Nazi nationalist rhetoric. This was the case in Munich with the war memorial (*Kriegerdenkmal*, 1924) in Hofgarten, designed by Karl Knappe, Bernhard Bleeker Thomas Wechs and Ulrich Finsterwalder, which commemorated the 13,000 Bavarian soldiers (their names were inscribed on memorial plaques) who died in the war.[31] The structure – a sculpture of a dead soldier in a crypt-like space located on a sunken plaza and enclosed by 12 massive pillars – was intended to link German First World War deaths to ideas of reinstating Frederick Barbarossa's medieval German Reich (Figure 1.1).[32] The reconstruction and replacement of the Sleeping Soldier spurred controversies, since the memorial was used by the Nazis during the Second World War. The explicit depiction of marching soldiers in one of

30 See Klaus-Jürgen Winkler and Herman van Bergeijk, *Das Märzgefallenen-Denkmal* (Weimar: Bauhaus-Universität Weimar, 2004).

31 See Gavriel D. Rosenfeld, *Munich and Memory: Architecture, Monuments, and the Legacy of the Third Reich* (Berkeley, CA: University of California Press, 2000), pp. 114–16.

32 Ibid.

Figure 1.1 War memorial in Munich's Hofgarten (1924), Munich; Karl Knappe, Bernhard Bleeker, Thomas Wechs and Ulrich Finsterwalder.
Photo: Almir Baždar

its reliefs was seen as a visual representation of the ideology of the myth of the eternal Reich. With the rise of fascism, this rhetoric became official.

Recognized for their power to convey political ideals, public monuments and war memorials became media for the establishment of the Third Reich's political outlook. German architect Friedrich Tamms described the vision of a commemorative structure worthy of the Nazi ideal:

> It must be rigorous, of sphere, clear, indeed classical form. It must be simple. It must have the quality of 'touching the heavens'. It must transcend everyday utilitarian considerations. It must be generous in its construction, built for the ages according to the best principles of the trade. In practical terms, it must have no purpose but instead be the vehicle of an idea. It must have an element of the unapproachable in it that fills people with admiration and awe. It must be impersonal because it is not the work of an individual, but the symbol of a community bound together by a common ideal.[33]

Monuments and memorials hence became popular venues for Nazi gatherings, as was the case with the New Guardhouse (Neue Wache) in Berlin, located at Unter den Linden, initially designed as a guardhouse for the guards of the Crown Prince of Prussia. After 1933, Nazis added a cross in

[33] Friedrich Tamms in 'The Law of Monumentality' (1944), quoted in Berthold Hinz, *Art in the Third Reich* (New York: Pantheon Books, 1979), p. 236.

the interior and the building became a focal point for official ceremonies of the Third Reich.[34] Commemorative structures answered Hitler's demand for immensity and political symbols in spatial design, of the kind demonstrated in Speer's 'Cathedral of Light' in Nuremberg that 'reached an apex in the art of influencing people'.[35] Here Mumford's distinction between monuments and modernity collapses completely. Similar zeal was invested in more permanent projects, for example the Honor Temples (*Ehrentempel*) or 'martyrs' temples' in Munich, designed by Paul Ludwig Troost, which were central points during many Nazi festivities.[36] The ideals of virtue and modesty, as expressed through landscape architecture in Volksbund cemeteries, were remodelled into a new type of burial place: the so-called *Totenburgen*, or fortresses of the dead. Even the commemorative practice of honouring the Unknown Soldier, based on the notion of equality of sacrifice, was transformed into a weapon for establishing the cult of military leadership, as exemplified in the appropriation of the Tannenberg Memorial (1927) in East Prussia. Hitler's orders for the redesign, after removing the tombs of the unknown soldiers, focused on the landscape and aimed to achieve an ideal of untouched nature. As a result, however, the artificiality of the work was apparent since 'natural' meant 'supporting nature in her insufficient attempt to produce a stage-like setting for architecture'.[37]

Comparable values were present in the commemorative architecture of fascist Italy, which also aimed to reinforce nationalistic political ideals through the exploitation of narratives of the past, be they mythical or historical. Experiments with a fascist style in various creative fields were encouraged, for instance in the exhibition of the 'Tenth Anniversary of the

[34] In 1969 the building was officially rededicated to the 'Victims of Fascism and Militarism' and received the function of a Tomb of the Unknown Soldier, with the remains of one Wehrmacht soldier and one German-fascist combatant interred together and topped with a glass cube with an eternal fire. Military statues of Prussian generals that used to stand in front of the building were all removed. In 1993, after the fall of the GDR, Chancellor Helmut Kohl dedicated the memorial to the 'victims of war and rule of oppression' ('Opfer von Krieg und Gewaltherrschaft'). See Koselleck, *Sediments of Time*, p. 243.

[35] Albert Speer quoted in Leon Krier (ed.), *Albert Speer, Architecture 1932–1942* (Brussels: Archives d'architecture moderne, 1985), p. 214.

[36] The two structures were erected in 1935 for the Nazi victims of the failed Beer Hall Putsch in Munich in 1923. Both temples were designed as roofless atria with a heavy cornice, containing black sarcophagi with the remains of the sixteen party members who had been killed. In 1946 the main architectural features of the temples were destroyed by the US army as part of the denazification program. In 2007 a small plaque was added explaining the original purpose of the temples.

[37] Brands, 'From WWI cemeteries', 240.

Fascist Revolution' opened in Rome in 1932.[38] Mario Sironi, a prominent artist at the time, had a significant role in designing the exhibition.[39] His *Galleria dei Fasci*, a monumental space in a sequence of spaces designed by different architects, was intended as a transition to the 'final rite of communion', leading to The Shrine of the Martyrs by Adalberto Libera and Antonio Valente. In line with the Fascistic tendency to produce ritual values through the use of technology, Libera worked under a motto 'the machine as a work of art' and explored religious traditions to help establish fascism as a 'religion of the State'. This part of the exhibition was laden with grandiose symbolism and heavy-handed theatrical effects. In the centre, a gigantic cross with the inscription 'Per la Patria Immortale' ('For the Immortal Homeland'), enclosed by a circular space composed of six horizontal bands lit from behind, rose from a 'pool of blood'. On the walls the word 'Presente' was inscribed,[40] in reference to martyrs who were, like their homeland, immortal. The theatricality of the exhibition, made possible by then-modern technologies combining lighting, music and other effects, was intended to evoke a cinematic experience and place the visitor as an actor on the stage. Here the very old was mediated by all the new technologies of the day.

Similarly, the Military Sacrarium of Redipuglia (1938) in the province of Gorizia, Italy, designed by Giovanni Greppi and Giannino Castiglioni, includes a rising set of steps evoking the scale of the loss, as well as a tomb containing thousands of bodies of fallen Italian soldiers. Each terrace progresses upward with the inscription 'Presente' above the list of names of the dead martyrs, evoking the old funeral rite in which the body of the deceased is surrounded by his comrades, upon which the eldest in the group pronounces the names of the others who confirm their presence by saying 'presente'.

Similarly, a purely symbolic space intended to communicate a higher purpose – the 1938 proposal by Rino Valdameri, director of the Brerra Academy in Milan, to create an institution that would serve as a

[38] See Francesco Garofalo and Luca Veresane, *Adalberto Libera* (New York: Princeton Architectural Press, 2002), p. 53.

[39] Sironi, a key figure in organizing the exhibition, was probably influenced by Ed Lissitzky's work for the side facade and the interior installation for the 'Pressa' exhibition in the USSR Pavilion in Cologne in 1928. See Garofalo and Veresane, *Adalberto Libera*, p. 30.

[40] The word 'presente' was used in other fascist memorials as well and symbolized the military virtue of obedience, for instance in the Sacrarium at Redipuglia, where the ubiquitous inscriptions of 'Presente' starkly represent the scale of death into which soldiers patriotically marched.

celebration of the great Italian poet Dante – was welcomed by the Italian government at the time as a project that 'possessed a dimension for the Italians that superseded political symbolism and patriotism'.[41] Giuseppe Terragni and Pietro Lingeri were appointed to make a model for the project after an audience with the Duce in November of the same year. Intended to transcend the tenets of fascism and the teachings of Christian philosophy, the 'Danteum' was planned to be built in Rome between the Basilica of Maxentius and Constantine, a symbol of ancient Rome, and the medieval Torre dei Conti, a symbol of the Middle Ages. Terragni and Lingeri strived to achieve a 'value of "absolute" geometric beauty'.[42] This resulted in a concept of *architecture parlante* with a succession of symbolic spaces isolated from the outside world. The plans for the project (never realized) show a vast, free-standing wall at the entrance, from which a passageway ascends towards the interior. Inside, a 'forest' of marble columns serves as an introduction to three temple-like spaces, arranged according to the *Divine Comedy*: Inferno, Purgatory and Paradise. In what seems to be a highly calculated, mathematical approach, it is surprising how much attention was given to spaces for contemplation and the psychological impact of the symbolically laden architectural elements on visitors.

The Inferno space in particular conveyed an 'atmosphere that influences the visitor and appears physically to weigh upon his mortal person, so that he is moved to experience the "trip" as Dante did'.[43] Passing through transitional spaces between the main rooms, one would proceed towards the Purgatory space in which a 'sensation of comfort'[44] pervaded as one looked up to the geometric openings that gave the spectator a view of the sky. The Paradise room opened with glass columns – contrasting with the rest of the building in its attempt at dematerialization. Here Terragni aimed at the destruction of materiality and architectural forms, rather than creating the 'absence of such forms'.[45] In contrast, his earlier works, namely the war memorial at Erba Incino (1932) and the Monument to Roberto Sarfatti in Col d'Echele (1935) – in which the throne becomes a memorial stone overlooking steps enveloped by the asymmetrical composition of a massive pedestal – display heavy materiality and use the

[41] Thomas L. Schumacher, *The Danteum: Architecture, Poetics, and Politics under Italian Fascism* (London: Triangle Architectural Publishing, 1993), p. 39.
[42] Ibid., p. 46.
[43] Ibid., p. 49. Schumacher quotes Giuseppe Terragni's *Relazione sul Danteum*, unpublished manuscript, 1938.
[44] Ibid., p. 53. [45] Ibid.

metaphor of the stairway as an element of the holy ritual of paying respect to the human sacrifice. The so-called scala santa was a favoured theme in Italian memorial designs after the First World War.

Italian experimentation being a notable exception, most nations and ideologies preferred timeless ancient forms for their public architecture commemorating the war dead. While designers and artists still grappled with the insurmountable trauma of the recent war, the threat of resurging nationalism and renewed warfare permeated every aspect of life. When, in 1933, Hitler was appointed as chancellor of Germany, the art of Käthe Kollwitz and numerous others was deemed 'degenerate'.[46] In this ominous atmosphere, the Swiss artist Alberto Giacometti presented in 1934 a large-scale, highly stylized female figure supported by a cage-like throne, with hands positioned as if holding an object. The object that the figure appears to be offering is missing, as indicated by the title of this Surrealist work: *Hands Holding the Void*. Descriptions of the work assert that the artist 'evokes a lost object, forever sought and never recovered'.[47] In an uncanny way, the subject of the work presaged many facets of commemoration in the years after the Second World War.

1.2 The Aftermath of the Second World War

Ruins, Concentration Camps, Civilian Deaths and the Search for Memorial Expression

Even though the actual scale of destruction in Europe only became clear decades after the war had ended, the commemoration of victims of the Nazi crimes in former concentration camps started before 1945.[48] In some cases, memorials were erected as spontaneous and impromptu reactions of liberated people, for example in Buchenwald, where a wooden obelisk was

[46] In November 1937, an exhibition entitled 'Entartete Kunst' (Degenerate Art) was organized in Munich by the Nazi Party. Over 650 works, including books, were exhibited with accompanying criticism and derisive text, in order to clarify what type of art was considered unacceptable. Most of the works had been confiscated from German public museums, including the works of artists like Marc Chagall, Wassily Kandinsky and Paul Klee.

[47] 'Hands Holding the Void (Invisible Object)' [gallery label text], Museum of Modern Art Collection, New York, available at www.moma.org/collection/object.php?object_id=81849, last accessed 30 October 2017.

[48] Kathrin Hoffmann-Curtius, 'Memorials for the Dachau concentration camp', *Oxford Art Journal*, 21.2 (1998), 21–44.

erected upon the liberation of the camp in 1945.[49] Most of these memorials were realized as memorial plaques and figurative sculptures, but also as experiential architectural spaces that were aimed at transnational audiences. These memorials had to address unparalleled and at times unanswerable questions as to the nature of what they had to commemorate. Artists, architects and other designers developed a new repertoire of symbols, forms and materials in their confrontation with these sites of suffering and mass death.[50]

The Holocaust marked the beginning of a new stage in the creation of commemorative edifices. A quest for new forms started in which survivors and states collaborated through international competitions inviting international proposals. One such example was the process of commemoration at one of the first Nazi concentration camps at Dachau in 1950. Commemorative efforts at Dachau began upon liberation with a project of staggering proportions, proposed by local officials in response to the American occupying powers' demand for a memorial on a nearby graveyard where corpses found in Dachau had been transported. The proposal, never realized, consisted of two 15 m-high columns, one crowned with a cross and the other with the Star of David.[51] In the same year, sculptor Karl Knappe presented a proposal for a 'monument of liberation', conceived as a space for contemplation and mourning.[52] Knappe's design offered a high platform with a view of the surroundings, and comprised an obelisk rising from a semi-circular base containing rooms with memorial plaques. There was no reference to the history of the site, since the designer believed that, to experience the memorial, it 'would have been sufficient to allude to the horrors in the large lower rooms, and not eternally block the road to freedom and salvation with remembrance'.[53] In spite of the collective feelings of denial that many Germans clung to at the time, the proposal was dismissed as unsuitable and reminiscent of National Socialist projects. Instead, propositions were made in favour of utilitarian structures as a

[49] In 1995 Horst Hoheisel's 'Warm memorial', consisting of a concrete ground plate warmed up to human body temperature, was placed on a spot where the temporary obelisk was standing.

[50] Harold Marcuse, 'Holocaust memorials: the emergence of a genre', *American Historical Review*, 115.1 (February 2010), 53–89, 54.

[51] Harold Marcuse, *Legacies of Dachau: The Uses and Abuses of a Concentration Camp, 1933–2001* (Cambridge: Cambridge University Press, 2001), pp. 189–91.

[52] Knappe was known as the creator of Munich's war memorial and for this project he used a monument to German Freikorps, in Upper Silesia, as a reference. See Hoffmann-Curtius, 'Memorials'.

[53] Marcuse, *Legacies of Dachau*, p. 191.

more positive way of honouring the dead, such as 'a residential settlement, a hospital or an orphanage for the survivors, coupled with a memorial grove and a simple monument'.[54] Notice the reference to pre-Nazi practices in this list of 'appropriate' forms of commemoration.

A courtroom for the trial of the Nazi leaders in Nuremberg illustrated the architectural and functional simplicity that in the immediate post-war period was considered proper for facing the mechanism of the defeated regime. The redesigned space integrated data and photographs of the Nazi camps, and was transformed into 'a kind of retrospective situation room, in which the victors took apart for the vanquished the mechanisms of their lost empire'.[55] Together with the start of a new rhetoric that promoted peace and reconciliation, the notion of *Mahnmal*, as a concept of commemoration that had to address the new totality of warfare which largely affected civilian victims, came to prominence in the post-WWII period. Since there were very few precedents for remembering civilian victims, discussions started taking place in the affected countries about appropriate commemorative forms.[56] Initially, priority was given to war ruins and their preservation, as tokens of warning against the carnage of war.[57] While responses to the tragedy of the war were significant in art, literature and philosophy, architects refrained from reflecting on the devastation left by war in general, and the Holocaust in particular.[58] The reconstruction of many demolished cities had priority, with some instances of leaving ruins untouched.[59]

[54] Ibid.

[55] Jean-Louis Cohen, *Architecture in Uniform. Designing and Building for the Second World War*, Canadian Centre for Architecture (New Haven, CT and London: Yale University Press, 2011), p. 386. The American architect Dan Kiley was commissioned by the Presentation Division of the Office of Strategic Services that had the task to set up the trial, which lasted from 20 November 1945 to 1 October 1946. Kiley's task was to rebuild the courthouse at Nuremberg.

[56] Monuments that glorified military tradition could not possibly serve such a role. In fact, in May 1946 a directive by the Allied Control Council ordered the demolition of all monuments that glorified war. See Stefan Goebel, *The Great War and Medieval Memory: War, Remembrance and Medievalism in Britain and Germany, 1914-1940* (Cambridge: Cambridge University Press, 2007), p. 293.

[57] Goebel, *The Great War*, p. 295. In 1944 an issue of *The Architectural Review* magazine under the slogan 'Save our Ruins' published the following argument: 'It is proposed that a few of the bombed churches in Britain be selected to remain with us as ruins, essential in the state in which bombing has left them, that they be laid out and planted appropriately, and that they be regarded as permanent places of open-air worship, meditation and recreation, as national war memorials of this war and focal points of picturesque delight in the planned surroundings of the post-war world.' Cohen, *Architecture in Uniform*, p. 385.

[58] Rosenfeld, *Munich and Memory*, p. 47.

[59] As was the case in Oradur-sur-Glane in France. Other well-known examples of commemorative efforts that involved the question of the preservation of ruins are the Kaiser Wilhelm-Gedächtniskirche in Berlin and Coventry Cathedral.

The names of the dead soldiers were added to the existing First World War memorials. This was also true for West Germany and the later GDR where many memorials were destroyed or altered by victors or left-wing groups. In West Germany, civilian deaths and later even deaths from concentrations camps were included in memorial inscriptions. While analysing typologies of German and French memorials to understand political veneration of the dead and its effect on the consciousness-forming about the two world wars in these countries, Reinhart Koselleck regarded this practice as a 'fundamental transformation in consciousness' arguing that 'war and terror came to be memorialized in conjunction, and this brought together different strands of identity whose minimal commonality consists only of a kind of despairing meaningless.'[60] Through a centralized perspective, both in France and West Germany memorials provided a continuous space of memory as a base for the future: by remembering liberators from fascism, victims of the concentration camps and resistance related to the workers' movement, as was the case with new memorials erected in West Germany.

In the immediate post-war years and with the Cold War gearing up, debates about the aesthetic of post-war monuments were marked by a distinct dichotomy between socialist countries and the West – the former preferred figural expressions, whereas abstract forms were more popular in the latter.[61] At the same time, significant experimental ways of commemoration started to emerge across Europe in response to the staggering scale of the overall destruction.[62] Conversely, in what began as a race with Nazi Germany towards gigantism, the commemorative efforts of Soviet architects continued to produce projects of enormous scale, rich in symbolic figuration and patriotism – Yakow Belopolsky's Soviet War Memorial at Treptower Park in Berlin (1949) is one example. Among them were several unrealized projects, such as design proposals yielded by a competition for a 'Pantheon of the Heroes of the Great Patriotic War' (1943) in Moscow.

[60] Koselleck, *Sediments of Time*, p. 223.

[61] Robert Burstow, 'The limits of modernist art as a "weapon of the Cold War": reassessing the unknown patron of the Monument to the Unknown Political Prisoner', *The Oxford Art Journal*, 20.1 (January 1997), 68–80.

[62] In Europe, 19 million civilians died in the war, not including over 6 million Jews and others killed in concentration camps. In the Soviet Union, 70,000 villages and 1,700 towns were destroyed; 75 per cent of Berlin was in rubble. Between the Soviet Union and Germany, 45 million people were homeless. In Poland, there were some 200,000 orphans. In Vienna, 87,000 women were raped by Soviet soldiers in the three weeks after the Red Army's arrival; more than that in Berlin. See Tony Judt, *Postwar: A History of Europe since 1945* (New York: Penguin Press, 2005), pp. 16–23.

A rare example of an early post-war effort in the Eastern bloc to commemorate the catastrophe in a different way was a project starting in 1948 for a modernist apartment complex, the quarter-memorial of South Muranów, on the site of the former Warsaw Ghetto, in close proximity to Nathan Rapoport's *Monument of the Ghetto Heroes* (1948).[63] The Polish architect Bohdan Lachert used the rubble, not uncommon in Warsaw at the time,[64] of the ghetto's former buildings, demolished by the Nazis during the uprising in 1943, for the foundations of a functionalist residential district–one of the last examples of Polish functionalism, which after 30 years of development was replaced by Stalinist monumental and eclectic socialist realism.[65] Lachert, an advocate of a break with traditionalism, was a member of a group of urban planners and architects appointed to work on a project on the grounds of the former Warsaw Ghetto. Works were initiated by the new Communist government, which aimed to display their triumph over both fascism and capitalism. Next to the use of detritus, the architect intended to leave the front of the building un-stuccoed, with the exposed dark red bricks as a symbolic reference to the blood of the ghetto's victims. On these grounds, the complex has been recognized as 'the boldest attempt in post-war Warsaw to bring Polish and Jewish suffering together into a single progressive, socialist memory'.[66] The original design was perceived as too monotonous and barrack-like by Communist party officials and was 'beautified' through the use of historicizing facade elements.

At the time, the architectural discourse was focused on the topic of monumentality, underlined by the wartime text of Sigfried Giedion, Fernand Léger and José Sert, entitled 'Nine points of Monumentality'. The manifesto stressed the importance of the communicative aspects of architecture, proposing that the need for symbols and monumental

[63] News of the Warsaw Ghetto Uprising reached Rapoport in the Soviet Union. Already in the summer of 1943, he began to conceive a monument which Stalinist officials proclaimed too Jewish and, therefore, rejected. The realized monument is an adjusted design and a result of a collaboration with the architect Leon Marek Suzin.

[64] See Katarzyna Uchowicz, 'Reading Muranów: memory of a place/memory of an architect. Commentary on the post-war work of Bohdan Lachert', *RIHA Journal*, 0108, special issue (31 December 2014), available at www.riha-journal.org/articles/2014/2014-oct-dec/special-issue-contemporary-art-and-memory-part-1/uchowicz-muranow-en, last accessed 31 October 2017.

[65] Wojciech Lésnikowski, *East European Modernism: Architecture in Czechoslovakia, Hungary, and Poland between the Wars 1919–1939*, 1st edn (London: Thames & Hudson Ltd, 1996), p. 293.

[66] Michael Meng, *Shattered Spaces: Encountering Jewish Ruins in Postwar Germany and Poland* (Cambridge, MA: Harvard University Press, 2011), p. 79.

expressions is, in fact, most natural to man. They called for a new monumentality that was different from the 'pseudo-monumentality' of the nineteenth century, thereby both subscribing to and subverting the position that Mumford developed.

After the war, however, monumental architecture seemed to oppose the democratic values promoted in the West. For example, during the 1948 *Architectural Review* symposium, 'In Search of New Monumentality', intimacy of architectural scale was preferred to the bombastic forms of the past.[67] Memorial structures were welcomed as transitional forms between architecture and sculpture. This attitude commanded a substantial following throughout the 1950s, when international discussions about the integration of arts and architecture proliferated.[68]

Arguments against traditional methods of commemoration were also dominant in the American context, where many were in favour of so-called Memorials That Live.[69] It was thought that memorial projects, like all architecture, had to be useful and serve community life. Designs considered to be purely symbolic were often dismissed on the basis of their uselessness. Lewis Mumford was among those who argued that the preservation of memory represents a higher purpose, and is only possible to achieve through specific projects of art, not through useful everyday structures. In this view, the notion of a modern monument had to be reconfigured.

In 1952, Herbert Read introduced his famous notion of the 'geometry of fear', and a year later the international competition for a Monument to the Unknown Political Prisoner, organized by the Institute of Contemporary Arts in London stirred international interest in the aesthetic of commemorative forms.[70] The number of projects submitted, a staggering 3,500, confirmed the significance of the subject. The contemporary penchant for

[67] See Gregor Paulsson et al., 'In search of a new monumentality: a symposium', *The Architectural Review*, 104.621 (September 1948), 117–30.

[68] Patrick Amsellem, 'Remembering the past, constructing the future. The memorial to the deportation in Paris and experimental commemoration after the Second World War' (unpublished PhD thesis, New York University, 2007), p. 204.

[69] This was the title of a widely used pamphlet on living memorials published by the American Commission for Living War Memorials (ACLWM) in 1944. The pamphlet served both as propaganda and as instruction for communities engaged with building living memorials. See Andrew Shanken, 'Planning memory: living memorials in the United States during World War II', *The Art Bulletin*, 84.1 (2002), 130–47, 133.

[70] The chosen theme of the competition was intended 'to pay tribute to those individuals who, in many countries and in diverse political situations, had dared to offer their liberty and their lives for the cause of human freedom'. See 'Reg Butler: the working model for "The Unknown Political Prisoner" 1955–6', in *The Tate Gallery 1978–80: Illustrated Catalogue of Acquisitions*,

crossovers between sculptural monuments and architecture was demonstrated in the winning design, by the British sculptor Reg Butler. In a tripartite, symbolically laden composition, the artist integrated traditional sculpture and abstract solutions, eschewing direct representation of the prisoner but instead implying the prisoner's sacrifice through the gaze of the sculptural group.[71] Butler was particularly concerned with the position of the spectator in terms of her interaction with the structure. The proposal was never realized, due to the political climate and the Soviet characterization of the competition as suspicious and in furtherance of the Cold War.[72] However, the results of the competition were invaluable for the development of later commemorative expression.[73]

For example, the entry by the Swiss architect and artist Max Bill reintroduced two aspects in memorial design: the relation to the context and engagement with the visitor through bodily experience. The memorial was designed as a composition of three cubes forming a central spatial triangle where a steel column was placed. Even though the competition brief did not offer a specific location for the future design, Bill's proposal was conceived in relation to a public space. Many interrelated elements of the proposal composed an interactive design in which the spectator would have been a participant and a contributor to the overall concept.[74] Conceiving the memorial as a structure of human scale, Bill reaffirmed the idea of space as an active realm, with the use of reflective material for the inner column, the materialization of the cubes as processional stairways, and the addition of benches that extended the memorial's space towards its surroundings.

There are two notable examples in Paris that also departed from triumphal commemoration, a common approach in official commemorative projects at the time, and instead encouraged quiet contemplation and active participation in the space of memory. These are the Memorial to

London, 1981, available at www.tate.org.uk/art/artworks/butler-working-model-for-the-unknown-political-prisoner-t02332, last accessed 31 October 2017.

71 The proposal for the monument consisted of: 'the rock' as a natural element that would serve as a platform for viewing, three female sculptures entitled 'the watchers' and a steel construction called 'the tower' – a symbolic reference to mechanisms of imprisonment. The treatment of space and steel structure in this work can be recognized in other works of the time, namely iron sculptures by Picasso and surrealist sculptures by Giacometti, for example *The Palace at 4 a.m.*

72 The proposed location for the memorial was on the border of West and East Berlin, which deepened the problem. See Michalski, *Public Monuments*, pp. 160–2.

73 In the post-war debate about figurative versus abstract design, the abstract was perceived as an antidote to Communistic and East European solutions. The ICA under art critic Sir Herbert Read conceived this competition as a 'multi-functional ideological weapon, furthering the ethos but also the forms of the West'. See Michalski, *Public Monuments*, p. 156.

74 Amsellem, *Remembering the Past*, p. 190.

Figure 1.2 Memorial to the Deportation (1962), Paris; Georges-Henri Pingusson. Photo: Author

the Unknown Jewish Martyr (1956) and the Memorial to the Deportation (1962) at the Île de la Cité. The first commemorates the Jewish memory of the war by using the universal symbolic language of First World War memorials, while the second is dedicated to 200,000 French martyrs and commissioned by the Le Réseau art committee.[75] While both memorials make use of underground space – each contains a crypt with the remains of an unknown victim – the deportation memorial is almost entirely invisible in the public space. Even though we can see the deportation memorial as a predecessor of many contemporary memorials, it was dubbed at the time an uninviting 'hidden crypt' that lacked the performative qualities of traditional national monuments (Figure 1.2).[76]

[75] The commissioning organization, Le Réseau du souvenir, created in 1952, was a small association of survivors and relatives of deportees. More than 200,000 people were deported from Vichy France to the Nazi concentration camps. The memorial contains the tomb of the 'Unknown Deportee from Struthof' – the only extermination camp on French ground. The memorial, like many others in post-war France, was intended to revive the nation by reinforcing the notion of resistance and thereby marginalizing the period of the Vichy regime.

[76] Amsellem, *Remembering the Past*, p. 38.

Installed in the vicinity of Notre Dame Cathedral and designed by Georges-Henri Pingusson, the memorial needed to respond to the location and the architectural elements that composed its 'architectural spirit'.[77] The head of the Le Réseau art committee, Jean Cassou, the prominent French writer and chief curator of the Musée National d'Art Moderne, argued for a connection to the site and an architecture with meditative qualities, believing that the memorial:

> Should not be built like ordinary statues or monuments, but instead should consider the site, whose lines present a harmony that is characteristic: it should not break away from the horizontality of the river and the point of the island ... it should invite the passerby to ... feel as though he should be welcomed into this space at once intimate and collective.[78]

In contrast to persistent contemporary demands for triumphal monuments to commemorate the French losses of the Second World War, the commissioner of the memorial desired a clandestine, quiet and meditative architecture. In addition, the memorial's non-appearance was in large part conditioned by the city council, which gave permission to build on this prominent location if nothing remained visible above the memorial's parapet.[79] The motif of a burial crypt particularly resonated with the 1953 Memorial to the Unknown Jewish Martyr that consisted of a cylinder at street level and an underground crypt.[80]

Experimentation: Italy and Yugoslavia

The focus on human scale was also clearly visible in some early post-war ideas in Italy discussed in international architectural journals, for example the Fosse Ardeatine Mausoleum in Rome and BBPR's 1946 Monument to the Victims of the Nazi Concentration Camps in Milan, installed at the Cimitero Monumentale.[81] Both represented a great contrast to traditional,

77 Shelley Hornstein, 'Invisible topographies: looking for the mémorial de la déportation in Paris', in Shelley Hornstein and Florence Jacobowitz (eds.), *Image and Remembrance: Representation and the Holocaust* (Bloomington, IN: Indiana University Press, 2003), pp. 305–24, p. 311.

78 Ibid.

79 Amsellem, *Remembering the Past*, p. 69.

80 The Memorial to the Unknown Jewish Martyr was elaborated on by Jean Cassou at a 1953 meeting of the Le Réseau art committee. Parisian underground ossuaries were the secret base for the resistance leader Henri Rol-Tanguy in 1944. The memorial probably had significant influence on Pingusson's design.

81 One member of BBPR's architectural office, Gianluigi Banfi, was a victim of the Mauthausen – Gusen concentration camp. The other three members – Lodovico Barbiano di Belgiojoso, who

Figure 1.3 Monument to the Women of the Resistance (1968), Venice; Carlo Scarpa and Augusto Murer.
Photo: Author

classicizing commemorative forms. Reactions to these new forms varied, as did the general outlook on Italy's contested past. One project that expressively combined traditional sculpture and architecture was the Monument to the Women of the Resistance (1968) on the shoreline of Venice. Commissioned to design a platform for a sculpture created by Augusto Murer, the architect Carlo Scarpa proposed a structure that would interact with the environment.[82] Scarpa designed an underwater dock framed by rectangular slabs of Istrian stone, emerging from the water at varying heights. In the centre of the dock a mobile platform for the sculpture was planned. The platform was to move with the water and thus create dynamic views.[83] As it happened, the idea was abandoned, and several other elements were added that considerably changed the original proposal (Figure 1.3).

was imprisoned in Mauthausen as well, Ernesto Nathan Rogers and Enrico Peressutti – designed the memorial while dealing with personal grief. For a detailed description and history of the memorial, see Amsellem, *Remembering the Past*, pp. 162–78.

[82] Initially, Scarpa argued for a quieter location that would allow for an 'appropriate visual relation between the viewer and the monument'. Francesco Dal Co and Giuseppe Mazzariol (eds.), *Carlo Scarpa: The Complete Works*, trans. Richard Sadler (New York: Rizzoli; Milan: Electa Editrice, 1985), p. 132.

[83] Ibid.

Other significant developments in Italy include several proposals for the 1962 competition for a Monument to the Resistance in Cuneo,[84] the Risiera di San Sabba (1975) in Trieste, and the Resistance Park in Ancona (1965). Aldo Rossi's design proposal for the Cuneo monument was particularly interesting and consisted of a cube containing stairways – a recurring element in his later designs – leading to an elevated platform from where it would be possible to see the exact place of the commemorated event. The memorial was imagined as a public space of seclusion: hence, the stairway narrowed towards the viewing platform, where the visitor is isolated from the outside world and permitted only a glimpse of the historical location. As such, the memorial echoed Terragni's complex destruction of cubic forms to offer an intimate space for reflection, visually orientated towards the site of memory.

In 1966 the city of Trieste organized an architectural competition that invited proposals for the commemoration of Risiera di San Sabba, a former detention camp. Protesting against the requirements of the competition, the architect Romano Boico decided to preserve the ruined structure where possible, arguing that ruins as symbols of destruction are sufficient for the process of remembering.[85] Next to this, Boico removed certain layers of the building in order to gain a better overview of the existing structure. In this approach of opening up the location for the process of remembrance, the architect carefully marked the history of space, for example by retracing the infrastructure of the crematorium, destroyed by the fleeing Nazis, with different materials embedded into the existing pavement. The most prominent element added to the site was the disquieting entrance that seems to introduce an atmosphere of impending danger (Figure 1.4). Similar additions became a common motif in former places of terror, perhaps most vividly executed in Wictor Tolkin's monument at Majdanek

[84] The winning design for the 'Concorso nazionale per il Monumento alla Resistenza a Cuneo' was by Umberto Mastroianni and featured diverse abstract elements suggesting powerful forces unleashed by the revolution. See Luciano Galmozzi, *Monumenti alla libertà. Antifascismo, resistenza e pace nei monumenti italiani dal 1945 al 1985* (Milan: La Pietra, 1986).

[85] Massimo Mucci, *La Risiera di San Sabba. Un'architettura per la memoria*, 6th edn (Gorizia: Libreria Editirice Goriziana, 2012), p. 39. Boico protested against the competition being planned for only a small portion of the site. His indignation was also expressed in the title of his entry, 'Assurdo'. The competition was closed in 1968 without a winner, but Boico's proposal and proposals by Costantino Dardi and Gianugo Polesello were chosen for further development. Dardi's proposal dealt with the creation of an 'emotional journey' through contemporary architectural forms that were supposed to dramatize the terror of the past, whereas Polesello made a strong argument for architectural contrasts between the old and the new, outside and inside. See ibid.

Figure 1.4 Risiera di San Sabba Memorial Museum (1975), Trieste; Romano Boico. Photo: Author

(1969) and its very similar, unrealized predecessor – Hans Hollein's Monument to the Victims of the Holocaust (1963).[86]

The method of isolating visitors while providing restricted glimpses towards the immediate surroundings was employed in several other Italian memorials from this period, such as the Monument to the Resistance in Udine (1969) by Gino Valle and Federico Marconi. The Udine memorial was significantly conditioned by its location – a prominent city square. The architects decided that the memorial needed to have both internal and external qualities, and therefore designed a rectangular slab structure raised above the ground by three plinths shielding an abstract winged sculpture by Dino Basaldella, visible from outside the memorial as well.[87] The front of the memorial opened towards the public space with a lowered,

[86] In 1968, Wiktor Tolkin's design was selected out of 130 submissions to be inaugurated for the 30th anniversary of the German invasion of Poland. Tolkin's design included three parts: the 'Road of Homage and Remembrance' that leads to the memorial, a mausoleum that now holds the victims' ashes originally collected by local civilians and a large abstract stone monument.

[87] Philip Cooke, *The Legacy of the Italian Revolution* (London: Palgrave Macmillan, 2011), p. 108.

Figure 1.5 Mausoleum Fosse Ardeatine (1949), Rome; Nello Aprile, Cino Calcaprina, Aldo Cardelli, Mario Fiorentino, Francesco Coccia, Giuseppe Perugini, Uga de Plaisant and Mirko Basaldella.
Photo: Samra Tanović

semi-circular fountain. The memorial was loaded with symbolic meanings, and its modernist purity was welcomed as 'expressivity without rhetoric'.[88]

The same aesthetics were applied in the Fosse Ardeatine Mausoleum (1949), one of the earliest examples of an extensive use of concrete – the material of the modernists. The enormous concrete block (hollow inside) appears to be hovering above the tombstones, a symbolic reference to the hardships of war that was popular in the early post-war period, and continued to be so in the following two decades (Figures 1.5 and 1.6). The project was an adjusted version of two winning proposals from a previously organized competition, which called for sarcophagi in the place where the Ardeatine massacre had taken place. The use of contemporary materials combined with a sensitivity for context impressed the critics, who praised the memorial for its attention to the psychological aspects of experiencing space, its anti-monumental appearance and its connection with the original site.[89]

Likewise, in Yugoslavia post-war memorial architecture was perceived as an invaluable part of urban planning and the modernization of post-war socialist society.[90] Ambitious commemorative projects pursued the construction of collective remembrance and identity around the People's Liberation War and the socialist revolution. Through a lens defined by a

[88] Ibid., p. 107. [89] Amsellem, *Remembering the Past*, p. 148.

[90] Sanja Horvatinčić and Beti Žerovc (eds.), *Memorial Production in Socialist Yugoslavia 1945–1990* (Berlin: Archive Books, 2019).

Figure 1.6 Mausoleum Fosse Ardeatine (1949): the tombs, Rome; Nello Aprile, Cino Calcaprina, Aldo Cardelli, Mario Fiorentino, Francesco Coccia, Giuseppe Perugini, Uga de Plaisant and Mirko Basaldella.
Photo: Samra Tanović

chronic selectivity, the new Yugoslav regime aimed to build relevant events into the cultural memory by a variety of means, memorial projects being one of them.[91] After 1948, when the Communist Party of Yugoslavia was expelled from the Cominform, the popular stereotypes that dominated Western perspectives on the Eastern bloc collapsed. The architectural production served as a valuable connecting bridge with the West, facilitating innovative commemorative projects freed from the monumental pathos pursued behind the Iron Curtain.[92] At the same time, designers adhered to the *Gesamtkunstwerk* (total work of art) by successfully combining 'a complicated technical process with avant-garde artistic thinking, dialectically sublating the opposition between technology and humanities'.[93] The Yugoslav architects Edvard Ravnikar, Zlatko Ugljen and Bogdan Bogdanović, for instance, explored archaic spaces devoid of historical or

[91] Amra Čusto, 'Bosnia-Herzegovina and the cultural memory of Bleiburg', *Croatian Political Science Review*, 55.2 (2018), 111–30.

[92] See Katharina Ritter et al. (eds.), *Soviet Modernism 1955–1991: Unknown History* (Vienna: Park Books/Architekturzentrum Wien, 2012).

[93] 'Socialist Modernism 1955–1991: Memory Park Kiev', available at http://socialistmodernism.com/memory-park-kiev, last accessed 30 September 2017.

Figure 1.7 Memorial Museum October 21 (1975), Kragujevac, Serbia; Ivan Antić and Ivanka Raspopović.
Photo: Archive of the Memorial Museum October 21

religious associations, in order to create an idiom that would communicate deeper meaning. Their aim was to transform the horrors of past war into spaces that both reflected mournful feeling and gave hope. Here we can find echoes of ancient mythologies and a strong relation to the occult origins of modernism. In their desire to create new symbols and meanings, Yugoslavian designers shared similarities with commemorative spatial logic and recognizable architectural features favoured in the West – for example, the use of landscape and processional routes can be seen in the design entries for the competition for the Roosevelt Memorial in Washington, DC, when the question was raised as to whether an affluent society can 'provide the background of emotional inspiration that can produce a monument'.[94]

Memorials were installed conventionally in locations where battles, massacres of civilians and other war atrocities took place. Here we also see early examples of memorial museums designed to commemorate the events in both their architecture and curatorial programme. One remarkable example of this new type was the Memorial Museum October 21 in Kragujevac, Serbia, designed in 1965 and realized in 1976. The windowless red-brick building is highly symbolic and monumental with elements evocative of the terror of the commemorated event (Figure 1.7).[95]

[94] Thomas H. Creighton, *The Architecture of Monuments: The Franklin Delano Roosevelt Memorial Competition* (New York: Reinhold Publishing Corporation, 1962), p. 13.

[95] See 'Museum 21st October', *Architecture and Urbanism*, 33–34 (1965), 39.

Figure 1.8 Monument to the Revolution (1972), Mt. Kozara; Dušan Džamonja. Photo: Author

The museum is a part of the memorial park established in 1953 on the site where, in October 1941, a few thousand citizens of various nationalities were shot in a reprisal by German soldiers.

Other Yugoslav memorial complexes also coupled architecture with sculptural monuments, but in a reversed order in which the centrepiece was usually a monumental sculpture with an adjacent museum, for example at the Tjentište memorial site (1971) and the Kozara memorial complex (1972), where the names of almost 10,000 partisans who lost their lives in the Second World War are listed (Figure 1.8). Some Soviet counterparts, such as the Ninth Fort Memorial and Museum (1984) in Kaunas, shared this typology.[96] The Maarjamäe Memorial (1958) in Tallinn is another example of a spatial landscape memorial that eschewed patriotic

[96] In some cases, a memorial is constituted of a large sculptural work housing a museum within – hence the museum becomes a sculpture celebrating the positive spirit of the resistance. For example, the 'Makedonium' in Kruševo by Jordan Grabulovski (1974), dedicated to the Ilinden uprising against the Ottoman Empire in 1903. There were other examples in Europe, such as the monument to the French resistance (1973) at the Glières Plateau by Émile Gilioli.

pathos manifested in gigantic forms typical for projects behind the Iron Curtain (the memorial was recently coupled with a new memorial dedicated to Estonia's victims of Communism). A better known example is the memorial to the victims of the Armenian genocide in Yerevan (1967), designed by architects Arthur Tarkhanyan and Sashur Kalashyan with artist Hovhannes Khachatryan, that originated after the Communist party of Armenia passed a resolution for its creation in 1965 to commemorate 50th anniversary of the genocide. The architectural solution of the memorial evokes destruction while providing hope in a circular space enclosed by slanted basalt slabs with the eternal fire at its centre to commemorate victims. An adjacent pillar symbolizes the rebirth of the nation (the memorial site was coupled with a memorial museum in 1995).

To commemorate the various events of the national liberation struggle, Yugoslavian leading architects adopted 'monuments in the West European sense' as a role model.[97] This was also the case in the 1955 urban plan for Sarajevo, which incorporated several distinct typologies for monuments and memorials. These included tower and obelisk-like structures for prominent traffic junctures, memorials as intimate mausoleums inspired by traditional architecture in the old part of the city, larger memorial spaces in the mountain terrains that echoed Italian interbellum memorial architecture, but also memorial museums such as the Museum of Young Bosnia, on the location of the 1914 assassination of Archduke Franz Ferdinand. Memorials that were planned for the city's public spaces aimed at promoting intimacy and seclusion.[98] Notwithstanding the inherent symbolic tension, especially with large national memorial complexes, designers of these memorial spaces focused on mediating feelings and the drama shared by numerous sites marked with post-war memorials and monuments. While doing so, they also addressed the topic of recovery from trauma and contemplation as a way to come to terms with the past. In many ways, Yugoslavian commemorative efforts, having been in recent years rediscovered for their aesthetic and formal qualities, signalled the

[97] Juraj Neidhardt, 'Spomenici (Monuments)', in Dušan Grabrijan and Juraj Neidhardt (eds.), *Arhitektura Bosne i put u Savremeno (Architecture of Bosnia and the Way to Modernity)*, trans. M. P. Moll and B. Vrčon (Ljubljana: Državna Založba Slovenije (Ciril Vidmar) under favor of the Government of the PR of Bosnia and Herzegovina and of the PR of Slovenia, 1957), pp. 430–41, p. 431.

[98] For instance, this is visible in an unrealized plan for a 'Monument of Marx and Engels' in the centre of Sarajevo, where the memorial space was imagined as a secluded green oasis. See Juraj Neidhardt, 'Monument of Marx and Engels on Marindvor', in Grabrijan and Neidhardt (eds.), *Arhitektura Bosne i put u Savremeno*, p. 429.

contemporary focus on the curative potential of architectural space. Spatial concepts such as 'empty space' and 'voided space' were introduced and explored through conceptual solutions, for example Zdenko Kolacio and Kosta Angeli-Radovani's winning proposal for the Monument to the Victims of Fascism (1958) in Jajinci near Belgrade and Ninoslav Kučan and sculptor Dušan Džamonja's proposal for the International Monument at Dachau competition (1959) entitled 'Deserted Cathedral'.[99] These projects, together with several projects from the former Soviet Union such as Ada Rybachuk and Volodymyr Melnychenko's unrealized design from 1965 to commemorate the Babi Yar massacre in Kiev, problematize the established West-dominated perception of the more or less homogenized experience of the Second World War by introducing heterogeneity of commemorative topics and representational strategies.

Holocaust Memorials and Museums

By the 1960s, Holocaust memorials were established as a new genre of commemorative art. Generally speaking, they were characterized by a minimal and unhistorical aesthetic, which frequently caused friction.[100] In several cases, and depending on the specificities of national discourse, survivors protested against highly intellectual designs that were perceived as too abstract and lacking spaces for private mourning. This happened in 1957, for example, when an international competition was organized for the commemoration of Auschwitz as a 'Monument to the Martyrdom of Polish and Other Nations'.[101] The competition brief asked for a monument that would eternalize the suffering of the victims of racial politics, and the artist Henry Moore was made the chairman of the Auschwitz Memorial Committee.[102] The memorial was to be placed on the site at the end of the

[99] On the Jajinci competition, see Sanja Horvatinčić, 'Povijest Nemogućeg Spomenika: Podizanje spomenika žrtvama fašizma u Jajincima', *Anali Galerije Antuna Augustinčića*, nos 32–33/34–34, special issue: 'Simpozij problem spomenika: spomenik danas: zbornik radova' (2012–15), 261–82.

[100] Marcuse, *Legacies of Dachau*, p. 190.

[101] The competition was organized by an international organization of Auschwitz survivors, based in Vienna, in cooperation with the International Union of Architects. On the International Auschwitz Memorial, see Jerzy Zachwatowicz, 'The international memorial at Auschwitz', *Poland* (January 1965), 11–13; Monica Bohm-Duchen (ed.), *After Auschwitz: Responses to the Holocaust in Contemporary Art* (London: Royal Festival Hall, 1995).

[102] The international jury included Odette Elina, a female French artist, the architects Giuseppe Perugini of Milan and Jacob Bakema of Rotterdam, August Zamoyski, a Polish sculptor living in France, and Pierre Courthion, a French critic.

Figure 1.9 'The Road' – Monument to the Victims of Fascism in Auschwitz-Birkenau (1957): on the right – a floorplan; left – a detail showing ruins of the crematoria; Oskar Hansen, Jerzy Jarnuszkiewicz, Julian Pałka, Lechosław Rosiński, Edmund Kupiecki, Tadeusz Plasota and Zofia Hansen; architectural scale model, 12 boards of cardboard and plywood. Long term loan from the Auschwitz-Birkenau Memorial and Museum, collection of the Museum of Modern Art in Warsaw.
Photo: César Delgado Martin

railways.[103] After reviewing hundreds of submissions, the jury selected seven proposals among which was the work of Alina Szapocznikow's team.[104] It depicted a rectangular slab with two monumental hands that seemed to be an enlarged version of Giacometti's *Hands Holding the Void*. Under the slab, a crypt with the ashes from the crematoria was planned. As the outcome of the second phase, the jury unanimously chose the non-figurative proposal of a Polish team led by architect Oskar Hansen. The proposal projected a 70 m-wide and 1 km-long black, tarmac road positioned diagonally across the former camp area. The rest of the site remained intact (Figure 1.9). It was designed along the principles of 'open form', a philosophical idea of shaping social space in such a way that there is room for interventions from audience and time.[105] In contrast to the traditional approach, which Hansen referred to as 'closed form', a memorial devised in this way would allow visitors to experience the site and confront oblivion at the same time, as he explained:

[103] Unlike many other sites of concentration camps, the buildings at Auschwitz were preserved, due to their sheer scale and complexity. Already in 1945, the camp premises in Oświęcim, the Polish name for Auschwitz, were placed under Poland's provisional government's Ministry of Culture and Art supervision for the creation of a museum, which was opened in 1947, the year when all the structures were pronounced national monuments by the Polish Parliament.

[104] The jury first met in Auschwitz to choose from over 400 designs, submitted by more than 600 sculptors and architects from 36 countries. Both figurative and abstract options were proposed. The seven shortlisted designs, after further refinement, were presented at the second stage of the competition in November 1958, at the UNESCO headquarters in Paris.

[105] The concept of 'open form' was described by Hansen at the International Congress of Modern Architecture (CIAM) in Otterlo in 1959.

> The road is the site for spontaneous gestures. If one should wish to leave a note with a name, or a figure of an Angel, one could do it by the road . . . The process outside the road was meant to be a biological clock. Already then trees were growing there, we saw running roe-deer and hares. We wanted to preserve the evidence on the road . . . in the way in which lava preserved Pompeii . . . Monument-the Road is the exploration of continuity. It departs from life, transgresses death, and returns again to another life. Life and death are defined through each other.[106]

Despite its popular reception, however, the project remained unrealized. It was too costly and, in fact, still too radical, since many existing structures would have to be demolished in order to build the proposed road – an act that was too problematic in the context of the West–East binary but also Poland's bifurcated view on the Second World War. Hansen's team withdrew from the competition when a compromise was offered, involving the addition of elements from another competition proposal. However, the most pronounced critique came from Auschwitz survivors themselves, who found the proposal too abstract and 'not in keeping with the literalness of their experiences'.[107] The argument was that the design lacked a focal point for commemorations, which the survivors found necessary. Indeed, in 1967 a figurative monument entitled 'International Monument to the Victims of Fascism' was erected on the site.

In the United States, the first public commemoration of the Holocaust took place as early as 1942, but it was not until the 1960s that a more organized approach developed, when Jewish focus on the Holocaust became 'a continuing liberal concern over racial and religious hatred and the forgetfulness of the political culture of the 1950s'.[108] Following the failure to realize a proposal for a memorial in New York by Erich Mendelsohn and Ivan Meštrović in 1951, a Committee for the Commemoration of Six Million Jews was organized. It came with its own Art Committee, including renowned professionals in the fields of art history

[106] Katarzyna Murwaska-Muthesius, 'Oskar Hansen and the Auschwitz "Countermemorial," 1958–59', *Art Margins*, 20 May 2002, available at http://artmargins.com/index.php/featured-articles/311-oskar-hansen-and-the-auschwitz-qcountermemorialq-1958-59#ftn_artnotes1_9, last accessed 31 October 2017.

[107] Young, *The Texture of Memory*, p. 136.

[108] Jeffrey Herf, 'How and why did Holocaust memory come to the United States? A response to Peter Novick's challenge', in Jeffry Diefendorf and Theodore Zev Weiss (eds.), *Lessons and Legacies VI: New Currents in Holocaust Research* (Evanston, IL: Northwestern University Press, 2004), pp. 457–74, p. 467.

and architecture. The organization appointed the architect Louis I. Kahn to design the first Holocaust memorial, to be erected in New York – the Memorial for the Six Million Jewish Martyrs. It was planned to occupy a spot in Battery Park in New York. The location was already cluttered with various monuments, ironically depicted in one of Claes Oldenburg's provocative drawings from 1965, featuring a giant vacuum cleaner clearing the site.[109] With his proposal, Kahn aimed to integrate the new memorial into the existing context by using glass – a material he explored in his concept proposal for a monument to Lenin (1932). He designed nine translucent glass cubes placed in a rectangular grid. The solution used the same aesthetic language as George Nelson's proposal for the Franklin Delano Roosevelt Memorial in Washington, DC (announced in 1961) in which Kahn also participated – tall glass cubes would allow neighbouring structures to visually pervade the space of remembrance.

Both proposals, though never realized, were a significant departure from the traditional monument, but Kahn's memorial in particular, concerning the topic it addressed. The architect considered the guidelines put forward by the commissioner, which were rather contradictory: the design was supposed to be of the highest artistic integrity, evoke the emotional, psychological and historical impact of the tragedy for future generations and while dealing with the horrendous past, it needed to express hope for a better future for all humanity, 'where man will not merely survive but prevail', in the words of William Faulkner's Nobel prize speech.[110] The elements in Kahn's design addressed these demands by introducing translucency and thereby dematerializing the memorial's structure, in order to create a stage where the visitor was free to explore and reflect in an atmosphere of light, hope and inspiration. Kahn also thought of placing the memorial to face three figures relevant to the American immigrant experience: The Statue of Liberty, Castle Clinton and Ellis Island. However, Kahn's proposal was criticized for its lack of direct symbolism and for its calmness; it was believed that the survivors would want to see 'some expression of their own lives, their own experiences, their seeming humiliation'.[111] The architect reacted to the critique by adjusting the

[109] In 1965 Oldenburg started working on drawings and projects for imaginary outdoor monuments, among them the Proposed Colossal Monument for the Battery, New York: Vacuum Cleaner.

[110] Mark Godfrey, *Abstraction and the Holocaust* (New Haven, CT and London: Yale University Press, 2007), p. 121.

[111] Ibid., p. 125.

design and imbuing it with a sense of ritual. Consequently, the initial design transformed into six blocks orbiting around a central pier – a symbolic chapel, raised on a black granite plinth. As Kahn explained:

> The Monument will get its mood from the endless changes of light and of night, the seasons of the year, the endless play of the weather, and even the sudden light of a flash of lightning. The drama of movement on the river will transmit its life to the Monument.[112]

This positive approach, accentuating recovery and hope instead of dwelling on the outcomes of the destruction, was typical for Kahn, who often argued for the power of light as a life-giving element.

Conversely, the unrepresentable realm of tragedy and horror was treated with silence. Denounced as too ambiguous and non-accusing, the memorial was never realized. At the same time, the need for 'spaces for healing' in memorial architecture was typical for the American context, where the 1960s were a time of turmoil with the ongoing battles over civil rights and the Vietnam War. By the 1970s, the debate about transmitting memory to future generations through evocative architectural forms and metonymic devices took a new turn. A new architectural genre started to emerge in the West – that of the Holocaust museum. The first Holocaust museum was built in Israel: the renowned Yad Vashem memorial complex was dedicated in 1957, with the central building, the 'Hall of Remembrance', inaugurated in 1961. It lends its timeless character to a combination of ancient commemorative symbolic and modern architecture. This mixture of past and present can be considered typical for the architecture of commemoration in Israel, a country unique for its number of memorials. Their duality is embedded in a specific order, the essence of which is the diametrical opposition of spatial forms, aimed to evoke contrasting experiences in visitors.[113] The principle extends to the juxtaposition of darkness and light, of horizontal and vertical, and so forth, and is widespread in Israel's memorial architecture. In Dani Karavan's Negev Brigade Memorial (1968), for example, its verticality contrasts with the overall horizontal composition of the memorial, while in David Anatol Brutzkus' Dakar Memorial (1971), placed on a military cemetery, the above-ground and underground composition of spaces augments the diametrical opposition

[112] Ibid., p. 129.

[113] Tula Amir, 'Life saver: typology of commemoration in Israel-architecture and society', in *The Israeli Pavilion*, curator Tula Amir, the 10th International Exhibition of Architecture, Venice Biennial, September–November 2006, pp. 12–17.

of qualities. Both memorials are composed on the principles of *architecture parlante* and are highly symbolic, as they tend to dramatize the story they are telling by using stark contrasts between outside and inside, incorporating a descent into the earth or long corridors as transitional spaces from one sequence to the other.

On the global scale, the interest in the Holocaust and the 'Final Solution' started to intensify with international media exchange. In West Germany, Holocaust curiosity was at its height by the 1980s, manifesting in three different discourses of memory production, with three specific representations. Consequently, the tension was inherited in the unified German collective consciousness as there was 'no single medium that united all Germans in reflection about their historical legacy'.[114]

1.3 After 1980: Filling and Creating Voids

The Vietnam Veterans Memorial, Washington, DC

The long discussion about abstract art versus figurative art began to wane in the early 1980s, coinciding with the creation of Maya Lin's canonical Vietnam Veterans Memorial (VVM) dedicated to those who were killed or missing in the Vietnam War – a product of a decade-long, bitter and divisive discussion in the United States. It is a convincing example of the viability of abstract forms as tools for supporting remembrance.[115] The designer, Maya Ying Lin, sought to materialize the unpresentable pain of loss as a scar:

> I thought about what death is, what a loss is . . . a sharp pain that lessens with time, but can never quite heal over. A scar. The idea occurred to me there on the site. Take a knife and cut open the earth, and with time the grass would heal it. As if you cut open the rock and polished it.[116]

114 Wulf Kansteiner, *In Pursuit of German Memory: History, Television, and Politics after Auschwitz* (Athens, OH: Ohio University Press, 2006), p. 332.

115 See Joan Marter, 'Postwar sculpture re/viewed' and 'The ascendancy of abstraction for public art: the Monument to the Unknown Political Prisoner competition', *Art Journal*, 53.4, special issue: 'Sculpture in postwar Europe and America, 1945–59' (1994), 20–2 and 28–36.

116 Maya Lin, quoted in Charles L. Griswold and Stephen S. Griswold, 'The Vietnam Veterans Memorial and the Washington Mall: philosophical thoughts on political iconography', *Critical Inquiry* 12.4 (Summer 1986), 688–719, 718. For a discussion about several analytical approaches to the memorial, see Gill Abousnnouga and David Machin (eds.), *The Language of War Monuments* (London and New York: Bloomsbury Publishing, 2013), pp. 66–72.

The memorial – very much a war memorial and not a monumental project – embodies some of the ideas that changed the perception of what a memorial should look like, an issue that never goes away. With a pronounced assertion towards the natural process of recovery, Lin's memorial invites participation on several levels and, despite its proximity to celebratory national monuments on the Washington Mall, manages to remain a contemplative and emotional realm, demonstrated by its ongoing acceptance and popularity.

The memorial was in line with strategies employed by the artists of the so-called environmental art movement from the 1960s and 1970s, who focused on reinforcing the *genius loci* of a given context. The memorial also reflects the tendency of predominantly environmental artists towards creating art as a negative form, exemplified in the landscape art of Robert Smithson or Robert Morris.[117] According to art critic Rosalind Krauss, what started as an exploration of negative space at the beginning of the nineteenth century, with Auguste Rodin's sculptures and later with Constantin Brâncuşi in the 1930s, was soon exhausted to the point where sculpture, *ergo* monument, was interpreted as pure negative form. Krauss went so far as to argue that 'modernist sculpture appeared as a kind of black hole in the space of consciousness, something whose positive content was increasingly difficult to define, something that was possible to locate only in terms of what it was not.'[118]

In this sense, the VVM can be classified in terms of its deviations from what the patronage and cultural production of an official war memorial normally entailed. At the same time, the memorial is strongly embedded in its monument-filled context, since it engages in dialogue with the adjacent structures: the Lincoln Memorial and Washington Monument prominently feature in the memorial space and one is constantly aware of their presence. The VVM, initiated by a Vietnam War veteran, was inscribed from the outset by ordinary people capable of 'reinterpreting the dominant ideological discourse for their own purposes'.[119] Following many futile efforts, it was also the first experimental memorial actually to be built, only to become the most visited memorial on the Mall a few years after its dedication in 1982.[120] Several earlier architectural projects were identified as possible sources of inspiration, among them the two French war

[117] Rosalind Krauss, 'Structure in the expanded field', *October*, 8 (1979), 30–44. [118] Ibid., 34.

[119] Albert Boime, *The Unveiling of the National Icons: A Plea for Patriotic Iconoclasm in a Nationalist Era* (Cambridge: Cambridge University Press, 1998), p. 309.

[120] Griswold and Griswold, 'The Vietnam Veterans Memorial'.

Figure 1.10 The Vietnam Veterans Memorial (1982), Washington, DC; Maya Lin. Photo: Willemien de Vries-Voet

memorials discussed above – the Memorial to the Deportation in Paris and Lutyens' Monument to the Missing of the Somme at Thiepval.[121] Others reinterpreted the memorial's aesthetic features in connection with art works such as Richard Serra's sculpture *Shift* (1972) or Judy Chicago's *Dinner Party* (1979).[122] Striking similarities can be found with some of the proposals participating in the 1961 competition for the Roosevelt Memorial in Washington, DC.[123] Other than the obvious departure from the typical historical and sculptural memorials present on the Mall, however, the highly minimalistic features of the VVM continue to escape stylistic categorizations. Determined by its ambiguity, the memorial remains a persuasive space that encourages public sentiment. The memorial's power of persuasion has been assigned to the following aspects: it violates the conventional form of war memorials, it assumes a welcoming stance, it provides little information to the visitor, it focuses attention to those who did not survive the war and it generates multiple references for its visual components (Figure 1.10).[124]

Appropriated as a space to contemplate and mourn, visitors continue leaving material offerings, most of which are catalogued and archived by the Museum Resource Center of the National Park Service. Imagined

[121] Hélène Lipstadt, 'Learning from Lutyens: Thiepval in the age of the anti-monument', *Harvard Design Magazine* (1999), 65–70.

[122] Boime, *The Unveiling*, p. 309.

[123] See Creighton, *The Architecture of Monuments.*

[124] Sonja K. Foss, 'Ambiguity as persuasion: the Vietnam Veterans Memorial', *Communication Quarterly*, 34.3 (1986), 326–40.

'not as an unchanging monument', but as 'a moving composition to be understood as we move into and out of it',[125] the memorial proved a successful design solution to a competition call that wanted 'no political statement about the war'.[126] It should be noted that although the VVM was considered by many as antagonistic to memorial concepts established in the 1980s, content-wise there was no attempt to include the names of the North Vietnamese civilian dead. This was done by the American artist Chris Burden in the art-work entitled *The Other Vietnam Memorial* (1991) that drew attention to the three million Vietnamese killed as a result of the American war. The names of the mostly anonymous dead – for the purpose of Burden's memorial, generated by computer software – were etched on copper plates and mounted into steel frames revolving around a central pole.[127] Maya Lin's battle, however, was to defend her design against attempts to tame her apolitically provocative design with traditional monuments, namely Frederic Heart's sculpture *The Three Soldiers*.

The Counter-Memory Movement

As international media exchange intensified in the 1980s, a revolution in West Germany's memory of the Third Reich produced a new paradigm conceived on 'more or less self-reflective routines of Holocaust remembrance' leading to the establishment of 'a new memory status quo that cut across political and generational divides'.[128] After 1985 the public was confronted with memorial projects that aimed to destabilize the very notion of memory. This so-called counter-memory or anti-memorial generation, with predominantly German artists, delivered numerous projects that aimed to encourage participatory acts by the visitor and employed contradiction as one of their artistic strategies. Sol LeWitt's work *Black Form Dedicated to the Missing Jews* (1987), for instance, contemplates the non-representational nature of trauma together with the exhaustion of the traditional repertoire of memorial expressions. *Black Form* was originally

[125] Maya Lin, 'Statement by Maya Ying Lin' (March 1981), *Vietnam Veterans Memorial Fund*, available at www.u.arizona.edu/~salvador/Spring%20thru%20February/Vietnam/Memorial%20history%202.pdf.

[126] Introduction to Maya Lin, 'Statement by Maya Ying Lin' (March 1981), *Vietnam Veterans Memorial Fund*, available at www.u.arizona.edu/~salvador/Spring%20thru%20February/Vietnam/Memorial%20history%202.pdf.

[127] Since the exact records of the dead were not available, Burden used a basic catalogue of Vietnamese names which he mixed and matched through a computer program to obtain three million names. See Boime, *The Unveiling*, pp. 329–33.

[128] Kansteiner, *In Pursuit of German Memory*, p. 316.

conceived for a location in front of Munster's castle, on the spot where an equestrian statue of the German Emperor William II stood, and was designed in tandem with LeWitt's *White Pyramid*, which was installed in the castle garden. *Black Form* recalls an enlarged sarcophagus, whereas *White Pyramid* cites pharaonic funerary monuments or Mesopotamian and Persian ziggurats, places of the divine.[129]

Endorsing counter-monuments, James Young argued that the most influential project, even the paradigm for a whole generation of artists and architects after the Holocaust, was the Monument Against Fascism (1986–93) in Hamburg-Harburg, Germany, by Jochen Gerz and Esther Shalev-Gerz.[130] This project is significant because it moved physical form into the realm of psychology and dematerialization. The concept of the disappearing monument, as introduced by the artists, tackled the meaning of a monument in general, but it also addressed the way in which a mourning process can develop. Here the psychological concept of 'working through' and 'coming to terms with the past' is translated quite literally into the physical form of a disappearing column. After being revealed to the public and inviting people to participate by writing on the column's metal surface, in the course of a few years, from 1986 to 1993, the column slowly vanished into the ground. Each participation or action of writing on the surface activated a specially embedded system which sunk the column further into the ground. What remained at the end is a memory object, the artefact of the sunken column, visible through a glass window at the lower street level. On the place where the column once stood, a plaque remains: 'Nothing can in the long run replace our own protest against injustice.' Thus, this interactive artistic installation asserts that building a monument is not sufficient; it is living with the memory of the events to which the monument refers and converting those memories into action which is at the core of the ethical purpose of commemorative art.

A similar but less interactive approach was used by the artist Horst Hoheisel, who designed the inverted Aschkroft fountain (1988) in Kassel and his more radical proposal to blow up the Brandenburger Tor in Berlin – a way to memorialize destruction with destruction. Equally radical was Daniel Libeskind's proposal for a competition to redesign

[129] The original conception of the two-piece work was sacrificed in 1988, when frequent vandalism led to the relocation of *Black Form* to Hamburg-Altona to serve as a monument for the missing Jews of Altona, while the White Pyramid was moved into the university's botanical garden.

[130] James E. Young, *At Memory's Edge: After-Images of the Holocaust in Contemporary Art and Architecture* (New Haven, CT and London: Yale University Press, 2000), p. 139.

Sachsenhausen concentration camp (organized in 1992) that was submitted as a counter-proposal to the competition call to design a mixed-use residential development on the site. Libeskind imagined partial flooding of the site with water to preserve the remains and offer something new.[131] In order to see the ruins, visitors would have to walk over dikes.

In pursuit of suitable modes to engage or even induce traumatic remembrance, several projects from this period were conceived as simple markings of places, for instance Gunter Demnig's brass blocks called *Stolpersteine* or *Stumbling Stones* (1992), installed in the pavement in front of the houses of people who were deported during the war.[132] You cannot just go on your way, since you will literally trip on the past, a past embedded in the sidewalks of cities.

Later examples adopted the notions of disappearance and reflection very literally, as was the case with Micha Ullman's poetically evocative Memorial for the Book Burning (1994) on Berlin's Bebelplatz, commemorating the infamous book burnings by the Nazis in 1933. The memorial consists of a subterranean white room with empty bookshelves, visible only through a transparent glass plate at surface level which hardly allows for any suitable viewing angles. Ullman's memorial employs the aesthetic concept of a voided space, explored by many other contemporary designers of memorial spaces. In a project entitled *Missing House*, for instance, Christian Boltanski used an existing architectural void in the urban tissue to create a memorial,[133] whereas Rachel Whiteread produced casts of voided spaces in order to emphasize the absence of the subject memorialized, for example in the Judenplatz Holocaust Memorial (2000) in Vienna.[134] Similar to

[131] See 'Project MoUrning Details', *Counterpreservation: Architectural Decay in Berlin since 1989*, available at https://signale.cornell.edu/media-details/1708/1639, last accessed 20 May 2019.

[132] The stones are installed in approximately 610 places all over Europe. They can easily be ordered online and the names are added to the generic text of the stones, which begins with 'Here lived. . .' Demnig cites the Talmud, saying that 'a person is only forgotten when his or her name is forgotten.' The text is quoted from the project's official website, available at www.stolpersteine.eu/en/home, last accessed 31 October 2017.

[133] The project was mounted for the exhibition 'Die Endlichkeit der Freiheit' (October 1990, Berlin). Here Boltanski sought to trace the people who lived in a building at Grosse Hamburgerstrasse from 1930 until it was destroyed by Allied bombing in 1945. Boltanski acquired photographs, letters and other documents belonging to the former inhabitants and placed them in archival boxes, together with maps of the neighbourhood. Nameplates were also hung on a side-facade of the adjacent building to identify the now missing inhabitants, Jews and non-Jews.

[134] The memorial is a result of an invited competition organized in 1996 at the initiative of Simon Wiesenthal, a concentration camp survivor and Nazi-hunter, who took on the role of spokesman for the public offence caused by the *Mahnmal gegen Krieg und Faschismus on Albertinaplatz* (1988) by Alfred Hrdlicka. See James E. Young, 'Memory, counter-memory,

Figure 1.11 The Holocaust Memorial at Judenplatz ('The Nameless Library', 2000), Vienna; Rachel Whiteread.
Photo: Šahin Šivšić

Ullman's 'hidden' library, Whiteread employed the symbolism of books to convey the meaning of the memorial (also known as the 'Nameless Library'), shaped as the inverted cast of a square library room with books whose titles we cannot read and a door we cannot open to enter (Figure 1.11). The memorial's large scale and its walls composed of inverted concrete books raised concerns about potential vandalism: the artist was less concerned and even welcomed such acts, as they would, in her opinion, reinforce the memorial's goal to 'invert people's perception of the world and to reveal the unexpected'.[135] While inviting participation by means of vandalism, the memorial remains an impenetrable mass – an inaccessible imprint of the absent.

Deconstructivism and the Holocaust

Treating voids as architectural spaces is a frequently employed approach in the design methods of deconstructivism, the best known proponents of

and the end of the monument', in Hornstein and Jacobowitz (eds.), *Image and Remembrance*, pp. 59–78.

135 Rachel Whiteread quoted in Kate Connolly, 'Closed books and stilled lives', *The Guardian*, 26 October 2000, www.theguardian.com/world/2000/oct/26/kateconnolly, last accessed 31 October 2017. Whiteread argued that: 'If someone sprays a swastika on it we can try to scrub it off, but a few daubed swastikas would really make people think about what's happening in their society.'

which are probably Peter Eisenman and Daniel Libeskind. Their breakthrough year was 1988, when the two architects were included in a New York exhibition entitled 'Deconstructivist Architecture'. In the same year, Libeskind won the competition for an addition to the Berlin Historical Museum, which was renamed thereafter the Jewish Museum of Berlin (2001).[136] The realized building communicates with the outside world by providing glimpses of it, through windows zigzagging across the zinc facade. The outer appearance of the museum is further dramatized by black diagonal lines, by now established as Libeskind's signature style.[137] In its layout the zigzag form,[138] defining the museum's appearance, intersects with a straight line running through the middle and, in that way, creates a series of voids or negative spaces. According to Libeskind, these spaces are places of both 'being and nonbeing' in which one can 'attempt to have access to it through names and addresses, through a kind of haunting quality of spaces through which the passage of absence took place'.[139] Libeskind's design was inspired by the erasure of Jewish notation on the tombs in the Weissensee cemetery in Berlin.[140] Consequently he sought to create spaces where there is nothing to be seen.[141] In this view, adding any content into these voids

[136] The existing building was designed by Philip Gerlach in 1735 as Collegienhaus. After surviving the heavy destruction of the Second World War, it was rededicated in the 1960s as the Berlin Museum. Originally, the 1988 competition invited proposals for an extension of the Berlin Museum with a Jewish Museum Department, but the entire complex later became the Jewish Museum of Berlin.

[137] Similar architectural patterns are used in Libeskind's project for the Felix Nussbaum Museum in Osnabrück (1998), his entry for Germany's national Holocaust memorial from 1998, entitled 'StoneBreath', his design for the Contemporary Jewish Museum of San Francisco (2008), and the Danish Jewish Museum in Copenhagen (2004).

[138] The origins of this layout are manifold. Libeskind derived the zigzag form by tracing imaginary lines on the map of Berlin which would connect streets where prominent Jewish people used to live. The title 'between the lines' implies that the meaning is to be derived from the intermediate space these lines create. There were also stipulations in urban planning that influenced the design. Libeskind was rejecting a logical organization and pursued fragmentation as the only true expression. The form can also be understood in light of a Jewish belief explained in Kaballah as God's creative process in which God broke his wholeness, hence as the negative act of *zimzum* – God's contraction of himself to create the universe. This aspect of Jewish mysticism was also an inspiration for Barnett Newman, for instance in his installation *Zim Zum* (1985), a zigzagged steel pavilion in Düsseldorf.

[139] Daniel Libeskind, 'Trauma', in Hornstein and Jacobowitz (eds.), *Image and Remembrance*, pp. 43–58, p. 44.

[140] Libeskind referred to marble tombstones without engravings, erected by wealthy Jewish families for future generations. The architect was struck 'by the fact that no members of these families could ever come back to see the emptiness of those slabs of marble'. Libeskind, 'Trauma', p. 44.

[141] Daniel Libeskind, *Jewish Museum, Berlin* (Amsterdam: G+B Arts International, 1999).

seemed contradictory.[142] Nevertheless, several artworks were installed and, as it is now, they affirm the architectural space and its meaning.

One of the voids is occupied by the artwork *Shalechet (Fallen Leaves)* by Menashe Kadishman. It consists of thousands of casts of schematic human faces which form a walkway. The encounter produces an engaging effect and transforms the 'void' into an interactive architectural device. Out of the seven voids, two are inaccessible to visitors. One of the voids is the so-called *Holocaust Tower*, a high space with a narrow slit at its highest point, allowing daylight and sounds to enter the space. Here the concept of voided space reaches its apex. The only part of the museum that is installed outside is the *Garden of Exile*, consisting of 41 concrete columns arranged in a strict grid and installed on sloping ground. The columns contain earth, and an underground irrigation system supports the willow oak planted inside to emerge at the top of the columns.[143] There is no level ground, only ramps and spaces that produce disorientation and discomfort.

A similar deconstructivist logic, based on significantly changing the existing setting with radical gestures, is also evident in Moshe Safdie's museum in Yad Vashem (2005). Conceived as an addition to an existing structure, the museum was designed as a triangular shaft approximately 180 m long. The longitudinal form perforates the landscape and eventually protrudes as a viewpoint console. Safdie referred to the Holocaust as a physical rupture, a story that is too terrible to be narrated in normal galleries. The architect sought to capture 'the feel of an archaeological remnant' and design a space that appears as if 'an earthquake ripped it apart'.[144]

Dedicated in the same year as Safdie's project, the Memorial for the Murdered Jews of Europe (MMJE) in Berlin is probably the best-known example of inversion and destabilization of the ground, a recurrent theme in this period (Figure 1.12). The project received building approval by the German Bundestag in 1999, five years after the first competition, whose winning design, proposing an enormous gravestone, was dismissed for its

[142] The construction of the museum was finished in 1998, but it took nine months to finalize the exhibition and its curatorial strategies, following a debate over whether to leave the museum empty, as a de facto memorial, or fill it with the exhibition and artefacts.

[143] Bernhard Schneider, *Daniel Libeskind, Jewish Museum Berlin: Between the Lines* (Munich and New York: Prestel, 1999), p. 40. In the winter period, the garden is usually closed to the public due to the slippery ground.

[144] Moshe Safdie, *Yad Vashem: Moshe Safdie – The Architecture of Memory* (Baden: Lars Müller, 2006), p. 97.

Figure 1.12 The Memorial for the Murdered Jews of Europe (MMJE, 2005), Berlin; Peter Eisenman.
Photo: Author

controversial symbolism and sheer scale.[145] The second competition was organized in 1997, following many fraught colloquia that questioned the very *raison d'être* of the future memorial as the main national memorial. It was feared that building such a memorial would be like creating a 'great burial slab for the twentieth century, a hermetically sealed vault for the ghosts of Germany's past'.[146] Notwithstanding the many doubts and pitfalls that are part of the process of making a memorial in the first place, the competition delivered two finalists: Gesine Weinmiller's 'Eighteen Scattered Sandstone Walls' and the collaborative project of Richard Serra and Peter Eisenman, 'Waving Field of Pillars'. Weinmiller's proposal depicted the location filled with 18 wall segments, a symbolic recall of life in Hebrew *gematria*, scattered over a sloping plaza. Seen from a specific angle, the wall segments formed the Star of David, which the jury found intriguing but too distracting at the same time. Similarly to the VVM, the proposal treated the space as a 'wound', a place where architectural features reinforced the sensory experience by introducing a

[145] The winning design by Berlin architect Christine Jackob-Marks consisted of a massive sloped surface, occupying the whole site, with eighteen boulders from Masada in Israel. The names of murdered Jews were to be inscribed on the memorial. The connection to Masada was problematic, as it was a historical site of the mass suicide of Jews during the revolt against the Romans. Among other things, the proposal was criticized for being 'too German'. James E. Young, who was part of the committee, argued that the competition brief was too ambiguous to begin with. Participants from the first competition were invited to the second, alongside newcomers like Peter Eisenman, Daniel Libeskind, Jochen Gerz, Rebecca Horn and Dani Karavan. Young, *At Memory's Edge*, p. 190.

[146] Young, *At Memory's Edge*, p. 194.

gradual descent towards the bordering walls, forcing visitors to engage in 'memorial-activity'.[147]

Serra and Eisenman's proposal, selected as the winner, shared the idea of visitor participation. The proposal comprised a thousand pillars, at first glance recalling a vast cemetery. There were several reasons for choosing this solution: its multiple forms would encourage individual involvement with the memorial without giving final messages or meanings; the designers saw memorialization not as static but as an ongoing process; the memorial's form and scale resisted reproduction through snapshots of cameras and thereby reinforced active participation; and, finally, the memorial imposed a sense of *Unheimlichkeit* – a sense of danger by destabilizing the visitor's position in space.[148] The design included two overlapping sheets of invented topographies on rectangular grids. These were placed above each other and undulated at different frequencies to determine the tilt of the pillars. The incongruent relationship of the two planes cannot be traced in practice, but only felt through its destabilizing effect. Even though Eisenman applied abstract elements in a rational approach to produce unpredictable results, reflected in the arrangement of the pillars, the architect resisted describing the memorial as abstract, instead referring to the design as 'indexical'.[149] Eisenman remained faithful to his conviction that instead of producing meaning, a memorial should question the conditions of horror by creating a 'powerful and evocative spatial experience that will precipitate discussion about the past . . . [so as] to ensure that . . . [it] will never [be] repeat[ed]'.[150] To do this, Eisenman used the tilted ground on which the pillars were installed as an element of displacement for two reasons: in opposition to the traditional notion of architecture as site-specific and ground-based, and as a reaction to the Nazi ideology of 'Blut und Boden' – the sanctity of German soil. Hence, decomposing the very basis of architectural form would counteract its

[147] Ibid., p. 205. [148] Ibid., p. 206.

[149] Godfrey, *Abstraction and the Holocaust*, p. 244. See also Rosalind Krauss, 'Notes on the index: seventies art in America', *October*, 3 (1977), 68–81.

[150] Gavriel D. Rosenfeld, *Building after Auschwitz: Jewish Architecture and the Memory of the Holocaust* (New Haven, CT and London: Yale University Press, 2011), p. 174. Eisenman's proposal for the 1995 competition for a Holocaust memorial in Vienna consisted of a plaza surrounded by wrinkle-like tall walls, a form derived from a series of overlapping maps from Vienna's ghettos from 1421 and 1678 with the map of the German Reich after the Nazi 'Anschluss' of 1938. His other proposal for the Jewish Museum of San Francisco (1996) was also developed around the notion of a powerful and disturbing spatial experience in which he was trying to evoke Auschwitz – 'a feeling of loneliness and being lost' (ibid., p. 176).

inherent ability to produce meaning.[151] The architect hoped to evoke the same feelings of loneliness and disorientation the survivors described to him during the research he conducted preceding the project.

Since the competition board wanted more space for commemorative events and at the same time feared that the memorial would become an uncontrollable labyrinthine space, the original design had to be adjusted. The revision of what became a one-man project, as Serra left it, unwilling to compromise, included a significant reduction of the number of pillars, adjustment of their height and spacing (the lowest pillars became higher) and the addition of a row of trees as a buffer between the city and the memorial. Once the design was approved, other practical issues came to the fore prior to its dedication in 2005: the possibility of vandalism and the desecration of the space by people climbing on the pillars.[152] While the first was a subject of controversy, the latter problem has never been resolved in spite of the official rules of behaviour installed around the memorial.

A final addition to the revised proposal, on the insistence of the minister of culture at the time, was an underground museum space called 'Ort der Information'. It was supposed to contribute to the pedagogical value of the overall concept. The extension needed to be integrated into the architectural language of the memorial, which was done by adjusting the Museum's distribution in such a way that the four rooms below would follow the layout of the field of pillars above. In this manner an inversed world was created, not unlike Libeskind's upside-down *Garden of Exile*, where the pillars could be interpreted as empty memorial plaques on unidentified graves. In reality, this observation remains in the domain of personal intellectual investigation.

In later years, two more memorials were realized in the adjacent Tiergarten park: the Monument to Homosexual Holocaust Victims (2008) and the Memorial to the Sinti and Roma victims of National Socialism (2012). While the first is a single impenetrable structure and aesthetically relates to Eisenman's memorial, the second memorial takes a different approach and offers a secluded realm for memory. Designed by Dani Karavan, it is separated from the rest of the park with a milk-glass fence on which a historical timeline is inscribed. The entrance gate is also a transitional passageway towards the other side, where a circular basin is inserted into the ground (Figure 1.13). In the centre of the basin, a small,

[151] Ibid.

[152] Eisenman argued that the text-less surfaces of the pillars were 'neither intended nor consecrated as tombstones'. Young, *At Memory's Edge*, p. 211.

Figure 1.13 The Memorial to the Sinti and Roma Victims of National Socialism (2012), Berlin; Dani Karavan.
Photo: Author

moveable triangular platform causes the water to spill over the basin's edge when elevated. Unlike the adjacent field of pillars, this memorial is precise in its address since the textual content serves an introductory purpose. The memorial hints at the currently re-emerging need for 'healing' spaces to replace the aggressive re-evocation of traumatic experiences.

1.4 Building Memory in the Twenty-First Century

Globalization and Spectacle

The so-called connective turn, reinforced by the abundance and immediacy of information, has certainly 're-engineered memory, liberating it from the traditional bounds of spatial archive, the organization, the institution'.[153] The traditional way of making memorial space, however, is as popular as ever. It takes considerable time to realize an architectural memorial project, for various reasons: contested views on a shared history, the absence of a satisfying representational vocabulary, or shortcomings related to the financial difficulties of a project. Despite these challenges, memorial architecture is a burgeoning design field. Our

[153] Andrew Hoskins (ed.), 'The restless past. An introduction to digital memory and media', in *Digital Memory Studies*, pp. 1–24, p. 1.

contemporary society is supported by the explanatory vocabulary for modernism's multiple wounds (total war, genocide, terrorism) and abundant anxieties (shell shock, survivor guilt, post-traumatic stress disorder).[154] Contemporary memorial projects can be seen as manifestations of this divergent and contested field of social and medical science. Many First World War memorials are still being built today, and the fact that 2014 marked the war's centenary certainly contributed to their proliferation. New Zealand's Tomb of the Unknown Warrior (2004), dedicated long after the many participating nation-states buried their unknown, also indicates the continued influence of First World War commemorative practices, in this case braided together with the Maori language of remembrance. Many established memorials and monuments standing on sites of First World War battlefields are currently being enlarged to satisfy contemporary requirements. The same is true for Second World War memorials, in particular Holocaust memorials, emerging across Europe and the United States.[155]

Among other reasons, this proliferation can be attributed to the growing, global social network and the ready availability of knowledge and information, conditioned by the internet.[156] The architectural network of contemporary memory projects and representations is affected by this process, which creates a sort of physical mnemonic system – a global theatre of memory.[157] Consequently, architectural forms replicate and end up commemorating different events in different parts of the word in similar ways. Some argue that the power of memorials rests precisely in their generalizability, the ability to provoke similar feelings in people from

[154] Doss, *Memorial Mania*, p. 131.

[155] T. G. Ashplant, Graham Dawson and Michael Roper (eds.), *The Politics of War Memory and Commemoration*, Routledge Studies in Memory & Narrative (London and New York: Routledge, 2000).

[156] Ashplant, Dawson and Roper discern the following key reasons for the contemporary proliferation in war memory: the intense emergence into public visibility of the Shoah; demands by social groups suffering injustice for public recognition; the enhanced profile of anniversary commemorations, for example to mark the beginning and ending of wars; and a new pattern of warfare, stimulated by the collapse of the Soviet Union and the Eastern bloc in Europe (1989–91), fought between peoples in the name of their differences. Ashplant, Dawson and Roper, *The Politics of War Memory and Commemoration*, pp. 3–5.

[157] Malcom Waters argued that globalization is defined by the relationship between social organization and territoriality, distinguished by three central functions of exchange: material exchanges localize, political exchanges internationalize and symbolic exchanges tend to become global. See Mark W. Rectanus, 'Globalization: incorporating the museum', in Sharon Macdonald (ed.), *A Companion to Museum Studies* (Oxford: Blackwell Publishing, 2011), pp. 802–37, p. 804.

different backgrounds.[158] Next to the numerous possibilities to learn about similar projects from various social and cultural contexts, memorial institutions, too, create networks and platforms through which they exchange information and knowledge. Hence, similar architectural expressions can be found in projects created in different parts of the world: South African memorials dedicated to a particular cultural narrative echo European projects that are built for very different purposes.[159] The memorialization of, for instance, the crimes of Apartheid in South Africa, genocide in Bosnia and Herzegovina or state terror in Argentina are widely relevant issues and are a constituent part of the global memory culture, directed by memory politics at both local and national levels. Cultural critic Andreas Huyssen has argued that 'memory projects may construct or revise national narratives, but these narratives are now invariably located in a space somewhere between the global and the local.'[160]

Memorial tourism, popularly called dark tourism, naturally relates to the issue of globalization, as many memorial sites compete in their offer of authenticity, while striving to transform locations into destinations.[161] While dark tourism is not an exclusively modern development and can instead be seen as permanent component of human life, we can recognize that today death is 'being reconceptualised as heritage'.[162] In the race for high visitor counts, authenticity is high on the list of demands. Some memorial sites aim to reify their offer by introducing theatrical effects, often confirming the statement that a 'society of spectacle turns sites of great battles into shows'.[163] For example, the Memorial to the Battle of Arras (2008) in the Wellington Quarry recreates the past into a permanent exhibit by using hi-tech, interactive, scenographic design incorporated into the authentic interior of the quarry where 24,000 soldiers lived between 1916 and 1918. The memorial is part of the 'Trails of Memory' route

158 See, for example, Sabine Marschall, *Landscape of Memory: Commemorative Monuments, Memorials and Public Statuary in Post-Apartheid South Africa* (Leiden: Brill, 2010), p. 116.

159 See, for example, the analysis of Freedom Park in Pretoria, South Africa, in Marschall, *Landscapes of Memory*, pp. 209–41.

160 Andreas Huyssen, *Present Past: Urban Palimpsest and the Politics of Memory* (Stanford, CA: Stanford University Press, 2003), p. 96.

161 See Rob van der Laarse, 'Beyond Auschwitz? Europe's terrorscapes in the age of postmemory', in Marc Silberman and Florence Vatan (eds.), *Memory and Postwar Memorials: Confronting the Violence of the Past* (New York: Palgrave Macmillan, 2013), pp. 71–92, p. 75.

162 Mattias Frihammar and Helaine Silverman, 'Heritage of death. Emotion, memory and practice', in Mattias Frihammar and Helaine Silverman (eds.), *Heritage of Death: Landscapes of Emotion, Memory and Practice* (London and New York: Routledge, 2017), pp. 3–20, p. 5.

163 Ragon, *The Space of Death*, p. 110.

mapped by the Nord-Pas-de-Calais region in northern France, where recently several memorials and museums have been dedicated to commemorate and develop the heritage of the First World War. Here, a visitor's experience is framed by the skilful implementation of acoustic and visual effects that accentuate the feeling of terror and suffering which permeated the war. Apparently, creating this memorial was justified by the growing interest of tourists since 1996, arriving from all over the world to experience the 'intriguing underground project and home for so many in the difficult circumstances of World War I'.[164]

The quest for exclusivity is not unfamiliar to acts of commemoration of important anniversaries. For example, the twentieth anniversary of the beginning of the Siege of Sarajevo was marked in 2012 with an installation called *Sarajevo Red Line*, which consisted of 11,541 red plastic chairs, each chair symbolizing one victim. The chairs were facing a stage where the commemoration ceremony was performed. With its red colour referencing a line of blood, reinforced by hundreds of small chairs that symbolized children victims of the siege, the installation produced a memorable visual effect.[165] In the same vein, the centenary of the First World War in Great Britain was commemorated with an art installation called *Blood Swept Lands and Seas of Red*, featuring 888,246 ceramic poppies, at the Tower of London. The symbolism of both projects is clear and instantly recognizable: using singular objects to demonstrate the scale of destruction is a common feature in commemorative projects. Apart from the aesthetic valorization of these projects and their artistic ideas, the installations raise numerous questions with regard to their context and the effect they have on the remembrance of the events. London's project successfully approached this issue by insisting on public participation (and employed artisans who experienced a personal loss in the war), based on the artist's idea that 'people should get involved in physically making things so that they mean something more',[166] whereas in Sarajevo's case this aspect was missing, and the red chairs were only meant to be observed as an absent audience.

164 La Carriére Wellington, *Mémorial de la Bataille d'Arras* (Carriere Wellington/@Studio K, 2008), p. 2.

165 A chair is a frequently employed element in memorial architecture, for example in the Oklahoma Memorial Museum. It communicates the absence of a person and at the same time the impossibility of grasping the other person's experience.

166 Paul Cummins quoted in 'People', *Leisure Management*, 4 (2014), 8.

Participation and Recovery

A competition in 1978 for a commemoration of the destruction of Lüdenhausen, Germany, in the Second World War yielded a proposal that involved citizens as both designers and owners of the design. The project, entitled 'Pro Memoria Garden' and designed by the Argentinian architect Emilio Ambasz, was devised as a labyrinthine garden with individually assigned gardening plots that needed to be nourished and cared for by the plot owners. In this way, the active participation would, the designer believed, symbolically keep the memory alive. Each plot would be assigned to a newborn and demarcated with a marble slab inscribed with that person's name. The proposed concept was that a person would own the assigned garden from the age of five until death, when the plot would be given to a new owner with a new marble slab placed next to the previous one. The architect hoped that from divided plots the labyrinth would grow into a common community garden and that, interacting in this way, the garden as a memorial in the making would teach people about the respect and value of life. As he argued: 'Children are taught the rudiments of gardening to prepare for a lifetime of responsible cultivation.'[167]

While this type of project was not a common practice in commemorative architecture at the time, today, more than two decades since the sinking of the Gerz column, the invitation for participation seems to be the accepted strategy in public monuments and memorials, even in national projects that are highly politically coloured. An example is the National Memorial to the Algerian War (2002) in Paris, dedicated to the memory of the soldiers who died for France in the Algerian War and during conflicts in Morocco and Tunisia.[168] The memorial consists of three aligned columns, approximately 6 m high, with alphanumeric screens running vertically along the front of each column. Next to the columns is a small computer terminal that allows visitors to search for a particular name which, when detected in the system, is displayed on one of the columns.[169] Similar to Gerz, the designer Gérard Collin-Thiébaut

[167] Emilio Ambasz, 'Pro-Memoria Garden (1978)', available at http://emilioambaszandassociates.com/portfolio/Pro-Memoria-Garden, last accessed 1 November 2017.

[168] The monument stands on the Quai Branly, close to the Eiffel Tower, and was inaugurated on 5 December 2002 by Jacques Chirac. The monument is controversial since it has been argued that the names of some known torturers are listed as well. At the same time, it represents a significant move for France towards addressing its difficult colonial heritage.

[169] The first column screens the names of 22,959 soldiers that scroll upwards in alphabetical order, separated by year of death. The central column displays a text which explains to whom the

employed columns, the most common iconography of war monuments, as a starting point in his quest to create a 'new type of memorial for the third millennium'.[170] More traditional employment of columns, however, can be seen in the Memorial to the Armenian Genocide (2006) in Lyon.

The tendency towards involving visitors not only physically, in the finished work, but also in the creation of a memorial seems to be more and more prominent in contemporary designs as well. One example is the memorial to Kornati Firefighters entitled 'Field of Crosses' (2010) on the island of Kornat in Croatia, which was almost entirely realized by volunteers. Its 12 dry-wall crosses of megalithic dimensions, accompanied by a circular chapel, were put in place by nearly 3,000 participants. It led to a general feeling of 'cathartic atonement'.[171] The broad participation in the construction of the memorial was recognized as crucial in terms of collective and individual witnessing, and of learning and recovering from the collective trauma created by the unfortunate event.

Similarly, Jochen Gerz's project, *The Square of the European Promise* (2015), takes participation as a key element. Surprised by the 1931 'Heroes Memorial Hall' in Bochum's Christ Church, where a memorial mosaic accusingly juxtaposes the names of enemy states with the names of local WWI victims, the artist, loyal to his signature approach, invited citizens to have their names engraved on memorial plaques to be added to this odd memorial. Next to offering their name, each individual was asked to make a private promise to Europe. The collected promises, symbolizing a shared future for all Europeans, remain invisible, as in Gerz's earlier *Square of the Invisible Monument* (1993) in Saarbrücken.[172] By adding names to existing memorial plaques, the artist indirectly refers to certain instances in which the dead of the Second World War were commemorated by their names being inscribed and added to existing WWI memorials. This was frequently seen as a cheap and convenient method of commemoration. The fact that Gerz's new list consists of living individuals remodels this practice to produce new meaning, as the artist argued: 'Europe can only exist if people want it to', and that 'to want Europe means to build upon

memorial is dedicated, and the third column's screen recommences when a name is depicted by a visitor in order to show it on the screen.

170 Robert Aldrich, *Vestiges of the Colonial Empire in France: Monuments, Museums and Colonial Memories* (New York: Palgrave Macmillan, 2004), p. 152.

171 Nikola Bašić, 'A Monument to Kornati Firefighters', *Pogledaj.to*, 27 November 2010, http://pogledaj.to/drugestvari/nikola-basic-a-monument-to-kornati-firefighters, last accessed 4 October 2018.

172 Also known as '2146 Stones-Memorial against Racism'.

the cultural patience, solidarity and imagination of those people, who have not forgotten misery and sorrow, whether they have suffered or caused suffering.'[173] Along this line, one could only wonder if Bochum's accusatory memorial plaque anticipated the destruction of Europe in the Second World War, and what kind of prophetic message might rest in Gerz's memorial to hidden promises of living memory.

Building for the Memory Boom: Electric Age between Amnesia and Permanence

The seemingly contemporary obsession with memory manifests itself in the continuously growing field of memory-studies and its expanding vocabulary including notions such as *countermemory*, *national memory*, *vernacular memory*, *spatial memory* and so forth. The main body of research problematizes the history–memory relationship, with French historian Pierre Nora's extensive volumes *Les Lieux de mémoire* being one of the ground-laying studies for Eurocentric perspective of memory studies. Critics of trends and perceptions shaped by research that attempts to historicize memory stress the connection of valorization of memory and crisis of identity arguing that our 'modern crisis of memory might not be as exceptional as we tend to assume'.[174] Monuments and memorials seem to fulfil the notion of a contemporary 'memory boom' as 'major modes of aesthetic, historical and spatial expression'.[175] According to Andreas Huyssen, the way Western societies remember at the end of the twentieth century can be defined as a 'hybrid memorial-media culture within which museums, monuments and memorials are again finding their *raison d'être*, helping society in a fight against amnesia and an "enlightened false consciousness"'.[176] Such hybrid memory projects are exploring the ways in which commodity culture remembers. At the same time, memory projects seem to regain their status due to their permanence, which, as Huyssen argues, attracts a public 'dissatisfied with simulation and channel-

[173] Jochen Gerz in '49th City Talks: Square of the European Promise. A speech by Jochen Gerz in Bochum Museum of Art, January 17, 2007', available at http://europeanpromise.eu/chronology/49th-city-talks, last accessed 20 December 2018.

[174] Kansteiner, *In Pursuit of German Memory*, p. 15.

[175] Andreas Huyssen, 'Monumental seduction', in Mieke Bal, Jonathan Crewe and Leo Spitzer (eds.), *Act of Memory: Cultural Recall in the Present* (Hanover, NH: Dartmouth College & University Press of New England, 1999), pp. 191–208, p. 191.

[176] Huyssen here paraphrases the German philosopher Peter Sloterdijk. Huyssen, 'Monumental seduction', p. 10.

flicking'.[177] From this point of view, memorials and other compensatory organs of remembrance such as museums, memorials, the study of the humanities, and historical preservations reappear as an alternative to the ruling electronic media of contemporary commodity and temporality generated by the quickening progress of media dissemination. A 'third memory boom' has been defined by 'more immediate, visceral and effervescent digital modes of representation, circulation and connectivity' that at the same time 'sits alongside but also clashes with those modes of representation consolidated by memory institutions and organizations'.[178] Meanwhile, projects like MEMO (Mass Extinction Monitoring Observatory), dedicated to remind us of the Earth's biodiversity and commemorate all the species gone extinct, are designed with the ambition of becoming truly global projects 'with authentic local roots'.[179] In the case of MEMO, this means also seeking its anchorage in space through a building made out of stone, as 'we have always built'.[180]

In reference to their social and political relevance (that normally also includes complicated emotional and psychological dimensions), some memorials constitute globally recognized anchor points in the work of remembrance. Examples include the 9/11 memorial in New York and the Jewish Museum and the MMJE memorial in Berlin. Perhaps lesser-known, but equally contentious is the discussion about commemorating the Berlin Wall that had already begun in 1990, the most prominent question being whether to reconstruct parts of the wall or not. The German Historic Museum, working on the site at the time, wanted to present it as a combination of an open-air exhibition, a museum and a memorial. One part of the preserved strip was to become a 1:1 scale reconstruction, the Museum proposing to complete it with authentic pieces from its own collection, to show what the Wall was really like.[181] This proved to be a highly problematic idea, and it was argued that personal memory would be

177 Andreas Huyssen, *Twilight Memories: Marking Time in a Culture of Amnesia* (New York and London: Routledge, 1995), p. 255. Huyssen refers to 'channel flicking' as a contemporary strategy of narcissistic derealization.

178 Hoskins, 'The restless past', p. 4.

179 MEMO is a collaborative project designed by architect David Adjaye to be placed on the Isle of Portland, on the south coast of Britain. *Mass Extinction Monitoring Observatory* (Weymouth: MEMO, 2014), available at www.memoproject.org/docs/MEMO-Brochure-2014.pdf, last accessed 16 June 2017.

180 Ibid.

181 Gabi Dolff-Bonekämper, 'The Berlin Wall: an archaeological site in progress', in John Schofield, William Gray Johnson and Colleen M. Beck (eds.), *Matériel Culture: The Archaeology of Twentieth-Century Conflict* (London: Routledge, 2002), pp. 236–48, p. 240.

in danger of being obscured by a ready-made image of the reconstructed parts. Those opposed to the reconstruction believed that 'authentic dread cannot be caught in such an installation because the terror was not bound to the objects but to the system' and, more importantly, that 'the dread belongs to those who experienced it – it is neither conservable nor can it be stimulated.'[182] The architectural office Kohlhoff & Kohlhoff decided to retain 60 m of the former no man's land between the two walls as a physical reminder, which is inaccessible to visitors since it is closed off on both ends with new stainless steel walls.[183] The sequence is only visible in its entirety from a viewing platform on the adjacent documentation centre. The rest of the memorial ground can be seen as an open-air museum with a continuous strip of memory in the public space, with the Chapel of Reconciliation rising from rubble, remnants of the former wall structure, some didactic content, a few markings and images of previous times, as well as the remains of torn-down houses. Along this path is a memorial to the victims.

In the American context, the embodiment of modern memory mania is the city of Washington, where a significant number of memorials and monuments have been inaugurated since 1995. According to art historian Erika Doss, memory mania reflects contemporary public feeling and is, as she explained, 'contextualized by a highly successful public art industry, burgeoning interest in "memory studies" and "living" or experiencing history and a shifting understanding of American national identity'.[184] Meanwhile, responses to the public's satiation with memory often take a satirical tone, particularly in contemporary art, as was the case with Claes Oldenburg's work and which can today be seen in the 15-min opera 'Memorial City', portraying a town obsessed with building memorials to everything, even to a person who choked on a pretzel.[185] The purpose of all that memorial-building seems to be forgetting, by chiselling the loss into the stone while architects and experts 'lavish solace on the town's angst-ridden population'.[186] It comes as no surprise then that the Mexican artist

182 Ibid.

183 The inscription on the northen wall reads: 'In Erinnerung an die Teilung der Stadt vom 13 August 1961 bis zum 9 November 1989 und zum Gedenken an die Opfer kommunistischer Gewaltherrschaft' ('In memory of the city's division from 13 August 1961 to 9 November 1989 and of the victims of communist tyranny').

184 Doss, *Memorial Mania*, p. 19.

185 A one-act music-theatre performance with text and drawings by artist Ben Katchor and music by composer Mark Mulcahy.

186 'Second thoughts on the memory industry', symposium, 7 May 2011, The New York Institute for the Humanities and The Humanities Initiative at NYU, press release, available at

Israel López Balan imagined a gigantic cube as a Monument to Fear (2014) in Mexico City, which would operate as an enormous *camera obscura*, large enough to reproduce the surroundings of the Plaza de la Constitución.

A frequently asked question is whether our contemporary culture, equipped with sophisticated and convenient data banks, encourages oblivion instead of active remembrance, as some sort of destructively efficient *pharmakon*,[187] and in the long run fosters oblivion and amnesia instead.[188] If monuments and memorials are built to be admonishments, the purpose of the admonishment remains enigmatic. Has the replication, and globalization, rendered the 'never again' too banal?

In this light, it is significant to ask to what extent memorial projects today, in a new context between the global and the local, are dependent on the social and cultural context they originate from. Discussing Karavan's *Passages* (1994) in Portbou, Shelley Hornstein stressed that if a memorial aims to reach wider audiences, it can achieve that only as an art object or a symbol 'with no relationship to that which it signifies, but needing to be learned in order to become a convention, as does language'.[189] Hornstein believed that by scattering parts of the memorial over the location in order to emphasize its specificity, the designer managed to communicate memory that is both 'local to Portbou and international'.[190] In a certain way, this logic resonates with the principle of remembering by mnemonists who created imaginary memoryscapes in order to provide a much-needed interpretation of the world – *clavis universalis*, or a master key, for understanding how the universe works.[191]

Undoubtedly, erecting monuments and memorials has been a profound human activity since the earliest civilizations. The monument genre was consistently used in processes of political legitimization by the erection of

www.nyu.edu/about/news-publications/news/2011/04/15/second-thoughts-on-the-memory-industrymay-7-.html, last accessed 29 January 2017.

187 In Plato's *Phaedrus*, the Egyptian god of writing Theuth, or Thoth, offers King Thamus writing as a remedy (*pharmakon*) that can help memory. Thamus refuses the gift on the grounds that it will only create forgetfulness because he perceived it not as a remedy for memory itself, but merely a way of reminding.

188 See Doss, *Memorial Mania*; Forty & Kuchler (eds.), *The Art of Forgetting*; Huyssen, *Twilight Memories*. The same questions are asked about the proliferation of museums after the 1970s. See Macdonald (ed.), *Companion to Museum Studies*.

189 Shelley Hornstein, *Losing Site: Architecture, Memory and Place*, Ashgate Studies in Architecture (Farnham and Burlington, VT: Ashgate, 2011), p. 17.

190 Ibid.

191 Paolo Rossi, *Clavis Universalis: Arti Mnemoniche e logica combinatorial da Lullo a Leibniz* (Milan: Ricciardi, 1960).

the new and the destruction or re-purposing of those of previous regimes. Periods when the work of construction was at its height, and when both official and unofficial commemorative projects proliferated, are often defined by significant cultural and social instabilities triggered by nationalistic political agendas and wars. Cities littered with monuments are a consequence of these prolific monument-building episodes when complex commissioning calls were organized, public discussions ensued and designers rushed to offer solutions, for example, during National Socialist and communist dictatorships (including former Yugoslavia) and after the collapse of the Soviet bloc in the newly created nation-states. There are other examples that precede the scope of this book (e.g. statuomania after the French Revolution). The memorial form came to prominence with the rupture of the First World War and continued to evolve after the Second World War, proliferating in the commemorative wave focusing on the two world wars since the 1980s.

Today, designers continue the quest of their predecessors, who had to find design solutions that would address the unprecedented number of the missing and dead soldiers in the First World War and the enormous number of civilian victims of the Second World War. While the debt to the dead seems to grow heavier with time as our knowledge about the wars and their casualties expands, it also means that we are now looking at scars that, at times, bleed because the wounds are reopened. The quest is equally challenging for designers who work on memorials caused by contemporary violence, faced in an atmosphere of shock and disbelief.

At the end of our survey, it seems that the major questions with which we are left are these: first, can contemporary architecture offer meaningful spaces for the bereaved and, if so, why do certain memorial spaces perform better then others? Second, can we learn from the twentieth century's processes of memorial-making and existing knowledge on the psychology of mourning in such a way as to create war memorials appropriate to our own time of post-national era violence and terrorism? And finally, does architectural commemoration help in the recovery of individuals and groups from trauma? Is there any evidence that visiting a memorial closes wounds or fosters forgiveness of the crimes of the last 100 years? These questions provide the axis of inquiry for the remainder of this book.

2 The Dual Role of Memorial Architecture

The Jews were not to be annihilated and then forgotten, but annihilated and then remembered.

Elisabeth Domansky[1]

We have no place to find. Nothing can be settled.

Idriz Merdžanić[2]

Will nicht narben.

Gertrud Riethmüller[3]

When British philosopher Bertrand Russell was invited to participate in a discussion with a proponent of fascist ideology in 1962, he declined with this famous response: 'The emotional universes we inhabit are so distinct, and in deepest ways opposed, that nothing fruitful or sincere could ever emerge from association between us.'[4] In the process of creating memorial architecture, however, it is the merging of such two distinct views that is in the essence of representing atrocities. In a way, Theodor Adorno touches upon this issue with an anecdote about an officer of the Nazi occupation forces who visited Picasso in his studio, inquiring whether he created *Guernica*. Picasso responded: 'No, you did.'[5] The irony present in this encounter is contained in most design efforts directed towards creating something that is at the same time visually appealing and evocative of terror.

[1] The Nazis planned to build a museum of former Jewish life in Prague which would celebrate the Final Solution. See Elisabeth Domansky, '"Kristallnacht", the Holocaust and German unity: the meaning of November 9 as an anniversary in Germany', *History & Memory*, 4.1 (1992), 60–94, p. 60.

[2] Idriz Merdžanić, survivor of Omarska concentration camp, quoted in Ed Vulliamy, *The War Is Dead, Long Live the War: Bosnia: The Reckoning* (London: The Bodley Head, 2012), p. xlii.

[3] Gertrud Riethmüller's inscription on the 'Hotel of Memory' memorial in Neue Bremm reads 'will nicht narben' ('does not want to heal').

[4] Shaun Usher (ed.), *More Letters of Note: Correspondence Deserving of a Wider Audience* (London: Canongate Books Ltd., 2015), p. 146.

[5] Theodor Adorno, 'On commitment', in Ronald Taylor (ed. and trans.), *Aesthetics and Politics: The Key Texts of the Classic Debate within German Marxism* (London and New York: Verso books, 1977), pp. 177–95, p. 178.

Designers of memorial spaces need to temporarily inhabit worlds of destruction in order to construct their representations. Even when commemorating positive examples of non-violent struggle, like the Zanis Lipke Memorial (2012) in Riga, Latvia, the focus on the conditions of destruction more often than not outweighs memories of defiance and humanity. Whether they choose to explicitly refer to the destruction or completely refrain from it, designers are expected to create structures that relate to a given context by adopting approaches that are beneficial for users. Since memorials, unlike other public buildings, are not utilitarian in measurable ways, it is challenging to evaluate their contribution in a precise manner. To tackle this issue, there are two significant points that need to be addressed here in relation to the construction of commemorative architecture today: the understanding of, first, the psychological implications of traumatic experiences and, second, the appropriation of a memorial space.

In the selective process of memorialization, usually constrained by many facets, it is not uncommon to ignore, twist or even alter historical information for the purpose of adding additional meaning to a place of memory. The danger of any representation, and especially the representation of war, is the creation of a myth.[6] A particular example is the so-called Trench of Bayonets at Verdun, where a group of soldiers died during a bombardment in 1916. French soldiers mistakenly interpreted the protruding bayonets (positioned upright by German soldiers who wanted to indicate to the French where the bodies of the dead soldiers were) as the heroic act of brave men who remained in their positions awaiting an awful death. The symbolic significance was instantly recognized, and shortly after the war ended the architect André Ventre, opting for a design that would last '500 years', created a memorial to mark the place and to protect it against 'the attacks of time or the cyclical pillage of the tourists'.[7] Regardless of the confusion of facts, the memorial's recognition as a highly symbolic representation of the human condition in war was significant for coming to terms with the tremendous loss of human life, and turned it into a site of collective mourning. Stressing the importance of such places, Jay Winter argued that

> the activity of remembrance, and the creation of places of collective experience, is irrepressible, expressing fundamental truths about the need

[6] See Jay Winter, *Sites of Memory, Sites of Mourning: The Great War in European Cultural History* (Cambridge: Cambridge University Press, 1995).

[7] Ventre quoted in Winter, *Sites of Memory*, p. 101.

> of ordinary people, of many faces and of none, to face the emptiness, the nothingness of loss in war, together.[8]

In the following chapter, the private and public role of memorial architecture will be addressed in respect of three relevant topics: collective remembrance and competing memories, the process of bereavement and the possibilities of architecture as an element of agency in remembering and dealing with a difficult past. Since rituals are articulated through space, we shall then turn towards a distinction of underlining spatial concepts that are essential in contemporary memorial architecture. The commemorative potential of cemeteries and landscapes will be explored in a brief analysis of the symbolic language and transitional qualities of both funerary and memorial architecture.

2.1 Collective Traumatic Memory and How It Is Constructed

The Materialization of Collective Memory

The controversial term 'collective memory'[9] was coined by the French sociologist Maurice Halbwachs (died in Buchenwald in 1945), who emphasized that memory endures only through the frameworks and spaces provided by social groups (*cadres sociaux de la mémoire*): memory is a socially embedded construct, its development only possible within specific social arrangements. Today, the term is widely scrutinized by scholars and new terms appear such as 'multidirectional memory',[10] 'memory of multitudes'[11] and 'collective remembrance'.[12] As forms of collective remembrance, official commemorations and memorials are the connecting tissue – they ask for participation and can evoke emotions in its participants.[13] In this way collective memories can influence or even become personal memories. Material objects and edifices, together with the visual arts, movies and literature, are carriers of cultural memory since they are

[8] Jay Winter, 'Remembrance and redemption: a social interpretation of war monuments', *Harvard Design Magazine*, 9, special issue: 'Constructions of Memory' (1999), 71 7, p. 77.

[9] Jeffrey K. Olick, 'Collective memory', in *International Encyclopedia of the Social Sciences*, 2nd edn (Detroit, MI: MacMillan Reference USA, 2007), pp. 7–8.

[10] See Rothberg, *Multidirectional Memory.*

[11] Hoskins, 'Memory of the multitude'.

[12] Jay Winter, *Remembering War: The Great War between Memory and History in the Twentieth Century* (New Haven, CT and London: Yale University Press, 2006).

[13] Nancy Scheper-Hughes and Margaret M. Lock, 'The mindful body: a prolegomenon to future work in medical anthropology', *Medical Anthropology Quarterly*, 1.1 (1987), 6–41; Rowlands, 'Remembering to forget', p. 133.

entangled with the process of remembering and are therefore considered immediate agents in the construction of identities. By being a medium for the externalization of memory, they support the imaginative reconstruction of the past and help in constructing one's own identity, in a process termed 'autobiographical memory'.[14] Scholars working in the fields of anthropology, sociology, cultural studies, literary studies and history interpret memory as a socially active agent, essential for the construction of identity. The German Egyptologist Jan Assmann explained collective memory as follows:

> The reusable and available texts, images and rites of each society, with the preservation of which it stabilizes and spreads its self-image; a collective shared knowledge, preferably (but not necessarily) of the past, on which a group's sense of unity and individuality is based.[15]

Inextricable from individual and collective memory, more precisely the construct of the two, cultural memory is a process, bound up with complex political stakes and meanings. Assmann makes a differentiation between potential cultural memories, representations of the past that are systematically preserved in archives and museums, and actual cultural memories that occur when the potentiality of the stored representations is adopted and explored in new contexts. In this process, representations of the past acquire new meanings and change their intensity and social relevance. While exploring the construction of collective memory through the construction of monuments in France after the First World War, Daniel Sherman explained the conventional character of culture as a collection of signs, constructed in a process of representation in order to interpret existing signs. As a result, a culture can be seen as a 'repository for the beliefs and values of a group of people and for the signs and interpretive strategies they share'.[16] Consequently, an artefact that is a product of the representational process becomes a sign of a particular culture.

Running parallel with the work of Halbwachs are the explorations of social memory by the German art historian Aby Warburg, materialized in

[14] Susan Schwartzenberg, 'Re-creating the past: notes on the neurology of memory', in Marc Treib (ed.), *Spatial Recall: Memory in Architecture and Landscape* (New York and London: Routledge, 2009), pp. 42–60.

[15] Jan Assmann, *Das Kulturelle Gedächtnis: Schrift, Erinnerung und politische Identität in frühen Hochkulturen* (Munich: Beck, 1992), p. 11. Quoted in Winter, 'Remembrance and redemption', p. 71.

[16] Sherman, *The Construction of Memory*, p. 6. Sherman refers to Terdiman, *Present Past.*

visual projects such as *Mnemosyne Atlas* (1924–29).[17] Recalling Mnemosyne, the mother of the muses who guarded the pool of memory in Hades, complementing the river of forgetting, Lethe, Warburg's utopian project consisted of a large constellation of symbolic images. These were aimed to animate the viewer's imagination and awareness of symbolical images, and the power they assert on the development of culture and thought. Intuitively charting images from Alexandrian Greece to his contemporaries in Weimar Germany, Warburg aspired to the creation of a dynamic 'thought-space' or *Denkraum*, where one would become aware of both subjective and objective forces that shaped Western culture. Influenced by new ideas about the psychology of perception, Warburg focused on the concept of *mimesis*, or the viewer's identification with the objects on display, where prominence was given to the notion of empathy as a 'force active in the generation of style'.[18] In order to obtain an emotional engagement with the object that would result in 'emphatic reciprocity', the mimetic process, according to Warburg, needs to be mediated by imagination.[19] Hence the employed images, as symbols of the unconscious, transform into logical 'dissociative allegorical signs'.[20] At the same time, Warburg understood social memory as a backdrop for this transformation, as he explained: 'the task of social memory emerges quite clearly: through renewed contact with the monuments of the past the sap should be enabled to rise directly from the subsoil of the past.'[21] In this sense, Warburg's work offered an example of understanding cultural memory through identification with its material legacy.

This theory echoed the seventeenth-century neo-Platonic mnemonists,[22] who created deeply embedded architectural constructions in their minds in

[17] *Mnemosyne Atlas* consisted of 63 wooden panels covered with black cloth, on which were pinned pictures from books, magazines, newspapers and other everyday sources in a non-discursive, frequently digressive character. Christopher D. Johnson, *Memory, Metaphor, and Aby Warburg's Atlas of Images, Signale: Modern German Letters, Cultures, and Thought* (Ithaca, NY: Cornell University Press and Cornell University Library, 2012), pp. 11–12.

[18] Matthew Rampley, 'From symbol to allegory: Aby Warburg's theory of art', *The Art Bulletin*, 79.1 (1997), 41–55, p. 44.

[19] Robert Vischer in his essay 'Über das Optische Formgefühl: Ein Beitrag zur Äesthetik' (1873) argued for art as 'an intensification of sensuousness' through which the mediating role of imagination, a 'fluid medium', could invest the emphatic object with an emotional content. Quoted in Rampley, 'From symbol to allegory', p. 45.

[20] Rampley, 'From symbol to allegory', p. 55. [21] Ibid., 52.

[22] In their search for the hidden structure of the universe, mnemonists Giulio Camillo and Giordano Bruno developed mnemonic techniques which were in fact designed architectural models. Camillo's mnemonic design was in the form of a memory theatre, appropriating an imaginary stage for all human drama to take place, while Bruno inclined towards the more

order to organize a large body of knowledge based on remembering, a method used by the Greek poet Simonides of Ceos in the first century BC.[23] Even though terms such as mnemonics, mnemonize or memorous have almost disappeared now, the mechanisms employed in these memory strategies still exist, for example in the so-called method of loci. Mnemonists structured their imaginary memoryscapes by attaching facts to emotionally evocative images and then categorizing the selected images within an architectural space that was already familiar. In that way, a dispersed body of knowledge was structured and evoked when needed, by a reference incorporated in the imagined, architecturally designed place. This process is echoed in the contemporary understanding of how remembrance works, as suggested by anthropological studies which indicate that in most cases the 'preservation of recollections rests on their anchorage in space'.[24]

Observing how the art of mnemonics works, historian Patrick Hutton recognizes something akin to Sigmund Freud's interest in the deep structure of the mind and human unconsciousness. Hutton connects Freud's theory about screen memories with the classic mnemonic code, the substitution of an image for an idea.[25] Still, the purpose of screen memories as mnemonic images that displace deeper, hidden memories, is described by Hutton as 'reverse mnemonics', because they help us forget traumatic experiences, rather than remember them.[26] Forgetting is a part of remembering; it can even be considered necessary, inevitable in every decision on what and how to commemorate. The demanding issue of exclusion and inclusion in remembering was elaborated already by French psychiatrists from the nineteenth century, who sought to understand precisely how much forgetting is beneficial before it could be regarded as a disease.[27]

complex design of a memory wheel, in order to provide a paradigm for all knowledge of heaven and earth. Frances A. Yates, *The Art of Memory* (London: Routledge & Kegan Paul, 1992). Originally published in 1966.

23 See Pim den Boer, 'Loci memoriae-Lieux de mémoire', in Astrid Erll, Ansgar Nünning and Sara B. Young (eds.), *A Companion to Cultural Memory Studies* (Berlin and New York: De Gruyter, 2010), pp. 19–25.

24 Nathan Wachtel, 'Memory and history: introduction', *History and Anthropology* 12 (1986), 207–24, p. 216.

25 Sigmund Freud, 'Screen Memories' (1899), in Gali S. Reed and Howard B. Levine (eds.), *On Freud's 'Screen Memories'* (London: Karnac Books, 2015), pp. 1–25.

26 Patrick H. Hutton, 'The art of memory reconceived: from rhetoric to psychoanalysis', *Journal of the History of Ideas*, 48.3 (1987), 371–92.

27 Théodul Ribot, the founder of the *Revue philosophique de la France et de l'éntranger*, Albert Guillon and Eugene Azam. See Michael Roth, *Memory, Trauma, and History: Essays on Living with the Past* (New York: Columbia University Press, 2011).

Apart from the clinical point of view on forgetfulness, Hutton based his argument on Foucault's notion of 'counter-memory', which concerns the proclaimed problem of oblivion and amnesia in modern times, demonstrated in the occurrence of counter-memorials.[28] In a similar vein, Pierre Nora argued that 'modern memory' is mainly archival and that it 'relates to the materiality of the trace, the immediacy of the recording, the visibility of the image'.[29]

Monuments and memorials are an indelible part of both collective and personal memory, since they provide a framework through which memories are localized, but it is the anthropological value of a commemorative structure that shapes its meaning. Cultural memory invested in, for instance, a memorial, is a kind of memory that expands in time and can be passed on to the next generation. The same applies to political memory, which is best reflected in institutionalized projects of memory, official monuments or consecrated places. Hence, monuments and memorials are an inseparable part of the dynamic memory process, as the prolific history of memorial architecture shows. As a representation of memory, commemorative architecture is symbolic and therefore open to interpretation. Reading monuments as symbols implies an understanding of their usually intricate background, since symbols stand for the most fundamental and at the same time vaguest concepts of human thoughts and ideas.

The Problem of Contested Memory and Generic Design

The issue of inscribing and reading memorial architecture is particularly contested in cases of difficult memory. If we understand commemoration as performative, or more precisely as a 'collective representation of a shared view of a past worth recalling',[30] the selection of narratives to be performed and commemorated is a far from easy task for any nation dealing with inglorious or traumatic events. Here too, decisions about what and how to commemorate are often contested, inevitably leaving out details and parts of the narrative.

The prolonged debates that accompanied plans for the MMJE in Berlin, popularly called the Holocaust Memorial, discussed in the first chapter,

[28] Michel Foucault, *Language, Counter-Memory, Practice: Selected Essays and Interviews* (Ithaca, NY: Cornell University Press, 1977).

[29] Pierre Nora, 'Between memory and history: les lieux de mémoire', *Representations*, 26 (1989), pp. 7–24, p. 13.

[30] Efrat Ben-Ze'ev, Ruth Ginio and Jay Winter (eds.), *Shadows of War: A Social History of Silence in the Twentieth Century* (Cambridge: Cambridge University Press, 2010), p. 20.

perhaps best illustrate how contested the contemporary perception of the form and use of a commemorative monument or memorial can become, due to selective remembrance. This is even more so because the memorial was intended to commemorate the genocide as a whole, on a site the historical significance of which was decidedly ignored in favour of a more general symbolism. Similarly, the Shoah memorial 'Binario 21' (2013) at Milan Central Station[31] grappled with this issue, in an atmosphere of indifference to the fact that Italy was an active participant in the Holocaust.[32] Some argue that the sudden interest in memorial architecture in Italy has to do with assuaging a sense of awkwardness, while avoiding the acknowledgement of guilt for an estimated 8,000 Jewish deportees.[33] At the same time, the veneration of the war criminal Rodolfo Graziani, a fascist commander also known as the 'Butcher of Fezzan', who was sentenced to 19 years of imprisonment for collaborating with the Nazis, has produced a mausoleum in Graziani's home town, to memorialize its 'famous son'.[34] The front of the Mausoleum, dedicated in 2012, reads 'Patria' and 'Onore', inscriptions that display a national pride which in this context directly refers to the darkest chapters of Italy's past.

The ethically complex issue concerning the representation of perpetrators is becoming a more prominent topic. For example, the serene landscape of the former transit camp in Westerbork, in the Netherlands, reveals little of its dark history to everyday passersby, since the camp's barracks were destroyed after its last residents, the Moluccans, left in 1971. The site of the former transit camp, now mostly used as a popular recreation site, is dotted with discretely dispersed monuments and

[31] The station (1931) was designed at the request of then Prime Minister Benito Mussolini to reflect the ideology of Italian fascism. The secret track used for the deportation of Jews in the Second World War, rediscovered in 1995, lies underground, at a short distance from the 24 regular platforms, to the east of the station's main entrance. Since 2002, there was a plan to build a memorial, the Memoriale della Shoah al binario 21, to commemorate the 7,000 Jews deported in 1944 from Milan to the concentration and extermination camps of Auschwitz–Birkenau or Bergen–Belsen, or to Italian collection camps such as Fossoli and Bolzano. The memorial, designed by Morpugo & De Curtis Architetti Associati and inaugurated in 2013, features a large inscription reading 'Indifferenza' at the entrance.

[32] Meanwhile, the Museum of the Shoah in Rome is planned to be constructed at Villa Torlonia, one of Mussolini's favorite retreats, and a National Museum of Judaism and the Shoah opened at the site of a former prison in Ferrara.

[33] Bridget Kevane, 'A wall of indifference: Italy's Shoah memorial', *The Jewish Daily Forward*, 29 June 2011, http://forward.com/articles/139293/a-wall-of-indifference-italy-s-shoah-memorial, last accessed 11 October 2017.

[34] David Willey, 'Italy memorial to fascist hero Graziani sparks row', BBC News, 15 August 2012, www.bbc.co.uk/news/world-europe-19267099, last accessed 16 October 2017.

Figure 2.1 Camp Westerbork – Commander's House (2015), Westerbork; Oving Architects.
Photo: Author

memorials. Concerned with the efficiency of the existing commemorative techniques, the managerial team decided to preserve a dilapidated house which belonged to the former commander of the camp. Even though the question of restoring and exhibiting the building as part of the itinerary, without endangering the historical narrative and its sense of place, remains much debated, since 2014 the officer's house is displayed as a museum artefact, covered by a large glass box (Figure 2.1). The strategy of preservation in Westerbork echoes the explanation given by the designers of Milan's Shoah memorial, who also struggled with ways of bringing the suppressed back to the fore. They had argued that 'you can't put the Shoah in a museum under glass. It's impossible.'[35] That this was done in Westerbork only underlines the fact that each place of memory comes with a unique context, and that certain design solutions can work in one place but not in another.

The erasure of barracks and other infrastructure was not unusual at the end of the Second World War, usually by the people who operated them. Since reconstruction can be seen as too problematic for multiple reasons,

[35] Guido Morpugo, of Morpugo & De Curtis Architetti Associati, argued: 'We had to try to bring to the surface some sign of something that was absolutely invisible in Milan. They didn't want a traditional museum. Here "the content and the container coincide."' Quoted in Jill Goldsmith, 'Memory in the making', *The New York Times*, 8 September 2011, www.nytimes.com/2011/09/11/arts/design/slowly-building-a-memorial-of-the-shoah-in-milan.html?_r=1&ref=design, last accessed 14 October 2017.

memorialization in such situations is mainly focused on demarcations of the original layout. In time, however, this strategy can prove too ambiguous, as the Westerbork example demonstrates. A case in point is the Jasenovac memorial site in Croatia, designed by the 'doomed architect' Bogdan Bogdanović. The setting of the former camp is accentuated in a more abstract, wavy landscape, similar to First World War battlefields but reminiscent too of primordial burial mounds. Among the dunes, each representing a specific building that once existed on the former camp site, stands a central monument, a so-called stone flower, the most dominant feature in the landscape. As an addition to the existing museum, the memorial marks the place in an uncanny way that is at once disturbing and comforting. The information about the numbers of deaths and the torture methods used at Jasenovac and its sub-camps are provided in the museum building at the entrance to the memorial site. For decades, the site has been the focus of a dispute initiated by Serbian and Jewish groups in Croatia who argue that the existing memorial serves as a political veil for the Croatian participation in the Second World War and the horrendous mechanisms of destruction established by the infamous Ustaša.[36] The accusations about historical revisionism at Jasenovac and the call for changes to the museum's exhibitions are becoming more prominent as the revitalization of the Ustaša regime seems to gain ground.[37] Bogdanović's poetic memorial remains in the background.

The matter of infamous colonial episodes is another highly contested arena that involves other European countries as well, perhaps equally disturbed and uncomfortable with questions concerning public acknowledgements and apologies. A closer look at contemporary memorials and museums dealing with this topic will demonstrate that there is a predominance of commemorative projects that promote ambiguity and are barely touching upon the actual reality of these contemporary issues. If we look at France's Memorial to the Abolition of Slavery (2012) in Nantes or Norway's Steilneset Memorial (2011) commemorating the seventeenth-century executions of people accused of witchcraft, there is an abundance of lamenting atmospheres to be discovered, but there are no significant attempts to address the current situation of millions of people suffering under similar conditions to those being commemorated. Their role then, as

[36] Estimates of the numbers killed at Jasenovac vary widely. Independent historians put the number of victims at between 80,000 and 100,000. Some Serbs put the death toll at more than 700,000.

[37] Van der Laarse, 'Beyond Auschwitz?'.

the most commonly used media for defining political battles in the public realm, should be to break the silence about repressed pasts. The limits of their agency, however, are foremost determined by the political will of their commissioners. On the other hand, if appropriated by their users, they can become active agents in the revitalization of relevant pasts.

The Destruction and Manipulation of Traumatic Memory

In 2003, Colin Powell, then United States Secretary of State, gave a speech to the United Nations Security Council making the case for war against Iraq. It will be remembered partly for the fact that UN officials hung a blue curtain over a tapestry reproduction of Picasso's *Guernica*, positioned at the entrance of the UN Security Council behind where Powell was to speak. The motives for covering up the artwork, with its powerful message about the carnage and destruction of civilians in war, remain controversial, in spite of official attempts to justify the act with the excuse that the sharp lines and grey tones of *Guernica* were inconvenient for television cameras. The irony of covering up *Guernica*, a globally known synonym for human suffering, within the chambers of the UN while considering the possibility of creating new carnage, is all too obvious. The carnage in the Basque region of Guernica in 1937 – something Europe witnessed for the first time in full description via daily media coverage – forewarned of the coming catastrophe of the Second World War.[38]

Covering it up only served to demonstrate *Guernica*'s power as an art object in the service of memory. As effective symbols for the revision of the past or the legitimization of previous political orders, architectural monuments are the most common targets for destruction in times of turmoil and war, prompted by a similar desire to 'cover up'. The rearrangement of commemorative monuments 'asserts the recurrence of national power and humiliates the former master because the destruction of a statue symbolically devaluates the commemorated person or event from sacred to profane'.[39] Architecture in general and commemorative monuments, together with sacred spaces and other architectural edifices of high

[38] See Gijs van Hensbergen, *Guernica: The Biography of a Twentieth-Century Icon* (New York and London: Bloomsbury, 2005).

[39] See Inge Melchior and Oane Visser, 'Voicing past and present uncertainties: the relocation of a Soviet World War II memorial and the politics of memory in Estonia', *Focaal-Journal of Global and Historical Anthropology*, 59 (2011), 33–50, p. 35.

identification value, become easy targets and tools for the dehumanization of 'the other'.[40] As such, the destruction of architecture as a signifier for the collective identity of the other can be linked directly to 'memoricide', a concept used by Robert Bevan to denote the destruction of cultural artefacts that enable a group of people to maintain their integrity and particular way of life. Monuments support the feeling of belonging to larger entities and they provide an illusion of permanence and stability.[41] They are thus material tools for the establishment of identity, encouraging the feeling of belonging and continuity, whereas the deliberate destruction of an architectural monument aims at humiliating the other and coercing forgetting. The destruction of their architectural edifices goes hand in hand with the dehumanization of that particular people. Such was the case with Kristallnacht in 1938, Mostar's old bridge in 1993, New York's twin towers in 2001, and many more examples throughout history and today that are destroyed in order to annihilate the people who created them. As Bevan puts it: '[t]he continuing fragility of civilized society and decency is echoed in the fragility of its monuments.'[42]

Along these lines, Bogdanović observed that the need to build runs parallel with the need to destroy. The Column of Trajan (107–13 AD), for example, materializes this assertion by representing both the destruction of Dacian buildings and the construction of Roman camps juxtaposed in one architectural edifice. Bogdanović understood that the contemporary destruction of architecture occurs due to 'modern barbarians', who in times of war have an opportunity to feed their latent hatred towards cities.[43] There is an abundance of historical records asserting this connection, going back as far as Rome's urbicide over Carthage,[44] the extensive

40 Here I refer to 'the other' as a notion that designates the different ethnic, religious or cultural background of a certain group of people.

41 Hannah Arendt argued that 'the reality and reliability of the human world rests primarily on the fact that we are surrounded by things more permanent than the activity by which they are produced.' Hannah Arendt, *The Human Condition: A Study of the Central Dilemma Facing Modern Man*, 2nd edn (Chicago, IL: University of Chicago Press, 1998), pp. 95–6.

42 Robert Bevan, *The Destruction of Memory: Architecture at War* (London: Reaktion Books, 2006), p. 8.

43 Modern barbarians are, according to Bogdanović, a semi-urban population that can't decide if they belong to a rural or urban area and therefore identify with neither. This opposition generates hatred towards cities as some unreachable ideal. Bogdanović also argued that the killing of the 'personality of the city' is an even bigger crime than its physical destruction. For more on Bogdanović's work, see Vladimir Vuković, 'Writing about cities: literary works of Bogdan Bogdanović about cities and urbanism', *SAJ*, 3.1 (2011), 1–14.

44 Famously, 'Carthage must be destroyed' was M. Porcius Cato's recurring admonishment in political speeches.

destruction of monuments during the French Revolution, and the same in the Soviet Union and Warsaw Pact states at the end of the Second World War. This is true even today, when we witness the outrageous destruction of cultural heritage in Mali, Syria, Palestine and other places. As a response to overwhelming destructive powers, some recognize that the pace of destruction exceeds that of the rituals provided by commemorative practices; this calls for some kind of new mnemonics in which monuments and memorials can become vital social figures.[45]

With a motivation to counteract the destruction that prevailed during the Second World War, the French philosopher Jean-François Lyotard stressed that 'one must, certainly, inscribe in words, in images.'[46] Rethinking the sense of representation after Auschwitz from a much-needed distance, during which time the events of the Second World War became clearer and better documented, Lyotard believed that the common ways of archiving memory, such as inscribing or recording, were insufficient since anything that is inscribed can be effaced.[47] The urgency and necessity to represent the event, the Holocaust in this case, were present, but a suitable form or medium in which this would be possible had to be found, beyond the conventional ways of representation, since the event exceeded them. In contemporary society these questions are equally relevant, and representations of memory constantly face dilemmas, such as whether it is possible to commemorate destruction with destruction, or with architecture that tries to recreate destruction by constructing spaces evocative of traumatic experiences. In both situations, destruction, with all its negative aspects, becomes a prequel to construction.

In response to these issues, many advocate small-scale commemorations and memorials, arguing that only these can be authentic to the memory-work of specific kinship groups. This approach is supported by memory studies that place kinship as a connecting part for all levels of memory processes. Small-scale commemoration, as Jay Winter points out, is more resistant towards the ulterior political motives of those in power, since these motives 'lead to a hijacking of the event and its deployment as a means of legitimating the current order'.[48] In other words, sites of mourning can easily be

[45] See Andrew Shanken, 'The memory industry and its discontents: the death and life of a keyword', in Treib (ed.), *Spatial Recall*, pp. 218–39.

[46] Jean-François Lyotard, *Heidegger and 'the jews'*, trans. Andreas Michel and Mark S. Roberts (Minneapolis, MN: University of Minnesota Press, 1990), p. 26.

[47] Ibid.

[48] Jay Winter, 'Thinking about silence', in Ben-Ze'ev, Ginio and Winter (eds.), *Shadows of War*, pp. 1–30, p. 28. See also Winter, *Remembering War*.

transformed into 'sites of mobilization' that facilitate the official commemorations of extremist political ideologies.[49] This occurred in Germany, where the commemoration of the First World War, developed under the democratic aspirations of the Weimar Republic, was gradually subsumed in exercises of nascent fascism. An unprecedented example of such mobilization could be seen in Italy during Mussolini's rule when monuments and memorials were reused or built as a reinforcement of fascist propaganda.

As we saw in the previous chapter, the search for appropriate ways and formal solutions for commemorating difficult pasts constitutes a tumultuous and, at times, impossible journey. In this quest, it is not uncommon that architecture falls victim to its faith in technology. While creating designs that need to satisfy demands for 'prosthetic' experiences, it takes skill not to fall into traps of banalization. With the occurrence of the genre of Holocaust museums, for example, some architects aimed to create emotionally evocative architecture by adopting, in true postmodernistic fashion, concentration camp iconography: barbed wire, crematorium chimneys, guard towers, and an extensive use of brick and stripped metal, as materials associated with the industrialized destruction of lives during the Second World War. In some instances, such references were employed to the point where comparisons with Disney Animation Studios were made.[50]

Still, we could argue that an absence of failed attempts to address difficult pasts in experimental ways would be an indication of architects and designers playing it too safe. The two ends of the spectrum are perfectly captured in Erwin Panofsky's reflection on contemporary art: 'While it is true that commercial art is always in danger of ending up as a prostitute, it is equally true that noncommercial art is always in danger of ending up as an old maid.'[51] Either way, in order to become valuable points of reference, memory and its traces need to be appropriated. If this is not the case, most likely the unclaimed objects of memory will be exposed to neglect, a process which is difficult to study and therefore remains neglected itself.[52]

The case of the Sarajevo Roses is a rather intriguing example of the slow pace of the destruction of memory traces which results in obscuring

[49] George L. Mosse, *Fallen Soldiers: Reshaping the Memory of the World Wars* (New York and Oxford: Oxford University Press, 1990).

[50] Rosenfeld compared strikingly similar features in the Holocaust Memorial Center in Michigan designed by Neumann/Smith and Associates, and Disney Animation Studios in Burbank, California. Rosenfeld, *Building after Auschwitz*, pp. 287–94.

[51] Erwin Panofsky in Emily J. Levine, *Dreamland of Humanists* (Chicago, IL and London: University of Chicago Press, 2013), p. 12.

[52] Shanken, 'Towards a cultural geography'.

remembrance. Imprints of the mortar shells fired during the Siege of Sarajevo were starkly present in the city's buildings, streets and pavements after the siege ended. At one point, the traces on the streets were filled with a red coloured resin, strongly suggestive of human blood. The designer, Nedžad Kurto, explained that this simple design gesture was intended as a silent reminder for those who remembered the explosions and their victims. Indeed, there are no plaques, or any other kind of explanation attached to the Sarajevo Roses. In the course of the following years, the Sarajevo Roses deteriorated as their red colour bleached or new layers of asphalt were added on top, leaving only a few roses visible at random locations. Kurto explained that the Sarajevo Roses are memorials of documentary significance. They do not need to be looked after and might disappear anytime; they are neither a monument nor a particularly stimulating innovation. Instead, they were intended to be a discreet signifier for the *loci* of commemoration.[53]

The preservation of shrapnel perforations is not new and has been practised in several places, for instance in Beirut, Budapest and Warsaw, as an immediate suggestive attempt to keep the cause of a severe trauma alive, as if preventing the perpetrator from escaping the place of a crime. But in the case of the Sarajevo Roses the essential question, related to their future existence, remains in the shadow of their appropriation. They are supposed to belong to the citizens of Sarajevo, but due to a highly complex political structure, a consequence of the Dayton Agreement which ended the war in 1995, Sarajevo's roses remain only a silent reminder destined to disappear, as the concept of 'belonging to the citizens' proved too ambiguous in the aftermath of the siege. In this way, the roses become a twofold assignment to contemporary memorial projects and their designers: to better understand the psychological aspects of difficult remembrance and to consider the importance of appropriation.

2.2 Coming to Terms with Loss and the Individual Mourning Process

Recent Developments in Western Mourning Practices

In the ancient world, commemoration and burial were extremely important rituals. If performed successfully, they would ensure the well-being of

[53] Nedžad Kurto, 'Memory of the dying city', in Azra Junuzović, *Sarajevo Roses: Towards Politics of Remembering* (Sarajevo: Armis Print, 2006), pp. 147–50.

the community and bring peace to the deceased person in the afterlife. It was strongly believed that ill fortune could come upon a community if the ritual was not performed well enough. This belief invigorated funeral rites in the ancient Mediterranean world, as a specific obligation and constituent part of collective memory.[54] Since ancient times, death and its commemoration were inextricable from community life and typically set in a religious context. The performance of the commemorative ritual was also intended to tame the feeling of loss and render it as a natural transition to the other world. In this way, the public ritual of 'taming death' created a sense of control, allowing its participants to overcome loss. Each individual was part of the community, while death was simply a transitional phase towards eternal life. Through the specific stages of these rituals, the community involved itself in the process of mourning, sharing the burden of death with the relatives of the deceased.

Some sociologists have argued that this conception of mourning as taming the unknown changed with the modernization and secularization of the West.[55] The main indication is the significant decline of mourning practices today when compared to mourning rituals up until the nineteenth century. While the burden of mourning shifted from the community to the individual, the practice of cremation contributed to a further separation of ritual and mourning, as crematoria often 'fail to meet the needs of both secular and religious mourners, and are sometimes seen as factories with conveyor belts, offering little in the way of spiritual meaning'.[56] The shift from collective to individual mourning developed throughout the course of a few centuries. As early as 1814, Benjamin Constant wrote about urban estrangement as a corollary of severed community bonds:

> Individuals, lost in an isolation from nature, strangers to the place of their birth, without contact with their past, living only in a rapid present,

[54] See for example Numa Denis Fustel De Coulanges, *The Ancient City: A Study of the Religion, Laws, and Institutions of Greece and Rome* (New York: Dover Publications, 2006), pp. 14–17. Originally published in 1874.

[55] On death as a topic of estrangement in modern society, see Philippe Ariès, *Western Attitudes towards Death: From the Middle Ages to the Present*, trans. Patricia M. Ranum (Baltimore, MD: Johns Hopkins University Press, 1974); Zygmunt Bauman, *Mortality, Immortality and Other Life Strategies* (Stanford, CA: Stanford University Press, 1992); and Michel de Certeau, *The Practice of Everyday Life* (Berkeley, CA: University of California Press, 2011).

[56] Pat Jalland, *Death in War and Peace: A History of Loss & Grief in England, 1914–1970* (New York: Oxford University Press, 2010), p. 260.

> and thrown down like atoms on an immense and levelled plain, are detached from a fatherland that they see nowhere.[57]

As a consequence, the focus was placed on understanding the psychoanalytic aspects of individual mourning. In this respect, French medievalist and historian Philippe Ariès has argued that the *invisible death*, which he defined as a biological transition from the world of the living towards a posthumous non-existence, is deprived of significance in contemporary society, in which the emphasis has been placed on the survivor's acceptance of death.[58] In contrast to the old social ritual that provided a framework for the suppressed emotions of the survivors, Ariès explained the new view of death as an 'embarrassingly graceless dying, which embarrasses the survivor because it causes too strong an emotion to burst forth'.[59] In this view, in the contemporary arid landscape of alienation, the public display of strong emotions is perceived as odd or even inappropriate.[60]

More recent studies, however, have argued that the relationship between modernity and religious decline is oversimplified. Even though the traditional ritual has lost its pre-eminence, the essentially human need to mourn still finds a way to channel itself through different modes of grieving. Agnostics and atheists in particular seem to place emphasis on memory as a 'prime consolation in the absence of religious faith and the loss of personal immortality in an afterlife'.[61] Recent developments are focused on a personalized design of cremation ceremonies, and on creating more room for public emotion, demonstrating that the dead are (again) merging with the space of the living. The topic of grief is becoming ever more prominent, especially so with art installations such as *An Occupation of Loss* (2016), a joint project by conceptual artist Tyron Simon and architect Shohei Shigematsu, which aims to tackle fundamental questions concerning ways of performing grief, the materialization of loss and the role of context in the process of mourning.

57 Benjamin Constant, *De l'esprit de conquête et de l'usurpation dans les rapports avec la civilization européene* (1814), in Benjamin Constant, *Oeuvres*, annotated with an introduction by Alfred Roulin (Paris: Bibliothèque de la Pleiade, 1957), p. 984, quoted in Anthony Vidler, *The Architectural Uncanny: Essays in the Modern Unhomely* (Cambridge, MA: MIT Press, 1992), p. 4.

58 Ariès points to invisible death as a contemporary concept of coping with death by perceiving medical personnel as masters of death who try to provide for their patients an 'acceptable style of living while dying'. Ariès, *Western Attitudes*, p. 89.

59 Ibid.

60 As Ariès argues, 'too evident sorrow does not inspire pity but repugnance, it is the sign of mental instability or of bad manners: it is morbid.' Ibid., p. 90.

61 Jalland, *Death in War and Peace*, p. 259.

As set forth in Chapter 1, the impact and influence of the First World War constructed new frameworks for contemporary commemoration practices. A vast number of war memorials built after the First World War can be understood as part of the mourning process, as psychological points of focus that enable the bereaved to mourn both individually and collectively. The nine million people who fought in the war, out of which four million were missing, urgently sought a kind of spirituality that religion and existing rituals were not able to provide. For example, the names of the dead, normally inscribed on tombstones within cemeteries, entered public space in the memorialization of the First World War, as a consequence of so many obliterated bodies without identities.[62] In all participating countries, feelings of loss and trauma were in need of a framework of mediation and were spontaneously channelled through novel forms, such as the Tomb of the Unknown Soldier. At the same time, the unprecedented scale of bloodshed was inevitably entangled with political interests that employed tradition as a meaningful source of understanding and continuity that had the potential 'to help people to restore and regain control over their lives'.[63] Jay Winter argues that in Britain, for instance, there was a mourning process that was marked by classical, romantic and religious notation informing public rituals and the erection of monuments to the dead.[64] Initially, most of these war memorials were conceived as monuments to victory; due to the needs of families in post-war societies, they quickly became monuments to suffering, particularly in the small villages and communities where 'the names on the memorial have faces for those who read them.'[65]

As a counter to the loneliness of individual mourning, many spontaneous gestures of mourning in the public sphere took place. A widely noted model was the dedication ceremony of Lutyens' Cenotaph in London. The Cenotaph, initially constructed as a temporary structure, was the centrepiece of the 1919 gathering that took place on the anniversary of Armistice Day in London, where a two-minute silence was introduced. Due to the public outburst of grief of around two million people, the Cenotaph was later remade in Portland stone and until this day serves as a key place for

[62] Layla Renshaw, 'The archeology and material culture of modern military death', in Sarah Tarlow and Liv Nilsson Stutz (eds.), *The Oxford Handbook of the Archeology of Death and Burial* (Oxford: Oxford University Press, 2013), pp. 763–80, p. 765.

[63] Goebel, *The Great War*, p. 286. Goebel discusses the mobilization of medievalism arguing that 'the dialectic of lamenting the human catastrophe and insisting on historical continuity was at the core of medievalist diction in war remembrance in Britain and Germany alike' (p. 288).

[64] Winter, *Sites of Memory*, p. 79.

[65] Ragon, *The Space of Death*, p. 108.

remembering the victims of the First World War: an emblem of timelessness – a three-dimensional form of silent mourning. It was the public that wanted the permanent form of the Cenotaph to 'record – to hold – the silence that was gathered within it and which, thereafter, would emanate from it'.[66]

A similar occurrence followed the death of Princess Diana in 1997, which provoked a massive public expression of grief manifested in the numerous objects left at the gates of Kensington Palace and other places, leaving authorities with the task of removing the piles of collected flowers and objects. In these cases, photographs of the victim are frequently offered, giving the whole ritual a sense of individuality and objecting to the inevitable fate of the victim becoming a statistic. These temporary memorials, or grassroots memorials, are one of the most common impromptu expressions of grief on sites of trauma and tragedy.[67] The importance of spontaneous memorials in contemporary culture lies in their essentially material existence, which signifies the process of mourning and intimates an individual's relationship with the deceased in the public space. By placing objects, notes or any kind of sign on a designated place, people instinctively identify that place as a place for mourning and establishing a connection with the dead. The American folklorist Jack Santino was possibly the first to use the term 'spontaneous shrines' to describe the process of public mourning for the victims of political assassinations in Northern Ireland. The locations of these events are transformed through the material objects produced by public mourning and, as such, are significant for understanding the process of bereavement. Santino termed the spontaneous offerings *performative commemoratives* because they 'display death in the heart of social life'.[68] They come to represent what cemeteries used to represent before the nineteenth century, when they were still part of the inner city and everyday public life. When cemeteries and mourning became more private and intimate, spontaneous memorials emerged as cultural phenomena, reviving the ritual of public mourning in new conditions.

66 Dyer, *The Missing of the Somme*, p. 24.

67 Christina Sanchez-Carretero and Carmen Ortiz, 'Grassroots memorials as sites of heritage creation', in Helmut Anheier and Yudhishthir Raj Isar (eds.), *The Culture and Globalization Series [4]: Heritage, Memory & Identity* (London: Sage, 2011), pp. 106–13.

68 Jack Santino, 'Not an unimportant failure: rituals of death and politics in Northern Ireland', in Michael McCaughan (ed.), *Displayed in Mortal Light* (Antrim: Antrim Arts Council, 1992), n.p.

Grief, Mourning, Trauma and the Role of Materiality

The concept of 'working through' grief can be traced back to Freud, who provided a framework for understanding the psychological aspects of mourning. Freud's work dealt with different types of processes: mourning related to the loss of a loved one, and a more abstract form of mourning which can occur with the loss of some higher ideal (such as the loss of a homeland, for example). In his watershed essay *Mourning and Melancholia* (1917), Freud argued that mourning was necessary for the grief-stricken to avoid melancholia when one can lack a point of focus, unable to put loss into perspective.[69] According to Freud, in the process of a 'psychical working out' two psychological liaisons play a role in mourning: one defined as libido, or strength of the attachment, and the other as object-love, or the attachment itself. This process was explained as an internal affair of constant invocation of painful memories, until both libido and object-love become neutralized. More recent scholarly work explaining reasons and forms of bereavement and grief recognized the renewed interest in the commemoration of the First World War in the 1990s as an unfinished process of mourning due to the vast number of missing soldiers.[70] The modern approach to trauma and victims of trauma displays a great deal of interest and research devoted to the concept of healing from traumatic events. Literature scholar Laura Tanner underlined the importance of a 'materiality of the body' in the mourning process. Tanner argued that Freud's model of mourning denies the mourner's need for materiality. Without the material component, according to Tanner, the bereaved 'witness that loss again and again as our minds construct the absent presence of bodies we can no longer hold through images we are unable to touch'.[71]

The process of mourning is a complex and delicate matter that is extensively studied. There are numerous examples that shed light on how both individual and collective mourning are performed and structured around material objects or spaces, in order to support the concept of working through the legacy of traumatic experiences. Since it is impossible

[69] Sigmund Freud, 'Mourning and Melancholia', in *The Standard Edition of the Complete Psychological Works of Sigmund Freud*, ed. and trans. James Strachey, vol. 14 (1914–1916) (London: The Hogarth Press, 1957), pp. 243–58.

[70] Stéphane Audoin-Rouzeau and Annette Becker, *14–18: Understanding the Great War* (New York: Farrar, Straus and Giroux, 2014).

[71] Laura E. Tanner, *Lost Bodies: Inhabiting the Borders of Life and Death* (Ithaca, NY: Cornell University Press, 2006), p. 13.

to briefly summarize its dynamics, for the purpose of this study it suffices to discuss the successive stages that are usually distinguished. Religious scholar Peter Homans schematizes the transformative process of mourning in the following relation:

> ATTACHMENT - LOSS - GRIEVING - MOURNING - REATTACHMENT.[72]

This scheme is incorporated in the context of a specific culture, thereby adjusted to particular needs and customs. Hence, grief and mourning are related but different notions in the sense that mourning is perceived as a symbolic action triggered by grief. Grief is an emotion, the capacity to express a specific feeling, while mourning is a process which enhances different abilities in human beings. Grief, as an individual emotional response to bereavement, is defined by the strength of the relationship with the deceased. A period of mourning is aimed at 'curing' a human being from the grief caused by a particular loss. Research has indicated that healthy oscillations are needed between 'dwelling on the death, the grief, and the emotions on the one hand, and dealing with the practical consequences on the other'.[73]

On the collective scale, it is still difficult to analyse this process through psychoanalytic or psychological categories due to the lack of appropriate methods that can scientifically discern the dynamics of collectives. Public outbursts of spontaneous mourning such as the ones mentioned above, however, correspond with the model of action-orientated mourning proposed by clinical psychologists. This model is based on several distinct steps that the bereaved have to take in order to cope with and adjust to the absence created by a specific physical or psychosocial loss. Echoing Tanner's stress on the importance of the materiality of the body in mourning, healthy mourning is defined by a constant re-experiencing and reviving. The essential part in the process of mourning is the 'emotional catharsis' which must take place together with a review and reintegration of past and present towards a revision of the assumptive world.[74] Due to the immediacy of their occurrence, from a psychological point of view spontaneous memorials can be recognized as material objects with a communicative value that help the transition from grief to mourning.

[72] Peter Homans, *Symbolic Loss: The Ambiguity of Mourning and Memory at Century's End* (Charlottesville, VA: University of Virginia Press, 2000), p. 3.

[73] Jalland, *Death in War and Peace*, p. 255.

[74] Therese A. Rando, *Treatment of Complicated Mourning* (Champaign, IL: Research Press, 1993).

Thus, the objects act as a transitional medium that guide the bereaved from sudden, extremely painful emotions towards recovery and acceptance.[75]

Particular forms of grief, with a set of specific grief-related symptoms, occur after events and situations where a traumatic loss takes place that exceeds the human coping capacity. Because the criteria for distinguishing boundaries between different psychological states keep changing over time, the understanding of these conditions is still a developing field of research.[76] Certain foundations have been established, however, including three variables that figure in the process: an objectively defined event, the person's subjective interpretation of its meaning, and the person's emotional reaction to it.[77] The diagnosis of post-traumatic stress disorder (PTSD) provided a basis for the further conceptualization of trauma as a stressor that is 'generally outside the range of usual human experience'.[78] Until recently it was believed that therapeutically re-experiencing trauma had little effect, since psychic trauma was considered too overwhelming to be grasped by the victim at the time it occurred, and therefore inaccessible.[79] Even though the re-enactment of a traumatic event was considered important in two ways, as testimony and as cure, witnessing trauma would imply witnessing incomprehensibility. The task of articulating trauma and transforming it into a narrative memory was approached with reservation because of the risk to 'lose both the precision and the force that characterizes traumatic recall'.[80] This standpoint has been challenged, as research has shown that survivors recall their traumatic experiences very well.[81] As a 'disorder of memory',[82] caused by the vivid remembrance of traumatic events, PTSD involves a complex state of instability that concerns the memorialization of traumatic events and is constantly reexamined to

[75] D. W. Winnicott (ed.), 'Transitional objects and transitional phenomena' (1951), in *Playing and Reality* (London and New York: Routledge, 2005), pp. 1–35. See also Avril Maddrell, 'Mapping grief. A conceptual framework for understanding the spatial dimensions of bereavement, mourning and remembrance', *Journal of Social & Cultural Geography*, 17.2 (2016), 166–88

[76] Paul A. Boelen and Holly G. Prigerson, 'Commentary on the inclusion of persistent complex bereavement-related disorder in DSM-5', *Death Studies*, 36.9 (2012), 771–94.

[77] Richard J. McNally, *Remembering Trauma* (Cambridge, MA and London: The Belknap Press of Harvard University Press, 2003), p. 78.

[78] Ibid., p. 8. PTSD was recognized in 1980 by the American Psychiatric Association and listed in the third edition of its *Diagnostic and Statistical Manual of Mental Disorders (DSM-III).*

[79] Cathy Caruth (ed.), *Trauma: Exploration of Memory* (Baltimore, MD: Johns Hopkins University Press, 1995).

[80] Cathy Caruth (ed.), 'Recapturing the past: Introduction', in *Trauma*, pp. 153–4, p. 153.

[81] McNally, *Remembering Trauma.* [82] Ibid., p. 9.

include a variety of possible traumatic triggers that do not necessarily include violent acts as a precondition for establishing a diagnosis.

The Importance of Public Recognition and Memorial Appropriation

When discussing the particularities of 'Jewish otherness', Lyotard went so far as to identify the repression of otherness as a main problem of memory in the modern condition.[83] A similar argument was already proposed by Theodor Adorno in his analysis of the dialectic of enlightenment and destruction. He argued that:

> Without memory, without reading the traces of the past, there can be no recognition of difference [Adorno called it non-identity], no tolerance for the rich complexities and instabilities of personal and cultural, political and national identities.[84]

Unstable identities of particular social groups are reinforced by a lack of acknowledgement from the 'outside', from other groups. With the development of human rights since the Second World War and the contemporary interest in memory, a political platform is created for marginalized groups to ask for public acknowledgements of their past and present suffering. Recognition of historical injustices has become a normative demand in global politics and our supposedly compassionate societies. According to some scholars, the instability characteristic of PTSD can be overcome through recognition by the 'other'.[85] However, the recognition of 'otherness', as ethical obligation self-imposed by Western theorists of trauma-theory discipline, proves increasingly difficult not only in reality, but in trauma-theory as well, especially when adhering to the traditional event-based model of trauma.[86]

With regard to emotional pain, it is proven necessary that individuals who have suffered need to have their pain and suffering recognized by

[83] Lyotard, *Heidegger and 'the jews'*.

[84] Adorno quoted in Huyssen, *Twilight Memories*, p. 252.

[85] In this respect, while discussing 'impossible witnessing', Caruth argued that 'trauma itself may provide the very link between cultures: not as simple understanding of the pasts of others but rather, within the traumas of contemporary history, as our ability to listen through the departures we have all taken from ourselves.' Caruth (ed.), *Trauma*, p. 11.

[86] Stef Craps, 'Beyond Eurocentrism: trauma theory in the global age', in Gert Buelens, Sam Durrant and Robert Eaglestone (eds.), *The Future of Trauma Theory: Contemporary Literary and Cultural Criticism* (London: Routledge, 2014), pp. 45–62.

other individuals (hence not necessarily cultural or ethnic others).[87] What constitutes one of the main factors in so-called complicated grief is the impossibility of understanding 'the other', which causes the accumulation of anger, a feeling of abandonment and severe anxiety disorders.[88] A psychotherapeutic approach when dealing with these and similar effects of trauma affirms the need for the acknowledgement of these issues, as a way to move towards the development of new relationships with objects and people. While the cognitive process of memorializing and remembering does not allow for the formation of coherent narratives, the bodily memory, apparently, recalls traumatic experiences accurately. People who experienced trauma can easily become 'hijacked' by unpleasant experiences that contain elements similar to those experienced in a past traumatic encounter, such as particular sounds, smells or visions.[89] The body instantly interprets the environment as unsafe or terrorizing. At the same time, environments can help in the transition from anger to acceptance, and this is particularly true for memorial spaces.[90]

On the other hand, since there is no consensus about what precisely constitutes a traumatic stressor, and the issue only appears to broaden, it is difficult to establish one unifying platform that could support representations intended to address trauma. The materialization of memory relies on individual memory, which is often unreliable and therefore an unstable point of reference for the creation of identity. In fact, any representation or recording of memory, both official and non-official, is produced with an ineluctable time distance from the lived experience and is therefore inevitably a process of negotiating the authenticity of the recreation. The paradox produced by the necessity to memorialize the past and the need to simplify and select, thereby sacrificing its authenticity, is contained in any archiving of memory or any design of a memory object: creating all too easily becomes forgetting.[91] Probably the most authentic representations of

87 Veena Das, 'Language and body: transactions in the construction of pain', in Nancy Scheper-Hughes and Philippe I. Bourgois (eds.), *Violence in War and Peace: An Anthology* (Oxford: Blackwell Publishing, 2004), pp. 327–33.

88 Jos de Keijser, 'Gecompliceerde rouw. Diagnostiek en behandeling', *Tijdschrift voor Psychotherapie*, 30 (2004), 60–9.

89 Van der Kolk, *The Body Keeps the Score.*

90 Nicholas Watkins, 'Mirror, mirror on the wall: ambiguous place attachment and the Vietnam Veterans Memorial', in Janice M. Bissell (ed.), *Proceedings of the Thirty-Eighth Annual Conference of the Environmental Design Research Association* (Oklahoma City, OK: EDRA 38-2007: Building Sustainable Communities, 2007), pp. 46–50.

91 See Paul Connerton, 'Seven types of forgetting', in Paul Connnerton, *The Spirit of Mourning: History, Memory and the Body* (Cambridge: Cambridge University Press, 2011), pp. 33–50.

grief are impromptu memorials that generally occur immediately after a tragic event or atrocity.

Art historian Harriet Senie stressed that the flourishing of spontaneous memorials and public grieving is related to the apparent need of having a private loss publicly acknowledged.[92] They are a relevant factor of social agency or even social change, since they inherently contain protest and indicate other emotions besides grief. Contrary to official monuments and memorials as fixed entities, spontaneous memorials are, according to Senie, a form of democracy in action. As such, they raise a range of critical questions for those commissioning and building permanent official markers. It is not uncommon that spontaneous personal gestures collide with official commemorative edifices, usually expressed through a violation of a monument or memorial or the removal of spontaneous shrines.[93]

Once the immediacy of the spontaneous expression of grief decreases in power, the mourning process continues, expressed in more or less the same way but less frequently. In many ways it transforms into a ritual similar to visiting a graveyard.[94] In this stage a memorial – if there is one available – becomes a transitional object and a holding space that is expected to create a safe environment for individuals who need to make sense of loss and deal with conflicting emotions. Hence, there is a silent demand from contemporary design concepts dealing with loss and grief to develop environments appropriate for rituals and the facilitation of a personal space for mourning. At the 11-M memorial in Madrid, which will be further discussed in the next chapter, the material offerings that initially expressed spontaneous mourning continued to be added to the memorial even after this possibility was excluded from the design. At the VVM in Washington, DC, on the other hand, a common scene is that of people tracing names with a piece of paper, or caressing the surface of the reflective granite walls, and leaving flowers and other objects. This is also true for many First World War memorials, where one can often see a poppy attached to a

92 Harriet F. Senie, 'Mourning in protest: spontaneous memorials and the sacralization of public space', *Harvard Design Magazine*, 9: Constructions of Memory (1999), 23–7.

93 For example, this was the case with a wooden cross originally situated on the western part of the Berlin Wall commemorating the death of Peter Fechter. After the fall of the Wall it became an obstacle for city development and was thus removed for 'later integration into a memorial for all victims'. In Polly Feversham and Leo Schmidt, *Die Berliner Mauer heute: Denkmalwert und Umgang/The Berlin Wall Today: Cultural Significance and Conservation Issues* (Berlin: Verlag für Bauwesen HUSS-MEDIEN GmbH, 1999), p. 146.

94 Anna Peterson, 'The production of a memorial place: materialising expressions of grief', in Avril Maddrell and James D. Sidaway (eds.), *Deathscapes: Spaces for Death, Dying, Mourning and Remembrance* (Farnham: Ashgate Publishing, 2010), pp. 141–61.

particular name. People perceive the memorial as their own, and thus the names of the dead become both of private and of national concern.[95] The sensory features of a memorial are normally intended to provide mourners with the necessary environment for facilitating the process of mourning, through the presentation, confrontation and recognition of loss.[96] Whether mourners use the memorial space as intended remains an open question, but keen observers of most visitors to memorial spaces argue that sensory features of abstract contemporary memorial spaces that lack 'denotative and connotative symbols' urge many to perform actions that appear hedonistic and self-indulgent.[97] As sociologist Jeffrey Alexander has argued, 'for an audience to be traumatized by an experience which they themselves do not directly share, symbolic extension and psychological identification are required.'[98]

A widely adopted hypothesis in the 'psychoanalytic version' of what Alexander terms 'lay trauma theory'[99] is that if not confronted and recognized, the denial of trauma and traumatic memories obstructs the recovery process and can lead to social death. It is by now a well-known hypothesis that suppressed difficult memories can become seeds able to destroy nation-states: for example, the disintegration of Yugoslavia, the consequences of which are clearly visible in the architecture of monuments and memorials in most of its former republics, now independent nation-states. In Bosnia and Herzegovina many monuments are purposely built to humiliate 'the other' while glorifying crimes and perpetrators.[100] Social death can be witnessed with concentration camp survivors living in northern Bosnia during the early 1990s who, denied their right to commemorate sites of atrocities, find themselves in an unimaginable situation lingering in the 'narrative void'[101] – a void that is felt even more strongly due to there still being thousands of people missing in the areas of former concentration

[95] Griswold and Griswold, 'The Vietnam Veterans Memorial', p. 709.

[96] Nicholas Watkins, Frances Cole and Sue Weidemann, 'The war memorial as healing environment: the psychological effect of the Vietnam Veterans Memorial on Vietnam War combat veterans' posttraumatic stress disorder symptoms', *Environment and Behavior*, 42.3 (2010), 351–75, p. 364.

[97] Quentin Stevens, 'Nothing more than feelings: abstract memorials', *Architectural Theory Review*, 14.2 (2009), 156–72.

[98] Alexander, 'On the social construction of moral universals', p. 8. [99] Ibid., p. 9.

[100] Rachel Irwin and Velma Šarić, *Call for War Memorials Divides Bosnia – Little Consensus on Whether Monuments Commemorating Wartime Help or Hinder Reconciliation Process*, International Criminal Tribunal for the former Yugoslavia, TRI Issue 673, 6 December 2010, available at http://iwpr.net/report-news/calls-war-memorials-divide-bosnia, last accessed 29 October 2017.

[101] Vulliamy, *The War Is Dead*, p. xlii.

camps such as the Omarska mine in the municipality of Prijedor. In their plight to create a space of memory on the site, London's ArcelorMittal *Orbit Tower* – a monumental structure designed by Anish Kapoor to celebrate the 2012 summer Olympics – was proclaimed a 'Memorial in Exile' due to the fact that material used for the *Orbit*'s construction also derived from ore from the mine at Omarska, where human bodies had been thrown.[102] As an attempt to influence the dominant politics of memory in their own country, the situation is exemplary of Judith Butler's conclusion on grievability: 'those whose lives are not "regarded" as potentially grievable, and hence valuable, are made to bear the burden of starvation, underemployment, legal disenfranchisement, and differential exposure to violence and death.'[103]

In cases like this, memorial architecture serves the purpose of collecting existing narratives related to living memories. It is also a sign of recognition of people's suffering, an escape from annihilation. Through creating memorial architecture, both public and intimate commemorations are invigorated. In this way a sense of continuity is created, and feelings of belonging are strengthened by offering a space for people to channel their emotions.[104] This was also true in the context of post-WWII Germany, when excessive and triumphal patriotic mourning was established as a counterbalance to fragile national self-esteem.[105] At the same time, we need to recognize that there is what Alexander called an 'interpretive grid' of particular cultures through which knowledge about specific trauma is mediated 'emotionally, cognitively, and morally'.[106]

Critiques, such as Wulf Kansteiner, also argue against an imprecise way of conflating traumatic and non-traumatic into an 'aestheticized, morally and politically imprecise concept of cultural trauma, which provides little insight into the social and cultural repercussions of historical traumata'.[107] Kansteiner voices his reservation about the use of psychoanalytic methods in collective memory studies and believes that nations 'can repress with psychological impunity; their collective memories can change without a

[102] See Andrew Herscher, 'In ruins: architecture, memory, countermemory', *Journal of the Society of Architectural Historians*, 73.4 (2014), 464–69.

[103] Judith Butler, *Frames of War: When Is Life Grievable?* (London: Verso, 2009), p. 25.

[104] See Rowlands, 'Remembering to forget'.

[105] Pieter Lagrou, *The Legacy of Nazi Occupation. Patriotic Memory and National Recovery in Western Europe, 1945–1965* (Cambridge: Cambridge University Press, 2000).

[106] Alexander, 'On the social construction of moral universals', p. 10.

[107] Wulf Kansteiner, 'Genealogy of a category mistake: a critical intellectual history of the cultural trauma metaphor', *Rethinking History*, 8 (2004), 193–221, p. 194.

"return of the repressed"'.[108] Believing that analysing the collective by emphasizing the human agency in the formation of collective memories is misleading, Kansteiner denounces researchers of memorialization processes who, for example, analyse museum designs assuming that 'the realized object and its meaning are prescribed by the maker's conscious or unconscious objectives.'[109] Theorists particularly point to the obliteration of historical specificities when discussing traumatic memories of the Holocaust, commonly evoked in discussions about representations of traumatic experiences, as a way to misleading generalizations and over-extensions of the victim-survivor concept.[110] At the same time, others argue that trauma-theory marginalizes other atrocities by focusing on the Holocaust, and more recently on 9/11, as paradigms of both individual and collective trauma. Likewise, critics indicate that Holocaust representation and education needs to be more inclusive and adapt to a universal and cosmopolitan view. However, the issue of inclusion inevitably relates to time management, and this is a general concern in most research and educational topics.[111]

The concept of homecoming is one way of dealing with trauma and therefore a relevant commemorative theme related both to grief and mourning. After the Vietnam War, US civilians used to greet Vietnam veterans with the phrase 'welcome home'. It was also exchanged between the veterans themselves when they would meet during commemorative ceremonies at the VVM in Washington, DC. Numerous Vietnam memorials erected across the country were symbolic, neutral and soothing, embodiments of homecoming, welcoming the soldiers back to a home from which they felt estranged.[112] In a different vein, but with similar intentions, the creation of the Tomb of the Unknown Soldier after the First World War commemorated the vast number of killed and missing soldiers as a result of brutal and mechanized warfare and responded to a strong need to comprehend, mourn and provide some kind of closure for the bereaved. Nation-states ritualized the burials of their unknown dead, honouring them on behalf of the nation and thus emphasizing the significance of their sacrifice. The fact that the tomb contained the body of an anonymous soldier provided the possibility for the bereaved to believe that

[108] Kansteiner, *In Pursuit of German Memory*, p. 17. [109] Ibid.

[110] LaCapra, *Writing History*.

[111] Michael Polgar, *Holocaust and Human Rights Education. Good Choices and Sociological Perspectives* (Bingley: Emerald Publishing Limited, 2018), p. 113.

[112] Patrick Hagopian, 'The commemorative landscape of the Vietnam War', in Wolschke-Bulmahn (ed.), *Places of Commemoration*, pp. 311–76, p. 314.

Figure 2.2 'Hotel of Memory' memorial at Neue Bremm (2004); Nils Ballhausen and Roland Poppensieker.
Photo: Author

that unknown may be their loved one. In this way, families deprived of the certainty that the burial of a body would normally provide found condolence in the possibilities opened up by the Tomb of the Unknown Soldier and its purpose to remember everyone by 'remembering no one in particular'.[113]

2.3 Designing Spaces for Traumatic Memory and Mourning

Spatial Memory and the Identity of Place

Along a road on the French–German border in Saarbrücken a large lenticular-print photograph depicting a happy family stands above a wall supporting a longitudinal, neon-blue sign saying 'Hostel' in different languages (Figure 2.2). As one passes, the photo appears and disappears, an uncanny apparition signalling that there is more to this place. Indeed, behind the wall and the photograph, historical information and remnants of the former Nazi torture camp are to be found. The Neue Bremm memorial (2004) is a demonstration of the Janus-faced character of memory, as it signals its presence behind the curtain of the familiar. Once behind this wall, the visitor is immersed in a different world, conjured up by artefacts, historical information and poignant commemorative monuments. Photographs of a few victims from the former camp are also

[113] John R. Gillis, 'Introduction: memory and identity: the history of a relationship', in John R. Gillis (ed.), *Commemorations: The Politics of National Identity* (Princeton, NJ: Princeton University Press, 1994), pp. 3–27, p. 11.

displayed on the facade of the adjacent hotel where the premises of a woman's camp used to stand. Designers Nils Ballhausen and Roland Poppensieker dubbed their project 'Hotel of Memory' – a 'counter-hotel' as a sign of a reality existing outside the reality inside the borders of the former camp.[114] Here the design follows memory traces and narratives in reaction to the obliteration of past and the commercial repurposing of the place.

Architecture is related to a place, while experiencing architecture is bound up with time. In other words, the space is a referential component, whereas time relates to the experiential aspect of the design. The Finnish architect and theorist Juhani Pallasmaa stressed that contemporary architectural settings are, as he put it:

> Usually experienced as having their origin in singular moments of time. They evoke an experience of flattened or rejected temporality. Yet, the existential task of architecture is to relate us to time as much as to space . . . The mental roles of these two fundamental existential dimensions are curiously reversed. In terms of space, we yearn for specificity, whereas in our temporal experience we desire a sense of continuity. Consequently, architecture has to create a specificity of space and place and at the same time, evoke the experience of temporal continuum.[115]

This is particularly true in memorial architecture, where a place is the defining context or even the construction material itself. In authentic places such as the remains of historically significant sites, architectural intervention is needed for its restoration as a *lieux de mémoire* and the 'sense of historical continuity' that permeates it.[116]

Furthermore, all material objects have a strong relationship with their context, as Ludwig Wittgenstein argued in the context of fin-de-siècle Vienna:

> Just as we can in no way conceive of spatial objects outside space or temporal objects outside time, we cannot conceive of any object outside the possibilities of its connection to others. Although I can conceive of the object in the context of the state of things, I cannot conceive of it outside the possibility of this context.[117]

[114] See Mark Landsman, 'Property and the banality of memory', *Cabinet*, 10: Property (2003), 94–7.

[115] Juhani Pallasmaa, 'The space of time', *Oz: Journal of the College of Architecture, Planning & Design, Kansas State University*, 20 (1998), 54–7, p. 54.

[116] Nora, 'Between memory and history', 9.

[117] Ludwig Wittgenstein, 'Tractatus logico-philosophicus', quoted in Benedetto Gravagnuolo, *Adolf Loos: Theory and Works*, Idea Books Architectural Series, US edn (New York: Rizzoli, 1982), p. 78.

While the interpretation of context varies according to scientific discipline, in architecture it normally refers to physical surroundings. Architecture in context presupposes visual and utilitarian relationships established with the surroundings. The relationship is based on the hypothesis that the context will benefit from architecture that engages in a dialogue with the specificities of a particular place. What problematizes this straightforward process is the fact that places are rarely inert, particularly places with difficult pasts.

The American philosopher Edward Casey noted that our memory is bound to a place through our experience of it: therefore, a place becomes a 'container of experiences that contributes so powerfully to its intrinsic memorability'.[118] People invest places with meaning, both social and cultural, and many have argued for the importance of place in the process of remembering. Through the cultural context and daily living, people transform places and create specific biographies of them. Cultural practice within culturally defined spaces forms and constantly reinforces social identities. As the composing tissue of cultural memory, places can be made sacred, as occurs with spontaneous memorials. What Casey called 'place memory' can be described as the embodied quality of a place, which can inform practice and produces particular expressions of place.[119] The biographies that places have acquired are more tangible if they are rooted in a material point of reference, which can be visited and experienced.[120] We can experience the history of a certain place and its meaning through space as a relational concept.[121] Phenomenological theory claimed that space is nothing but the relationship between objects while place is space which has meaning, derived from personal and collective remembrance and identity.[122] Space designed as a strong holding environment can elicit the sense of place.[123]

At the end of the twentieth century, an interdisciplinary interest developed around the urban condition of cities, leading to new ideas about space and its production. One of the key figures shaping the debate on

118 Edward Casey, *Remembering: A Phenomenological Study* (Bloomington, IN: Indiana University Press, 1987), p. 182.

119 Casey defined 'place memory' as 'the stabilizing persistence of place as a container of experiences that contributes so powerfully to its intrinsic memorability'. Ibid., p. 186.

120 See Charles Tilley, *A Phenomenology of Landscape: Places, Paths and Monuments* (London: Berg, 1993), p. 33.

121 Christian Norberg-Schultz, *Genius Loci: Towards a Phenomenology of Architecture* (New York: Rizzoli, 1991).

122 See Haim Yacobi (ed.), *Constructing the Sense of Place: Architecture and Zionist Discourse* (Aldershot: Ashgate Publishing, 2004).

123 Elizabeth Ellsworth, *Places of Learning: Media, Architecture, Pedagogy* (New York: Routledge Taylor & Francis Group, 2005).

'spatial theory', Henry Lefebvre introduced a distinction between 'representations of space' and 'spaces of representation'. The first involves a system of abstract and dominant codes, whereas a space of representation is a resistant space, offering possibilities for imagination and invention. Lefebvre stressed that an unrepresentative space or 'passive representational space' can be transformed into a dynamic site of ideology.[124] In reverse, a place becomes part of an identity through experience and peoples' reaction to that place. This interaction is a dynamic process in which both people and places evolve, as 'space and the political organization of the space express social relationships but also react back upon them'.[125] The choice of a site for the Tomb of the Unknown Soldier, for example, was of great importance for the nation-states involved in the First World War, both on the collective and the individual level. These sites gained an almost mythical status, resembling a symbolic rebirth of the state embodied in the Unknown Soldier as a national hero.[126] Once the space was officially dedicated, it became an incentive for social memory. These physical spaces communicate a certain meaning which changes during the course of time due to the inevitable contestation that comes from cultural and political influences. Becoming a type of mnemonic construct, empowered with the emotion of the narrative connected to them, they reinforce the identification of people with the national context. While arguing that 'sites of memory' are places where 'people affirm their faith that history has a meaning', Jay Winter reminds us that these sites also vanish if not sustained by ritual action.[127]

Hence, a place is never inert; rather, it is in a constant state of flux and a constituent part of forming an identity. Consequently, our attachment to a place is never inert either: it changes depending on our perception of a place, which is modelled by our emotions, beliefs, behavioural changes and

[124] Henry Lefebvre, *The Production of Space* (Oxford: Blackwell Publishing, 1991), p. 39

[125] Ibid., p.8.

[126] The sites of the Tomb of the Unknown Soldier occupied prominent places: in France, under the Arc de Triomphe in Paris; in England, Westminster Abbey in London; in Italy, the Monument to Victor Emmanuel in Rome; in Belgium, next to the Colonnade of the Congress in Brussels. See Carole Blair, V. William Balthrop and Neil Michel, 'The arguments of the tombs of the unknown: relationality and national legitimation', *Argumentation*, 25 (2011), 449–69.

[127] Jay Winter, 'Sites of memory and the shadow of war', in Astrid Erll, Ansgar Nünning and Sara B. Young (eds.), *Cultural Memory Studies: An International and Interdisciplinary Handbook* (Berlin and New York: De Gruyter, 2008), pp. 61–73.

other factors. This relationship that is so highly susceptible to change has been termed the 'ambiguous place attachment'.[128]

The importance of Lefebvre's representational space is recognized and practised by contemporary urban planners, who often design public 'event places' rich in symbolism and historical narrative. Memorial projects such as the MMJE in Berlin or 'Memento Park' in Budapest belong to the contemporary trend of restoring places with destructive histories as representational spaces. They restore the historical narrative through architectural design on a large scale, aiming at the integration into the everyday life of a local community. They are meant to support the historical memory of the local community, create popular public spaces, attract tourists and, perhaps, set straight the historical record. In practical terms, the great risk that lingers over these projects and the historical memory they carry is that they tend to become popular playgrounds. While some might see this as a positive development, tension inevitably rises between the need to be historically and morally responsible and an ambitious eagerness to produce a successful public space. In this way, a design has to respond to a wide range of public interests, while the initial purpose of the place remains hidden. For example, when observing the public life and usage of the space of the MMJE, it is clear the public is largely ignorant of the purpose of the memorial. As a public space, it is rather an appealing place to play hide and seek, take selfies, jump over the large concrete cubes, have lunch, sunbathe, or even conduct fashion shoots.[129] The ambiguity of the memorial has to do with many factors, such as unclear goals in its very conception phase, but also the choice of a location that was a 'no man's land' between East and West Berlin.[130] In line with Musil's observation in the 1930s about the invisibility of monuments, this memorial's purpose may almost be invisible in contrast to its physical presence. Similar arguments were raised in relation to the controversial National Monument of the 1956 Hungarian Revolution and War of Independence, unveiled in Budapest in 2006, with regard to its abstract appearance and its ignoring of the historical heritage of the location.[131]

128 Watkins, 'Mirror, mirror', p. 50.

129 See Quentin Stevens, 'Waarom het Holocaustmonument in Berlijn zo'n geliefd speelterrein is' ('Why the Holocaust memorial is such a popular playground'), *Oase*, 77: Into the Open (2008), 71–9.

130 Carrier, *Holocaust Monuments*, p. 102.

131 The location of the memorial is the Felvonulasi Square where a statue of Stalin was toppled in the uprising on 23 October 1956, leaving only one part of the monument standing – Stalin's boots (a replica of which can be found today in the Budapest Statue Park of Communist Sculpture). Next to this, there used to stand a statue of Lenin and a giant cross. See Sharon Macdonald, *Memorylands: Heritage and Identity in Europe Today* (London: Routledge, 2013).

Wittgenstein's attention to context echoes the idea Loos expressed about the tomb as a special, even religious, precinct. A tomb makes one immanently aware of the presence of a real body or artefact and therefore erases the distance of representation which is normally created by an act of representation. Thus, a tomb signals the immediacy of death. A site of tragedy is a sign itself – a terrorscape,[132] as was the case with Ground Zero in the aftermath of the 9/11 attacks in New York, when the clearing of the site was accompanied by widespread claims for its sanctity: it was often referred to as a place 'permanently marked by tragedy'.[133]

Conversely, the power of representation of a commemorative site that is not 'marked' depends upon the rhetorical force of the representation strategy, since the meaning of the project needs to be metaphorically summoned.[134] In other words, the symbolic content of memorial projects occupying non-authentic sites are expected to be added through the design.[135] However, the same can be argued for authentic places. Design is of no less significance in bringing those places into the present, either by marking them or by narrating their history. In Catalan collective memory, the Grave of the Quarry (*Fossar de la Pedrera*, 1986), adjacent to the Montjuïc cemetery in Barcelona, is a place of emotional strength, emphasized by an architecture that tells the story of thousands of victims executed in the 1940s under the Franco regime. The architecture designed by Beth Gali carries carefully planned stages of experience, preparing the visitor for each new encounter with the site's narrated history.

Former places of terror and suffering are in many ways unique. First World War battlefields, for instance, quite literally 'remember', since their morphology was remodelled by heavy artillery, as masterfully depicted in *Der Krieg* (1924), a series of etchings by German artist Otto Dix. The landscape of the First World War is recognized as the most important 'last witness' – reshaped by the ravages of war, a container of the war's traces and invaluable archaeological remains.[136]

[132] See Terrorscapes, a transdisciplinary, international network of scholars and professionals, of which the official website is available at www.terrorscapes.org.

[133] Michael Sorkin, *Starting from Zero: Reconstructing Downtown New York* (London: Routledge, 2003).

[134] Richard M. Sommer, 'Time incorporated: the romantic life of the modern monument', *Harvard Design Magazine*, 9: Constructions of Memory (1999), 38–44.

[135] See Michael A. Stern, 'The national cemetery system: politics, place, and contemporary cemetery', in Wolschke-Bulmahn (ed.), *Places of Commemoration*, pp. 107–30, p. 108.

[136] *The Great War Centenary (2014–2018)* (Brussels: VisitFlanders, Flemish Government, 2011), available at www.vlaanderen.be

Once harrowing, the lunar landscape of First World War battlefields is today covered up with vegetation, giving it a soft, uncanny character. Through the memorialization and the creation of cemeteries on these sites, considerable effort was invested in transforming these sites of trauma into pristine panoramas with soothing characters.[137] Inevitably, a century of nature's influence also helped to reverse the images of horror into serene landscapes with cemeteries as salient guardians of memory. The slow transformation towards tranquil and meditative natural surroundings inevitably erases the horrors of the past. Today, however, and also in the context of the 'perilous landscapes'[138] of numerous former Nazi camps and trauma sites in general, the natural change of landscape and the blurring of the sites' former infrastructure is perceived as a threat to memory-work. For this reason, landscape design and choices made about the ways and forms of commemorating are of the utmost importance in conveying the meaning of a particular site, since the site itself rarely transmits its own past and its meaning can easily become veiled by natural changes. There are numerous examples to illustrate the ongoing struggle between forgetting and remembering in such places, where nature in large part determines the pace of representation.[139]

Hence, when the physical traces disappear, the sense of place usually needs to be enhanced by architectural elements, composed around archaeological remains to help visitors trace the historical narrative. These sites can be perceived as special kinds of cemetery, in which the emphasis is placed on the disturbing feeling of anticipation that permeates the space. For the survivors of these places, they carry a sense of terror or a distinct presence to which they return to revisit difficult feelings.[140] For future generations this appears to be true as well, since such places represent a palpable material connection to their ancestors.[141] In terms of transitional justice, these sites are central for providing an opportunity for democratic

[137] Ana Carden-Coyne, *Reconstructing the Body: Classicism, Modernism and the First World War* (New York: Oxford University Press, 2009).

[138] Sybil Milton, 'Perilous landscapes: concentration camp memorials between commemoration and amnesia', in Wolschke-Bulmahn (ed.), *Places of Commemoration*, pp. 257–68.

[139] Art historian Detlef Hoffmann argued that Dachau concentration camp did not appear overnight, and that a part of the commemoration process should be to preserve its evolution. In his opinion, a history of a site also involves the periods of neglect prior to its safekeeping as a memorial. See Young, *The Texture of Memory*, p. 71.

[140] Paul Adams, Steven Hoelscher and Karen Till (eds.), *Textures of Place: Rethinking Humanist Geographies* (Minneapolis, MN: University of Minnesota, 2001).

[141] Cathy Caruth, *Unclaimed Experience: Trauma, Narrative and History* (Baltimore, MD: Johns Hopkins University Press, 1996).

engagement through public involvement. By designating them as 'sites of conscience' they are approached as 'a primary terrain on which diverse constituencies address the enormous and challenging complexities of a traumatic past'.[142]

Architectural Representation and Its Limits

In the Memorial to the Deportation at the Île de la Cité in Paris, Georges-Henri Pingusson developed a project rich in symbolic meaning and focused on two spatial strategies: transition and separation. With an aim to create a 'violence of contrast', Pingusson extended the symbolism to the use of building materials: for example, instead of using normal concrete, he used so-called artificial stone made out of aggregates of stone mixed with a white concrete.[143] This mix was composed from aggregates of stone taken from different mountain ranges across France, to symbolically reinforce the national character of the memorial. Relying strongly on his knowledge of religious rituals and liturgical spaces, the architect developed several stages that together constituted the overall experience of the memorial. The first was an intermediary space, the 'phase of silence', that employed the existing park – which was now transformed into a 'preparatory reflection'. The following sequence, the 'phase of estrangement', constituted a descent towards the sunken plaza of the memorial, past monolithic concrete walls with only a single opening towards the River Seine, framed by a portcullis of symbolic iron spikes. Finally, beyond the opening, the narrow entrance to a crypt was intended as the last stage of the experience, the 'phase of presence' where the visitor faces memory.[144]

All the elements of the memorial were designed with the intention of dramatizing the experience, in order to communicate the 'hardship of oppression'.[145] The crypt is a hexagonal space that consists of a long corridor lit by 200,000 small glass beds installed on side walls and two niches on the sides, each containing an empty prison cell – symbols of a prisoner's passage through the camps (Figure 2.3).[146] The walls of the interior contain engraved names of different concentration camps, accompanied with texts by authors who had been involved in the resistance.[147]

[142] Brett et al., *Memorialization and Democracy*, p. 1.

[143] Amsellem, *Remembering the Past*, p. 97. [144] Ibid., p. 90. [145] Ibid., p. 100.

[146] 'War Memorial Paris', *The Architectural Review*, 133.793 (March 1963), p. 186.

[147] Texts by Antoine Saint-Exupéry, Louis Aragon, Robert Desnos, Paul Éluard, Jean Augustin Maydieu, Jean-Paul Sartre and Vercors.

Figure 2.3 The Memorial to the Deportation (1962), Paris, Georges-Henri Pingusson. Photo: Author

When designing the Memorial to the Deportation in Paris, Pingusson believed that architecture alone is not sufficient in communicating the history of Second World War deportations. He argued for the importance of a textual component to be an integral part of the memorial. His inquiry resulted in a permanent exhibition, installed on the upper floor above the crypt. The addition, even though never opened to the public, provoked strong reactions, as it was believed that any sort of textual and didactic content would only rob the space of its meditative qualities. Pingusson, however, designed the addition as a continuation of the orchestrated experience that was imagined as developing in a one-way circulation pathway, including both shocking exhibits and meditative spaces. For example, Pingusson planned to install a winter panorama of Auschwitz and reinforce the image by applying an unusual treatment of the concrete in the circulation path. In order to shock the visitor, he planned to install an image of a dead deportee at the exit. In a more recent project, the Holocaust Museum in Ottawa (2017), Daniel Libeskind adopted a similar approach that reinforces architectural space through large-scale photographs of Holocaust sites painted onto the concrete walls of the memorial – a noteworthy addition to his recognizable architectural language. The same intervention was performed in a project called 'Recycled Memory' by Hoheisel and Knitz at the 1970s dilapidated Soviet memorial in Kaunas, where they installed photographs of the Kaunas Jewish Ghetto that existed on the site between 1941 and 1944.

In the global culture of memory – a contemporary construction developed through the worldwide network of print and image media which drastically changed traditional ways of remembering – architectural forms can be easily replicated. The international success of a project inevitably influences aesthetic perceptions and the public's expectations of another, regardless of the context. In regards to this point, many have argued that the unofficial language of Holocaust memorial art is abstract art – a type of art, as one critique pointed out, which 'does not allow us to interpret it with reference to what is depicted'.[148] In the context of complicated mourning, then, it is perhaps understandable why abstraction and minimalism are dominant in memorial representations. Abstract art seems to appropriate Lyotard's notion of 'presenting the unpresentable', stressing that the representation's subject or content is less accessible, but not absent. The memorialization of a traumatic event through abstract forms and ambivalent meanings appears to be recognized as an effective way to deal with the topic. Early examples, as we have seen, are Lutyens' design solutions for the commemoration of the First World War, which aimed to address the all-encompassing character of the war and therefore relied on universally recognizable forms to confront the ubiquity of loss.

[148] Briony Fer, *On Abstract Art* (London and New Haven, CT: Yale University Press, 1997), p. 5.

The architectural historian Alberto Pérez-Gómez argued that the historical and societal role of an architect is to design a theatre of memory, as he explained:

> A theater of memory for culture, capable of embodying truths that, however culturally diverse and specific, makes it possible for humanity to affirm life and contemplate possibilities of a better future.[149]

In this way, Pérez-Gómez believed, an architect can create the possibility for experiencing order, as opposed to anarchy or tyranny. Ironically, this is precisely what Adolf Hitler's personal architect and Minister for Armaments, Albert Speer, achieved for the Nazi Party Rally Grounds in Nuremberg. Here the 'Cathedral of Light' was installed in 1938 – Speer's first major project, which consisted of 130 anti-aircraft searchlights, placed at 12-m intervals and aimed skyward. When contemplating the seductiveness of the immaterial architecture of light in his project, Speer summarized these aspirations as follows:

> The actual effect far surpassed anything I had imagined. The hundred and thirty sharply defined beams, placed around the field at intervals of forty feet, were visible to a height of twenty to twenty-five thousand feet, after which they merged into a gentle glow. The feeling was of a vast room, with the beams serving as mighty pillars of infinitely high outer walls. Now and then a cloud moved through this wreath of lights, bringing an element of surrealistic surprise to the mirage. I imagine that this 'cathedral of light' was the first luminescent architecture of this type, and for me it remains not only my most beautiful architectural concept, but after its fashion, the only one which has survived the passage of time.[150]

Speer's deliberations display a concern that is inherent in architecture's aspiration as a medium for elevating the spirit towards the timeless and the sublime, the cradle of civilization. In this ongoing search for the effective and the beautiful, the moral and ethical aspects of a design are often ignored in the face of opportunity. It is not uncommon for architects to turn a blind eye to reality in their drive to realize their creative visions if given the chance. Speer's work is perhaps the best example of

[149] Alberto Pérez-Gómez, 'The architecture of Richard Henriquez: a praxis of personal memory', in Howard Shubert (ed.), *Richard Henriquez, Memory Theatre* (Montreal: Canadian Centre for Architecture, 1993)), pp. 9–29, p. 9.

[150] Albert Speer, *Inside the Third Reich: Memoirs by Albert Speer* (New York: Simon & Schuster, 1970), p. 59.

this: from a theatre of 'order', the 'Cathedral of Light' transformed into a symbol of tyranny and destruction. The powerful effect of searchlights, however, continued to be explored and used in commemoration projects for the Second World War, for example in the immediate post-war years,[151] in 1995 for a 'Peace Sculpture' project along the west coast of Jutland, Denmark, and finally in the commemoration of 9/11 in New York.

The duality created by the fusion of the terrible and the beautiful echoes some of the principles Étienne-Louis Boullée employed in attempting to achieve the feeling of the sublime and the melancholy of the natural world, in order to create a framework for potentially didactic experiences. As seen in numerous examples of funerary architecture and representations of death, architects commonly aspire to the sublime and the spiritual, but inevitably meet the limitations of the physical. The architect and theorist Bernard Tschumi has questioned the modes of representation used by architects, arguing that in spite of their generativity and precision these representations are logical reductions of architectural thought 'caught in a sort of prison-house of architectural language'.[152]

In projects dealing with difficult memories, the search for the 'beautiful' fuels controversy. Often these structures are expected to reflect their abysmal topics: if the very architecture provides pleasurable feelings, it would betray its purpose. In such cases, a design is expected to convey a sombre past, and every gesture can either enhance the historical narrative or lead to misinterpretation or misleading information. Such considerations recall Adorno's famous assertion about the impossibility of writing poetry after Auschwitz. When discussing this particular requirement of works of art dealing with the Holocaust, Adorno pointed to Samuel Beckett's play *Endgame* as a work of art that manages to meet the impossible by not addressing the Holocaust directly. Beckett's play is situated in a post-apocalyptic context in which 'the violence is mimicked by the timidity to mention it.'[153] Adorno's fears are illustrated in the verbatim utilization

[151] In 1946 André Bloch, known as Bruyère, proposed a setting for a memorial rally in Compiègne that would have consisted of a 20 km long path along the river Oise defined by anti-aircraft searchlights. Cohen, *Architecture in Uniform*, p. 417.

[152] Tschumi quoted in Tina di Carlo, 'Bernard Tschumi. The Manhattan Transcripts Project, Episode 1: The Park, New York City, New York', in Matilda McQuaid (ed.), *Envisioning Architecture: Drawings from the Museum of Modern Art* (New York: Museum of Modern Art, 2002), p. 204.

[153] Theodor Adorno, 'Trying to understand *Endgame*', in Brian O'Connor (ed.), *The Adorno Reader* (Oxford: Blackwell Publishers, 2000), pp. 319–52, p. 324.

of forms alluding to the infrastructure of Nazi camps, such as crematoria chimneys. While this was the case with some of the earliest commemorations after the Second World War (usually initiated by the survivors),[154] ironically, this strategy has become common practice in commemorative designs for the Holocaust, especially in the United States, where chimneys and wires are constituent symbolic elements for some of its postmodernist *architecture parlante*.[155]

The United States Holocaust Museum in Washington, DC (USHMM, 1988–93) by James Ingo Freed, for example, tries to recreate a journey many had to undertake when forced to leave their everyday life only to end up in ghettos. Historian Edward Linenthal argued that the mood of the exhibit spaces offered not only aesthetic but also moral direction. Visitors are expected to take this journey with a heart and soul 'heavy and dark', like the space itself.[156] The museum's evocative language balances between abstract and direct symbolism, with a basic layout consisting of two parts connected by steel bridges. A rich palette of sensory materialization supports the architectural narrative, such as clanking metal staircases, glass walkways that invoke the sensation of stepping into a void, and a variety of unsettling textures and smells in the part where piles of clothes, hair and shoes are exhibited.[157] The museum was received as a great masterpiece of architecture, successfully producing a *dark architecture parlante*.[158] The art commissioned for the museum, a topic in its own right, included works by renowned contemporary artists and added another layer to the building's story. One of the initial reasons for including non-figurative artworks was to create a counter-balance to the narrative of the museum.[159] Fearing that the

[154] A chimney of Flossenbürg (1946) is one of the earliest examples. The chimney memorial, 27 m tall, stands in the Neuengamme former concentration camp site near Hamburg and was placed on the initiative of the survivors, who even proposed a colossal chimney-like tower turning the space into an experiential event. The first memorial erected in Neuengamme (1953) was, however, a neutral cylinder 7.5 m high with the simple inscription 'To the Victims 1938–1945', modelled on the examples in Belsen and Hamburg-Ohlsdorf. However, the survivors wanted a different memorial, which would represent human suffering. Therefore, in 1965 a much taller, rectangular, instead of cylindrical, memorial replaced the old one and a sculpture depicting a fallen 'deportee' by Françoise Salmon was added at its foot. See Marcuse, 'Holocaust memorials', p. 70.

[155] See Rosenfeld, *Building after Auschwitz*.

[156] Edward T. Linenthal, *Preserving Memory: The Struggle to Create America's Holocaust Museum* (New York: Penguin Group, 1997), p. 170.

[157] Adrian Dannatt, *United States Holocaust Memorial Museum: James Ingo Freed* (London: Phaidon Press, 1995), p. 21.

[158] Rosenfeld, *Building after Auschwitz*, p. 268.

[159] Godfrey, *Abstraction and the Holocaust*, pp. 199–237.

museum risked becoming an isolated world, a hermetic container for the display of horror with only glimpses to the life outside, the architect acknowledged these abstract artworks as a more direct connection to the contemporary world, giving the museum 'a kind of legitimacy'.[160]

It comes as no surprise that many contemporary designers choose a more taciturn position and create memorials as background architecture that does not communicate straightforwardly or try to depict the absence of meaning or context as a consequence of the memorialized topic. Some authors have criticized this approach as a contemporary trend that borders on 'reflecting amnesia', or the demonstration of an inability to address loss.[161] At the same time, a parallel development in memorial architecture is characterized by a curative sensibility focused on the concept of 'working through' trauma.[162] Doss recognized this as a dominant approach in memorials dealing with the memorialization of traumatic events:

> Many terrorism memorials employ a redefined minimalism that manipulates normal understandings of space and time in order to evoke trauma's dissociative effects of fear and anxiety. Towering monoliths, angled walls, recessed forms, reflective surfaces, and gridded units strewn throughout enormously scaled sites lend these memorials their purposely disconcerting impressions. Pits, voids, and an aesthetic of 'absence' further their destabilizing sensibility; tensions between their overwhelming spatiality and their simultaneous emphasis on intimate experience heighten their anxious affective conditions.[163]

Since the architecture of memorials is at the same time symbolic and narrative, experimenting with representations of memory borders on an act of violence, as Friedrich Nietzsche had argued about art.[164] In line with Loos' recognition of memorial architecture as art, architecture can degenerate into a violent intervention in space, in cases when the architectural language is more telling about the designer than about the context. This brings with it the debate about monumentality versus modesty: do our

[160] Godfrey has argued that the abstract works 'interrupt the narrative and punctuate it, refusing to represent the Holocaust through graphic images and steady narratives' (ibid., p. 236).

[161] Doss, *Memorial Mania*, p. 145. Doss argued that loss connotes destruction and disappearance, whereas absence suggests vacancy and lack, or 'non-presence' and the anxious possibility of reappearance.

[162] Ibid., p. 137. [163] Ibid., p. 146.

[164] Friedrich Nietzsche, 'Book three. Principles of a new evaluation. IV. The will to power as art', in Walter Kaufmann (ed.), *Friedrich Nietzsche: The Will to Power*, trans. Walter Kaufmann and R. J. Hollingdale (New York: Vintage Books, 1968), pp. 419–57.

memorials need to be big to reference the scale of atrocity?[165] Like in any architectural endeavour, understanding a given context and then establishing a strategy of approach by, for example, choosing a subtle anchorage in space or a strong authoritarian presence, seems only logical – architecture is not solely an aesthetic power but has moral obligations as well. Whether architecture respects the hierarchy of a given situation or aims to establish a new order, the depth of its morality derives from its service to the society. The choice of the design is immediately a straightforward intervention, in the sense that it inevitably influences the landscape of memory.

With all this in mind, memorial architecture in general and that of memorial museums in particular take up the role of a precisely designed scenography, set on the stage of a designated historical fact for the visitor to experience through different levels of participation. The process of creating is, like any architectural project, restricted by funding and resources. Again, designing and building a memorial space is further complicated by a number of tasks that go beyond regular projects – as wells as, more often then not, having to address strong emotions and sentiments. When it comes to realization, conceptual ideas will inevitably be challenged by both practical and social issues – the rules of a construction site alone will call for compromises. It is precisely here, in the vacuum between the intangible and tangible realms, between the imagined and the real, where potential lies: to create meaningful and emotional spaces is to understand the limitations and ambiguities of present and historical realities. Working with and adapting to these boundaries is where the full potential of a design comes to fruition.

The role of the designer is a difficult one, because his guidelines for designing are not utilitarian in their origin but are rather elusive. Taking architectural space as a precondition for fostering memory, the designer takes on the responsibility for the representation of memory, while at the same time affirming to understand the elusiveness of it. As to the question of the actual realization of a concept proposal, it is often the case that many valuable proposals remain unrealized, overruled by the ultimatums of popularity. For example, the New England Memorial in Boston was the result of a transparent architectural competition that was unique because it included public opinion in the decision-making process.[166] However, whether this inclusion had any influence on the final outcome is not clear.

[165] See Franziska Bollerey, 'Modesty versus monumentality: the quieter way of speaking about Holocaust in Europe', *Ezelsoren: Bulletin of the Institute of History of Art, Architecture and Urbanism*, IHAAU, 1.2 (2008), pp. 25–43.

[166] Young, *The Texture of Memory*, pp. 321–8.

Instead, the final choice was determined by what seems to be a common strategy in similar competitions – 'the better known the winner the easier it would be to garner public and political support for the monument's construction.'[167] This logic, however, failed in the process of creating a Holocaust Names Memorial or 'Namenmonument' in Amsterdam, where the commissioner appointed the star-architect Daniel Libeskind without an open call for the memorial's design. Harsh criticism of Libeskind's concept proposal and the commissioning process led to the issue going to, and being resolved in, court.

Educating the Public through Memorial Design

Commemorative monuments are commonly understood as didactic; they are constructed to inform us. The information monuments are intended to share is often inscribed on the monument and augmented by the choice of representation. As places of experience and learning, they are perceived as fixed entities in space: hence, the knowledge they provide is interpreted as factual and thereby static. This is contrary to the purpose of a monument as depicted by Françoise Choay, who argued that 'it is not simply a question of informing, of calling to mind a neutral bit of information, but rather of stirring up, through the emotions, a living memory.'[168] Even if memorials manage to achieve this, the arrival of new generations and ever-changing context urge for up-to-date approaches.

Artists like Krzysztof Wodiczko and Shimon Attie focused their work on reanimating historical monuments or bringing forgotten places of memory back into the present by temporal recreations of related events and political messages. With his *Memorial Projections*, starting in the 1980s, Wodiczko aimed to provoke the established knowledge provided by a monument, whereas Attie, also using projections, rediscovered the hidden pasts of places and buildings, transforming them into sites of memory.[169] Advocating interrogative design while exploring issues of xenophobia, social violence, militarism and other contemporary topics, Wodiczko argued that 'the meaning of our monuments depends on our active role in turning them into sites of memory and critical evaluation of history as well as places of public discourse and action', and he adds that 'this agenda is not only social or political or activist, it is also an aesthetic mission.'[170] In a

[167] Ibid., p. 328. [168] Choay, *The Invention*, p. 6. [169] See Young, *At Memory's Edge*.
[170] Krzysztof Wodiczko, *Critical Vehicles: Writings, Projects, Interviews* (Cambridge, MA: MIT Press, 1999), p. 62.

similar approach, Hoheisel and Knitz went a step further than Ullman's Memorial for the Book Burning (1994) with a project entitled 'Book-Mark' (Lese-Zeichen, 2013) commemorating the book burning of 10 May 1933 in front of Bonn's town hall. A bronze slab with the titles and names of the authors whose books were burned was sunk into the cobbled square while underneath the slab is a space that contains copies of these books. The slab is planned to be opened on every anniversary of the book burning, when copies of the books will be given to passersby.[171]

In much the same way, the Polish artist Lukasz Surowiec, who participated in the Seventh Berlin Biennale with his project *Berlin-Birkenau* (2012), explored the issue of interaction in art projects that deal with burdensome and transnational memory. Surowiec transported several hundred young birch seedlings that were growing in the area around the former Auschwitz–Birkenau concentration camp to locations in Berlin.[172] In an effort to create a sort of a 'living archive' by returning to Germany a part of its past and thereby addressing issues of trauma, reconciliation and memory, the artist used trees as a medium to involve individuals and social bodies, such as park commissions.[173] Surowiec's attempt to create a monument that not only 'needs to be protected from destruction, but is something that you need to actively care for', speaks about the need to work with memory by addressing the responsibility attached to it.[174] Belonging to the third generation after the Second World War, this project also raises a question about the ways memory is transmitted to future generations on the familial and national level. Replanting trees that grew in soil rich with the ashes of Auschwitz victims in Berlin can be understood as a test for the resilience of this specific memory, but at the same time it is an intimate engagement with memory for every individual involved with the project.

171 See Horst Hoheisel and Andreas Knitz, *Kunst der Erinnerung, Erinnerung der Kunst. Zermahlene Geschichte. Kunst als Umweg*, 2015.

172 'Berlin-Birkenau, Lukasz Surowiec', The Seventh Berlin Biennale Archive, available at http://artmuseum.pl/en/archiwum/archiwum-7-berlin-biennale/2034?read=all, last accessed 8 October 2017.

173 The birches were planted in public parks and spaces such as Wuhlheide Park in Treptow-Köpenick, on the grounds of schools, and also in places that have a historic connection to the Holocaust and deportation, like the memorial site Gleis 17 in Grunewald. In each location, a plaque with the following inscription can be found: 'In November 2011, the Polish artist Lukasz Surowiec brought 320 birches from the area around the former concentration camp Auschwitz–Birkenau to Berlin, to work against forgetting. The trees are spread over the whole city. They were planted with support from the 7th Berlin Biennale for Contemporary Art.'

174 Interview with Lukasz Surowiec by Daniel Miller, 27 March 2012, available at http://blog.berlinbiennale.de/en/comments/an-interview-with-lukasz-surowiec-26719, last accessed 16 October 2017.

The transnational character is also recognizable in the field of Holocaust education, which seems to be experiencing 'innovation and profound developmental transformations'.[175] Memorial museums in particular, with their advanced technology and expanding archives, are supposedly helping in the transformation of the Holocaust from a European memory to a global event. With a hypothesis that Holocaust education can be useful in promoting human rights and civic education, universalization of the Holocaust paradigm can hypothetically assist nations in achieving positive national and international transformations, 'a process that can, with potential risk to historical focus and accuracy, generate cosmopolitan, though less culturally focused forms of historic memory'.[176] The current state of Holocaust education, however, is constantly challenged. Particularly in regard to the use of the digital medium, critiques refer to the established ways of memory transmission as 'the dinosaur of Holocaust memory' that prefers and offers 'sterile, homogenous, and uninspiring platforms of Holocaust education'.[177] The didactic potential of this and other media, in this view, urges for more self-reflective and transparent exploration. Initiatives like *The Vienna Project* (interactive performance 2013–14), for example, use social media and available technologies to promote 'differentiated inclusivity' and commemorate victims of different groups through exchange and collaboration – a controversial concept in Holocaust memorialization in today's Austria.[178]

Other explorations of different ways of learning share this point of view, stressing that knowledge is 'dead' if defined, taught and used as a given, or made into an object because it is no longer true to its character as a 'thing in the making, continuously evolving through our understanding of the world and our own bodies' experience of and participation of that world'.[179] Hence, the pedagogical force is strengthened through the experience of a space and in the way our body inhabits that space through the 'affective somatic responses' it creates.[180] This aspect of learning through experience is intuitively recognized by designers, but at the same it is

[175] Polgar, *Holocaust and Human Rights Education*, p. 118. [176] Ibid., p. 117.

[177] Wulf Kansteiner, 'The Holocaust in the 21st century. Digital anxiety, transnational cosmopolitanism, and never again genocide without memory', in Hoskins (ed.), *Digital Memory Studies*, pp. 110–40, p. 111.

[178] Karen Frostig, 'Activizim and citizenship. Performing memory and acts of memorialization in Austria', in Corey Dzenko and Theresa Avrila (eds.), *Contemporary Citizenship, Art, and Visual Culture: Making and Being Made* (New York and London: Routledge, 2018), pp. 145–57.

[179] Ellsworth, *Places of Learning*, p. 1. [180] Ibid., p. 4.

influenced by the contemporary trend to create experiential spaces. In many recent memorials, we can find in-between spaces, transitional spaces, non-representational events based on movement and rhythm and so forth. These all aim to involve users into their pedagogical intent. Of particular interest is that the design concept of a transitional space is comparable to the anthropological notion of *liminality* – as defined by the early-twentieth-century ethnologist Arnold van Gennep in a work entitled *The Rites of Passage*.[181] Van Gennep analysed rites of passage as universal demarcations of a specific period in the life of an individual or group and distinguished three stages in a rite of passage: separation, transition (a phase of ambiguity) and incorporation. He illustrated his theory with the example of territorial journeys, as they always consist of a departure, travelling and arriving. In this way, rites of passage are liminal and have their prototype in crossing over a physical border from one environment to another, for instance when passing through a portal or moving across a square.[182] According to van Gennep, the transitory experience, an act of crossing defined by a certain period of time spent in a so-called neutral zone, creates possibilities for the deeper understanding of a ritual.[183]

Similar to spaces in cemeteries, transitional spaces are recognized as powerful didactic spaces that create a certain potential for learning through experience. It is a space that exists around a defined content and its purpose is to encourage the feeling of connection between two realities, personal and factual. Thus, creating an interrelational environment, which offers the opportunity for one to act and be acted upon, arguably represents a powerful didactic model. In such an environment, the body is encouraged to experience the space through the sensation of movement

[181] See Arnold van Gennep, *The Rites of Passage*, trans. Monika B. Vizedom and Gabrielle L. Caffe (London: Routledge, 2004). First published in 1909.

[182] The concept of liminality refers to the actual crossing of thresholds (in Latin *limen* means threshold) which van Gennep used to describe the rites of separation as pre-liminal rites, liminal and post-liminal rites. Robert Herz argued that liminality refers both to the mourner and the diseased, meaning that each subject has to pass the transitional phase in a sort of parallel journey. See Robert Hertz, *Death and the Right Hand*, trans. Rodney and Claudia Needham (Aberdeen: Cohen & West, 1960). Originally published in French as 'Contribution à une étude sur la représentation collective de la mort', L'Année sociologique (1896/1897–1924/1925) 10e Année (1905–6), 48–137, and as 'La prééminence de la main droite: Étude sur la polarité religieuse', *Revue Philosophique de la France Et de l'Etranger*, 68 (1909), 553–80.

[183] Neutral zones refer to physical spaces that are in some way ambiguous or in between clearly defined territories, for example deserts, forests or other types of no-man's land. Van Gennep observed rites of initiation in tribal societies as a liminal phase that was performed by actual seclusion. The complete transition van Gennep explained as a 'rite of the threshold'. See van Gennep, *Rites of Passage*.

Figure 2.4 Red Location Museum: 'Memory Boxes' (2005), New Brighton, Port Elizabeth; Noero and Wolff architects.
Photo: Noero Architects

and duration, providing a better understanding of the pedagogical intent of the space.

In the Red Location Museum of the People's Struggle (2005) in South Africa, the idea of a transitional space is quite literally translated into architecture in the form of hallways of 'twilight memory'. These hallways run between units of space designated as memory boxes, each containing the documents and life stories of those who fought Apartheid, arranged in a non-hierarchical fashion (Figure 2.4). Whether or not one enters these boxes and in which order remains a personal choice; they do not present a linear historical narrative. In that way, the memory boxes act as 'a laboratory in which the museumgoer must actively participate in weaving together the various stories of Red Location'.[184] The transitional hallways create their context in a physical sense, as a buffer space in which the perceived information needs to settle and find its place.

[184] Andreas Lepik (ed.), 'Red Location Museum of Struggle', in *Small Scale, Big Scale: New Architectures of Social Engagement* (New York: Museum of Modern Art, 2010), pp. 53–62, p. 54.

Figure 2.5 Srebrenica Memorial Room (2007), Potočari; Christoph Hinterreiter, Gerd Wochein, Armin Sepić, Isra Tatlić.
Photo: Author

Alfredo Jarr's installation *Real Pictures* (2005) also engaged the theoretical concept of learning by willingly becoming a witness. It consisted of a darkened room with several black linen boxes, labelled to explain that they contain the artist's pictures of the Rwandan genocide. In eight different configurations of these boxes, the top of each box was silk-screened with a text in white letters that described the images buried within. The installation was proclaimed a 'tomb for the media' and interpreted as a critique of the images of violence regularly employed in media reports, causing an unbridgeable distance from the real experience and thereby lessening the impact of real events.[185] To emphasize this, Jarr's installation invited visitors to open the boxes and, in that way, deliberately choose to become witnesses, or more elaborately – 'to witness witnessing themselves'.[186] Similarly, in the Srebrenica Memorial Room (2007), Bosnia and Herzegovina, two black towers sit in the dilapidated Yugoslavian-era factory that served as a UN headquarters during the 1992–5 war: one displays a documentary film about the course of the genocide that took place in 1995; the other contains personal items and showcases the stories of twenty of those killed (Figure 2.5). Installed in an overwhelming authentic place,

[185] Jane Blocker, *Seeing Witness: Visuality and the Ethics of Testimony* (Minneapolis, MN: University of Minnesota Press, 2009), p. 55.
[186] Ibid.

the two dark cubes act as connotative anchors of meaning. These examples seemingly go against the popular practice of, especially in memorial museums, creating a scenography that strategically imbues the visitor with content aimed towards emphatic and emotional responses.

For a long time now, the concept of education through experience and participation has been recognized and explored as one of the most important tasks of museums. However, not all experiences are educative, or more precisely, routine experiences that are not stimulating for the mind and hence do not support the growth of further insights are not useful in a learning process. It is not sufficient for the experience to be only simulating and lively, if there is no planned educational base.[187] Several key factors for creating a successful museum experience have been suggested, among them the following:

Curiosity – the visitor is surprised and intrigued;
Confidence – the visitor has a sense of competence;
Challenge – the visitor perceives that there is something to work towards;
Control – the visitor has a sense of self-determination and control;
Play – the visitor experiences sensory enjoyment and playfulness;
Communication – the visitor engages in meaningful social interaction.[188]

In memorials and memorial museums, the emphasis is placed on the creation of social space, places for dialogue about what is memorialized and how it relates to the experiences of young people today.[189] In most cases exhibitions are structured in chronological order with well-defined educational content. For example, in Kazerne Dossin in Mechelen, discussed in Chapter 4, the exhibits develop gradually over several floors and are aimed at schoolchildren. To put the story in a wider context, references to other similar affairs and crimes against humanity in the world are provided. Interactive screens and other technical supplements are presented to establish an engaged relationship with the theme through discovering more about a particular victim or event. Authentic photographs are often employed as powerful didactic tools that can contribute to the overall design. As a result, it has become a common strategy to juxtapose large prints of documentary images and the present situation, to display the history of a place. Photographs and audio-visual testimonies are added to existing monuments and memorials in order to reinforce

[187] George E. Hein, *Learning in the Museum* (London: Routledge, 2002), p. 2.
[188] D. L. Perry, 'Designing exhibits that motivate', quoted in Hein, *Learning*, p. 152.
[189] Brett et al., *Memorialization and Democracy*, p. 15.

their meaning, for example at the Interment and Deportation memorial (2008) in Royallieu.

Next to their documentary value photographs can become powerful design tools when manipulated to augment the architectural space, as we have seen in the case of the Neue Bremm memorial in Saarbrücken. This method was used in Alfredo Jarr's *Geometría de la conciencia* (2010), a work dedicated to the victims of Pinochet's regime and installed in a room adjacent to the Museum of Memory and Human Rights in Santiago, Chile. Jarr blurred some 500 faces from the photographs to the point where the faces became silhouettes, organized in a geometric grid which appears endless due to the reflection produced by mirror walls. As the grid suddenly lights up, the darkened room transforms into an infinite screen which at the same time multiplies the image of the observer. The *Geometría* creates an effective holding environment for experiencing, but its meaning can only be addressed in the context of the museum's exhibit.[190]

Stimulating the sensory-cognitive relationship in memorial designs is essential in strengthening the educational potential in memorial spaces. This symbiosis delivers dynamic transitional environments in architectural design that suggest movement through space and time. It is therefore not surprising that they are a common feature of memorial architecture. We can see attempts of this merging already in Pingusson's memorial, but also in several Soviet memorial projects, such as Salaspils memorial (1967) in Latvia, where a metronome installed in a black cube resembles heartbeats, or Khatyn memorial (1969), Belarus, where the periodic sound of bells breaks the silence of the place. The Salaspils memorial additionally embodies the notion of passage and motion in reference to the mechanism of industrialized killing.

In the Tyne Cot war cemetery, close to Ypres, one enters the newly built visitor centre from a long descending slope, while the names and ages of the soldiers buried in the cemetery are narrated from hidden speakers. As such, the visitor hears several names on approach to the information centre. Poignant and supported by the experience of the slow descent and peaceful surroundings, this is a strong introduction to the cemetery one is about to enter. Maya Lin employed both sound and touch in the Civil Rights Memorial (1989) in Montgomery, Alabama, creating a 'vehicle for education'.[191]

190 See Estefane Andrés, 'Materiality and politics in Chile's Museum of Memory and Human Rights', *Thresholds*, 41 (2013), 158–71.

191 Southern Poverty Law Center, Civil Rights Memorial, available at www.splcenter.org/civil-rights-memorial, last accessed 30 October 2017.

Here the sensory and the cognitive merge in what is literally a moving work of art and memory. Three decades later, Montgomery received the National Memorial for Peace and Justice (2018) by MAAS Design Group – a space of remembrance that is conceived not only as a sensorial design, but is actually an active catalogue of the ongoing work of memory. At this memorial site, 800 monuments are waiting to be appropriated and installed on locations in different counties and states where racial terror lynching took place.[192]

2.4 Fundamental Elements of Engagement

Death and Architecture

As twentieth-century architectural historian Howard Colvin summarizes it, 'architecture in western Europe begins with a tomb.'[193] The fascination with the realm of death always occupied a prominent place among architects who explored the dialectic relationship between the permanency of architecture and transience of life. Before the First World War, in an attempt to make a clear distinction between utilitarian and non-utilitarian forms, Adolf Loos declared that 'only a very small part of architecture belongs to art: The Tomb and the Monument.'[194] This frequently quoted statement demonstrates that designing for occasions concerning dying and death remains a source of inspiration for architects. For Loos, a work of art is never conservative, and it is created with the intention to make us feel uncomfortable without having any responsibility to please or comfort anyone. As he bluntly put it:

> A work of art is concerned with the future and directs us along new paths, a building is concerned with the present. We love anything that adds to our comfort, we hate anything that tries to pester us into abandoning our secure and established position. We love buildings and hate art.[195]

[192] See 'The National Memorial for Peace and Justice', https://museumandmemorial.eji.org/memorial, last accessed 25 May 2019.

[193] Howard Colvin, *Architecture and the Afterlife* (New Haven, CT and London: Yale University Press, 1991), p. 1.

[194] Adolf Loos quoted in Colin St. John Wilson, *Architectural Reflections: Studies in Philosophy and Practice of Architecture* (Oxford: Butterworth-Heinemann, 1992), p. 57.

[195] Adolf Loos, 'Architecture' (1910), in *On Architecture*, selected and introduced by Adolf and Daniel Opel, trans. Michael Mitchell (Riverside, CA: Ariadne Press, 2002), pp. 73–85, pp. 82–3.

A tomb as the last meaningful space – and as Loos argued more than a century ago, 'a genuine expression' – persists today despite the technological advancements that provide us with imaginative possibilities of preserving and recalling the past in contemporary modes of commemoration. In September 2016 during a three-day-long event entitled *Good Grief* at Highgate Cemetery in London, a temporary and modified enactment, dubbed a 'pop-up tomb', of Loos' unrealized mausoleum for Max Dvorák (1921), served as the centrepiece for discussions about the reasons for and purposes of memorials in contemporary society, which one critic described as a 'gullible tragedy-hungry memorial culture'.[196] The glass structure, which was symbolically built as a 'memorial to a memorial', was conceived without additional commemorative purpose; instead, its short existence was directed towards imagining 'other possibilities, altered presents and alternative futures'.[197]

Already Etienne-Louis Boullée, who embodied Enlightenment ideas in his work, moved past the figurative character of commemorative architecture towards a symbolic design, which usually imitated principles of nature. With the Cenotaph to Sir Isaac Newton (1784), Boullée strived to create an architectural concept that would project the memory of Newton as the very essence of Enlightenment. A way to achieve this in architecture, as elaborated in Edmund Burke's 1757 essay on the sublime,[198] was preconditioned by large dimensions and infinity.[199] As Burke argued, the *artificial infinite* consists of two elements: succession and uniformity of parts. Succession is the requirement that the parts in question may be continued in such a way that they offer the imagination an idea of their progress beyond their actual limits, as in the way columns are arranged in ancient temples. Uniformity of the participating parts is necessary to

[196] Jon Astbury, 'As good as grief gets', *The Architectural Review*, 1436.240 (November 2016), 37–8, p. 37.

[197] Amy Frearson, 'Sam Jacob erects Adolf Loos-designed mausoleum in Highgate Cemetery', *Dezeen*, 14 September 2016, www.dezeen.com/2016/09/14/sam-jacob-adolf-loos-mausoleum-tomb-highgate-cemetery-london-architecture-foundation, last accessed 14 September 2016.

[198] Edmund Burke's essay, 'A philosophical enquiry into the origin of our ideal of the sublime and beautiful', was first published anonymously on 21 April 1757 by R. and J. Dodsley, London, who issued a new edition every third year for 30 years, amounting to about 7,000 copies during Burke's lifetime. See Paul Langford, T. O. McLoughlin and James T. Boulton (eds.), *The Writings and Speeches of Edmund Burke: Volume I: The Early Writings* (New York: Oxford University Press, 1997), p. 185.

[199] Richard A. Etlin, 'Architecture and the sublime', in Timothy M. Costelloe (ed.), *The Sublime: From Antiquity to the Present* (Cambridge: Cambridge University Press, 2012), pp. 230–74.

continue the progression of the succession and create an effect of infinity.[200] Boullée's appropriation of the *artificial infinite* is displayed in the memorial to Newton, in the immense spherical surface and one fixed focal point in the whole design – Newton's sarcophagus. A spectator standing at the 'center of gravity', represented by the tomb, would see the uninterrupted vast surface of the circular dome with neither beginning nor end, and would feel obliged to remain in the centre next to the tomb as the sole material object, until the moment of epiphany is achieved and the spectator becomes one with Nature and the Tomb, together representing the sublimity of the genius.[201] Sublimity as an architectural concept is described as a trigger of 'inner movement', normally provoked by an overwhelming space that creates confrontation with 'a seeming nothingness, with rooms with a vast extent or of the most severe barrenness, as well as the experience of being submerged in total silence, extreme darkness or blinding light'.[202]

Devoid of mundane activities, spaces of death are spaces of absence, a constituent part of so-called deep structure, which architectural historian Richard Etlin explained as a primal space of 'particularly intense experiences in which sentience, the feeling of vital life, takes on a particularly intense coloring of life'.[203] Seeking to understand this source of inspiration in primordial and ancient expressions concerning death and the afterlife, Etlin made an effort to categorize architectural responses to the quest for a symbolic space to dwell on the absence of the deceased into eight types: Temple-like Enclosures, the Descent into the Earth, the Gaping Tomb, the Impenetrable Mass, Staircase to Heaven, Matter into Spirit, the Hovering Roof and the Architecture of Shadows.[204] For Etlin, these spaces are paradoxical places of absence, for they are 'neither of this world nor of the next'.[205]

200 Edmund Burke, 'A philosophical enquiry into the origin of our ideas of the sublime and beautiful', in Langford, McLoughlin and Boulton (eds.), *Writings and Speeches*, pp. 185–321.

201 Richard Etlin, *Symbolic Space: French Enlightenment Architecture and Its Legacy* (Chicago, IL and London: University of Chicago Press, 1994), p. 122.

202 Alban Janson and Florian Tiggers (eds.), *Fundamental Concepts of Architecture. The Vocabulary of Spatial Situations* (Basel: Birkhäuser, 2014), pp. 314–15.

203 Etlin, *Symbolic Space*, p. xx. Etlin makes a distinction between three different types of symbolic spaces as codes of order humans use to organize their world: (1) the primal, experiential space of 'deep structure', (2) the hierarchically organized space according to social codes, (3) the multiple, simultaneous layering of meaning given to a particular space.

204 Ibid., p. 172.

205 Ibid., p. 173. Etlin argues that the space of absence derives from the spiritual outlook of the Enlightenment, when empty spaces were designed and dedicated to specific abstract concepts so that by entering those spaces, man could commune with higher ideals.

The last category, Etlin's 'Architecture of Shadows', is the embodiment of a space of absence. This particular type originates from Boullée's eagerness to represent the uncanny feeling inspired by certain shadows and silhouettes of nature. If applied in architecture, Boullée believed, shadows created by different forms and shapes placed against the light could reproduce the sense of dreadful and strange familiarity. In order to translate the melancholia dominating the natural end of life into funerary architecture, Boullée developed concepts of an architecture of shadows, buried architecture and naked architecture, three principles that together constituted a 'new genre in architecture'.[206] Never realized, these concepts served as inspirational guidelines for future designers such as Henry Latrobe, whose starkly abstract rows of cenotaphs designed for the Congressional Cemetery in Washington, DC (1816) provoked the congressman of Massachusetts, George F. Hoar, to proclaim that 'the thought of being buried beneath one of those atrocities brought new terror to death.'[207]

The descent into the earth is commonly associated with the realm of the dead or unseen of Hades. The passage from the world of the living to the world of the dead is often represented as a symbolic facade, a labyrinth, a staircase, a ladder, or similar concepts, among which are the 'space of fire' and the 'space of water' seen by particular cultures as privileged spaces of crossing.[208] The symbolism of the facade of the 'other' world can be compared to that of the theatre backdrop, as 'both hell and theater are worlds peopled by shadows, phantoms and illusions – akin to those of the houses of living, yet which gives onto chambers that are dark and bare.'[209] For the soldiers symbolically marching into the ground, as seen in various war memorials, earth becomes a facade of the arid space of death, destitute of any further meaning. By accentuating the absence of human versatility, the form turns into absence itself, hence its own subject.

From this perspective, architectural representation resonates with the argument that modern art introduced nothingness as its subject and 'forgot

[206] Richard A. Etlin, 'In the face of death: calming the mind, mining the soul', in Claudia Denk, John Ziesemer and International Council on Monuments and Sites (eds.), *Der bürgerliche Tod: städtische Bestattungskultur von der Aufklärung bis zum frühen 20. Jahrhundert = Urban Curial Culture from the Enlightenment to the Early 20th Century; Internationale Fachtagung des Deutschen Nationalkomitees von ICOMOS in Zusammenarbeit mit dem Bayerischen Nationalmuseum, München, 11–13 November 2005*, ICOMOS: Journals of the German National Committee no. 44 (Regensburg: Schnell & Steiner, 2007), pp. 35–45, p. 40.

[207] Keith Eggener, *Cemeteries* (New York: W.W. Norton & Company, 2010), p. 129.

[208] See Ragon, *The Space of Death*, pp. 65–71.

[209] Pedro Azara, 'The house and the dead: on modern tombs', in Mónica Gili (ed.), *The Last House* (Barcelona: Editorial Gustavo Gili, 1999), pp. 24–39, p. 26.

about the wound and concentrated on the knife'.[210] As we have seen, it is in the very core of human nature to mourn, contemplate and somehow reunite with the dead, even though grief and the desire to 'die with our dead' are the potentially most self-destructive psychic crises.[211] This aspect is poignantly explored in John Hejduk's memorial to Jan Palach that consists out of two cubes: the 'House of the Suicide' and the 'House of the Mother of the Suicide', set apart by a few meters. The observer can enter only one cube, the 'House of the Mother', where a small platform, set in a cramped dark space with a small opening, permits one to gaze outside. The other cube is impenetrable. By allowing the gaze but omitting the possibility of entering the other structure, Hejduk touched upon the notion of witnessing trauma at a remove, unable to reach the subject physically. The gaze of the observer becomes the gaze of the mother, fixed on the act of the suicide, distant and unreachable and therefore evocative of trauma.[212]

For Loos, revoking the irrevocable was possible with the tomb and the monument as abstract symbols that represented 'irreducible architectural form'.[213] In a similar logic, the space of a mausoleum, released from functional obligations, is a space of memory and transition, a podium for intimate expression. Loos explored this potential when designing his own tombstone – a simple white cube – and in his unrealized concept for a mausoleum for Max Dvorák, its projected black Swedish granite giving an impression of a well-grounded, heavy cube topped with a three-level stepped pyramid, while the interior was supposed to be decorated by Oskar Kokoschka's frescoes. The outside appearance and the simplicity of its form reflected the notion of death as a heavy and introverted subject, confined within the walls of its primitive construction. It would have been only in the interior of the mausoleum that the space would become a holding environment for intimate feelings, as Kokoschka's art was invited to 'depict the emotion aroused by the commemoration inside the tomb'.[214] Thereby the private experience of the artist, as portrayed in his art, would

210 Paul Virilio, *Art and Fear*, trans. Julie Rose (London: Continuum, 2003), p. 16.

211 Robert Pogue Harrison, *The Dominion of the Dead* (Chicago, IL: University of Chicago Press, 2003), p. 55.

212 Mimi Zeiger, 'John Hejduk's The House of the Suicide structures get new life in Prague', *Architects Newspaper*, 19 January 2016, https://archpaper.com/2016/01/hejduks-house-suicide-structures-get-new-life-prague, last accessed 30 October 2018.

213 Panayotic Tournikiotis, *Adolf Loos* (New York: Princeton Architectural Press, 2002), p. 21. See also Burkhardt Rukschcio and Roland Schachel (eds.), *Adolf Loos: Leben und Werk* (Salzburg and Vienna: Residenz Verlag, 1982).

214 Gravagnuolo, *Adolf Loos*, p. 170.

become 'a design for an unconscious archetype in which personal memory is blended with the collective one'.[215]

Spaces of Transition

In reference to the transitional period through which a mourner has to pass before he or she is able to return to society, Loos' mausoleum can be seen as one of the three distinctive spatial concepts that together form an engaging environment: entrance, room and a path. An entrance can be defined as a spatial condition that involves movement and creates the potential for the unfolding of subsequent spaces. Apart from merely being a barrier, the gate of a cemetery, for example, is also an element of transition, a highly complex threshold that is at once 'the limit, the boundary, the frontier that distinguishes and opposes two worlds - and at the same time the paradoxical place where those worlds communicate, where the passage from the profane to the sacred world becomes possible'.[216] Next to its obvious function, to distinguish the space of a cemetery, the entering sequence is a preparation for the awaited experience, provided architecture offers a scenic framework. Potentially, it also gives a sense of expectation, curiosity and a sense of thrill.[217] The fascination with cemetery gates as symbolic passageways, a transition to the realm of death, is illustrated in the paintings of Caspar David Friedrich, who was himself consulted about the designs of cemeteries. Friedrich's dramatic deathscapes reflected the changing attitude towards death at the time, when the 'great fear of death' was replacing what Ariès called 'tamed death'. Friedrich's response to this change of feeling had a nostalgic character that was shaped by 'looking back to the past, to a medieval tradition of taming death through spirituality and ritual'.[218]

Similarly, Le Corbusier recognized the significance of thresholds in his concept of the architectural promenade, arguing that the placement of a door in an architectural space influences the overall feeling and the

[215] Ibid.

[216] Mircea Eliade, 'The sacred and the profane' (1957), quoted in Kenneth T. Jackson and Camilo José Vergara, *Silent Cities: The Evolution of the American Cemetery* (New York: Princeton Architectural Press, 1989), p. 72.

[217] See Grant Hilderbrand, *Origins of Architectural Pleasure* (Berkeley, CA: University of California Press, 1999).

[218] In Karl Whittington, 'Caspar David Friedrich's medieval burials', *Nineteenth-Century Art Worldwide*, 11.1 (2012), available at www.19thc-artworldwide.org/index.php/spring12/whittington-on-caspar-david-friedrichs-medieval-burials, last accessed 20 October 2017.

perception of the space: hence the entrance or door becomes an element of transformation and revelation, as he argued: 'depending on the way you enter a room that is to say depending on the place of the door in the wall of the room, the feeling will be different. That is architecture.'[219] The entrance is the first stage in the ritual procession, and for the mourners it is the first encounter with the space.

A good example of a design that displays a concern with the ritual procession and the time needed for experiencing the architecture is the Igualada Cemetery (1996) near Barcelona, designed by Enric Miralles and Carme Pinós. The design was based on the idea that a cemetery, in addition to being a transitional space, is also a transient form, just like human bodies are. Commemorative plaques and furniture in the cemetery are made of materials that are susceptible to deterioration and thereby serve as a constant reminder of the passage of time and the continuity of a life cycle. In an unexpected proposal, the designers sought to materialize their idea that 'life itself makes the cemetery die.'[220] The cemetery becomes the intentionally impermanent memorial to death – a natural part of life. The entrance, positioned on a higher level than the rest of the site, allows an overview over the cemetery valley. Before descending into the valley, a former quarry, the visitor passes an entering sequence composed of different layers of soil and plants that accentuate the natural change of context and reinforce the feeling of immersion into a different world. It is also possible to access the cemetery through another entrance, which is incorporated into the building itself: it creates the complete opposite effect, as it encloses the visitor into an arid architectural space with openings towards the sky. In contrast to the first part of the cemetery, this sequence is a searing concrete space – a counteract to nature (Figure 2.6). Here we find a clear demonstration of how significant design choices are in creating the entering sequence, a prototype for van Gennep's rite of separation.

As an archetypical concept in the construction of symbolic and experiential space, the formal materialization of a path frames how the subject will interact with the environment. Opposite to the effect produced by a descending ground level, an ascent usually communicates a path of initiation, as we have seen with Italian sacrariums. The progression from the earthly to a higher point is often a central metaphor in contemplations

[219] Flora Samuel, *Le Corbusier and the Architectural Promenade* (Basel: Birkhäuser, 2010), p. 86.

[220] Anatxu Zabalbeascoa, *Igualada Cemetery: Enric Miralles and Carme Pinos (Architecture in Detail)* (London: Phaidon Press, 1996), p. 19.

Figure 2.6 Igualada cemetery (1996), Barcelona; Enric Miralles and Carme Pinós. Photo: Author

about death, and it usually employs the symbolism of steps or stairways. In the Partisan Memorial Cemetery (1965) in Mostar, designed by Bogdanović, a winding, ascending road leads towards terraces containing gravestones of fallen partisans. At the highest point, a water basin designated as a cosmological circle, a symbol of life, overlooks the amphitheatre of death beneath – a city of the dead faced with the city of the living.

For the artist Louise Bourgeois, steps were a symbol of a dualistic possibility: a path that leads towards a better place, what Etlin categorized as a 'staircase to heaven', or suggestive of a nihilistic purpose manifested in the repetitive motion of climbing steps that lead nowhere, as demonstrated in her installations *No Escape* and *No Exit* (1989). In this work, Bourgeois identified with Albert Camus, for whom stairways were a metaphor for the essential nature of human existence, inviting engagement, since 'action is always a necessary gesture, no matter how futile.'[221]

In Bourgeois' work, however, the steps lead to no particular physical object, but instead to a space opening up to one of two possibilities: hope or futility. If translated to a funerary context, it can be argued that Bourgeois' art 'negates traditional sculpted funerary moment and its customary message, "may he or she rest in peace"'.[222] Hence the ascent is a symbol of the futility of hope. The same uncanny twist is materialized in Aldo Rossi's

[221] Terrie Sultan, 'Redefining the terms of engagement: the art of Louise Bourgeois', in Charlotta Kotik, Terrie Sultan and Christian Leigh (eds.), *Louise Bourgeois: The Locus of Memory, Works 1982–1993* (New York: Harry N. Abrams, 1994), pp. 28–50, p. 49.

[222] Alex Potts, 'Louise Bourgeois: sculptural confrontations', *Oxford Art Journal*, 22.2 (1999), 37–53, p. 53.

Modena ossuary (1971), a cubic building with an arid interior which the architect referred to as an 'unfinished house'.[223] The metal staircases connecting the galleries of the ossuary only augment the sombre, prison-like mood of the interior, in which one has a feeling as if the dead are abandoned and destined to observe, in perpetuity, the unreachable sky, visible through a roof opening. Originally designed as one end of a long axis in the San Cataldo cemetery – the other end would have been a large conical form (a common grave) – the ossuary embodies Rossi's ideas of a cemetery as a reflection of a city, and reflects his notion of death as a solitary journey *contra natura*, defined by emptiness and hopelessness.[224] The unrealized common grave was imagined as a truncated space with a circular opening towards the sky, once again distant and isolated.[225] In opposition to the approach of accepting and taming death, adopted in Mostar's Partisan Memorial Cemetery, for example, here the architectural typology was chosen to fit Rossi's configuration of the cemetery as an empty house being 'the space in the memory of the living.'[226]

In line with the Loosian argument about the spiritual realm of architecture signifying death, the basic architectural typology of the room translates into a space that encapsulates feelings that come with loss. Within the confinement of four walls, these rooms are temporary shelters for the grief stricken, much like the shelter buildings in First World War cemeteries.[227] They are reminiscent of the mausoleum, a permanent last house for the departed and a temporary realm of seclusion for mourners. For Louis Kahn, a room was the beginning of architecture, a place of mind, as he illustrated in his 1971 drawing *Architecture Comes from the Making of a Room*.[228] Handwritten on the drawing are Kahn's ideas about the room, in which he stressed the scale and the possibilities of interaction that a room

[223] Aldo Rossi, 'Cemetery of San Cataldo, Modena, 1971', in K. Michael Hays (ed.), *Architecture Theory since 1969* (Cambridge, MA: MIT Press, 2000), pp. 68–72, p. 69.

[224] See Tina di Carlo, 'Aldo Rossi: Cemetery of San Cataldo, Modena, Italy', in McQuaid (ed.) *Envisioning Architecture*, pp. 160–1, p. 160.

[225] See Rafael Moneo, 'Aldo Rossi: the idea of architecture and the Modena cemetery', trans. Angela Giral, in Hays (ed.), *Oppositions Reader*, pp. 105–34.

[226] Aldo Rossi, 'L'azzurro del cielo', *Controspazio*, 10 (1972), 4–9, p. 5. Quoted in Moneo, 'Aldo Rossi', p. 119.

[227] The shelter buildings in war cemeteries were designed to offer a place of mourning for the bereaved. They were initially planned for all cemeteries, but after calculating costs for the first three built, shelter houses were restricted to larger cemeteries. Tim Skelton and Gerald Gliddon, *Lutyens and the Great War* (London: Frances Lincoln, 2008), p. 119.

[228] 'Louis I. Kahn: The Making of a Room', Arthur Ross Gallery, University of Pennsylvania, available at www.arthistory.upenn.edu/themakingofaroom/catalogue/section1.htm, last accessed 16 September 2017.

Figure 2.7 Crematorium 'Uitzicht' (2011), Kortrijk; Souto de Moura Arquitectos & SumProject.
Photo: Author

could provide: 'In a small room one does not say what one would in a large room. A room with only one other person could be generative. The vectors of each meet.'[229]

At cemeteries and crematoriums, particular attention is given to the importance of having a space for the private intimation of death, set apart from the ritual space, where families can have a moment in private contemplation. Naturally, when funerals are planned on a tight schedule, it becomes a challenging task to provide enough spaces that are both secluded and lofty. Such is the case with the 'Uitzicht' crematorium in Kortrijk, Belgium. Upon descending into the building, we see the crematorium's chimney ahead of us (Figure 2.7). Once in the entrance hall, the space directs one's view towards the valley. As the stages of the burial ritual progress, the space turns introspective by omitting any visual connection with the outside world. At the end of the ritual, the same view is reintroduced at the exit, a design gesture that augments the symbolism of the relationship between the view and the ceremony. However, the connection with the outside is only possible from spaces not related to the ceremony, namely an auditorium and the so-called family rooms which have

[229] Ibid.

Figure 2.8 Tulach a'tSolais memorial (1999), Wexford; Ronald Tallon and Michael Warren.
Photo: Brian Heffernan

openings in the ceilings to provide daylight. This enhances the sensation of being underground.

In a more forward-looking manner, and with the goal of creating 'a modern Stonehenge', the Tulach a'tSolais memorial in Wexford, Ireland (1999), is a mound with an interior room designed on the principles of the golden section. Referring to the ancient tradition of burial mounds as spaces where the living communicate with the dead, the designers positioned the structure in accordance with the passage of the sun and the summer solstice (Figure 2.8). The mound is cut in half, creating a skylight for the memorial room. Given the weather conditions that day, on 21st June the room is induced with the 'light of resurrection', further augmented by the use of white concrete for its 'pallor of death'.[230]

[230] Scot't Tallon Walker Architects, Tulach a'tSolais Memorial, available at www.stwarchitects.com/project-information.php?p=09672, last accessed 31 October 2017.

Next to the symbolic features of the memorial design, such as the alignment with the sun and the view towards the adjacent hill where the commemorated event – the 1798 United Irishmen uprising – took place, the fundamental idea here is that by inducing stillness into the recess room, the space becomes an emptiness that is filled with light, quiet and stillness – as the designers have argued, not very different from the condition of a prayer in its purest form. Here, in this specific form of tension augmented by the division of the mound, all men are equal in the light of the European Enlightenment it seeks to commemorate. Thus, unlike memorial voids that memorialize the loss of meaning and absence of being, the room at Tulach is imagined as a transformative journey that encourages the contemplation of meaning in a space that aims at elevating spirits. In many ways similar to some of the examples discussed so far (Kahn's Holocaust memorial, for example), where architects believed in the transformative possibilities of architectural spaces through the use of immaterial substances such as light, the Tulach a'tSolais memorial speaks about the essence of designing and building a memorial as a space that attests to the validity of life. Regardless of their subjects of commemoration, the vectors of these memorials meet in providing memorial spaces that are essential in their form and hope-giving in their meaning.

The Mnemonic Power of Landscapes

Landscapes in general, and cemetery landscapes in particular, have the potential to become spatial mnemonic devices in the production of a narrative.[231] Similar to literary narratives, landscape narratives are constructed through tropes, such as metaphor, metonymy, synecdoche and irony.[232] With regard to this, the architect and theorist Marc Treib suggested that there are four levels of conveying meaning in a landscape design, distinguished by the applied method and the directness of communication.[233] The first level implies the modification of the natural order of a landscape, in order to suggest human presence: through the newly established relationship between the original elements, they are invested with meaning. An ancient example of this is found in megalithic sites around

[231] Matthew Potteiger and Jamie Purinton, *Landscape Narratives: Design Practices for Telling Stories* (New York: John Wiley & Sons, 1998).

[232] Ibid., p. 34.

[233] Marc Treib, 'The landscape of loved ones', in Wolschke-Bulmahn (ed.), *Places of Commemoration*, pp. 81–105, p. 95.

the French village of Carnac. If these natural elements, such as stone boulders, are then remodelled by human effort, for example by added inscriptions, they constitute the second level of commemorative landscape. At this point, the meaning of the original setting, now reconfigured in a non-natural order, is invigorated. As an example of this level of conveying meaning, Treib discusses the memorial landscape of Kongenshus Mindepark by landscape architect C.-Th. Sørensen and architect Hans Georg Solvgaard, on Jutland, Denmark, built between 1945 and 1953. The site, a tract of 1,200 hectares of heath, is defined by boulders bearing the inscriptions of 1,200 names of the people who worked on this site – and who initiated the preservation of the site as a memorial – in poor life conditions. The arrangement of these boulders symbolically refers to the past, such as the circular space which recalls the funerary tradition of ship settings found in Jutland, and in the Viking period when such constructions were considered a symbol of eternity.

The third level of commemorative landscapes introduces architectural structures into a given landscape composition. The insertion should not rely on any explicit references or information, but instead aims to engage the visitor in a deeply individual experience through a perceptual program. We can see this approach in most of Bogdanović's memorials but also in Edvard Ravnikar's 1953 Memorial Complex at Kampor on the Island of Rab in Croatia. Situated next to the site of a former Second World War Italian concentration camp, the memorial is composed of basic elements of architecture – columns, platforms and walls – in order to convey the sacredness of the place. Influenced by the Jože Plečnik – a proponent of the origins of architecture being transformed into a new symbolical language – Ravnikar ardently 'translated' elements of the antique funerary typology, such as a funerary urn in the entrance, containing samples of soil collected from the native homes of the prisoners, and the memorial's pavements which possibly refer to an ancient sacred way or the mythological River Styx.[234] Clear hierarchy, the interplay of the various elements within the precise architectural grid and its materialization turns the memorial cemetery into a highly transitional space.

The more influential example is found in the Woodland Cemetery (Skogskyrkogården) in Enskede-Stockholm (realized between 1920 and 1940), a landscape that 'modulates comportment' and in which

[234] William J. R. Curtis, 'Abstraction and representation: the memorial complex at Kampor on the island of Rab (1952–3) by Edvard Ravnikar', in Aleš Vodopivec and Rok Žnidaršić (eds.), *Edvard Ravnikar: Architect and Teacher* (Wien: Springer, 2010), pp. 33–50, p. 38.

'the retrieval of memory derives equally from the actions of the individual and his or her associations'.[235] A collaborative design project between Erik Gunnar Asplund and Sigurd Lewerentz, the cemetery is possibly the first landscape that introduced a new perspective in powerfully exploring mnemonic codes, situated within architecturally defined episodes: Entrance, Hill of Remembrance, Resurrection, Woodland and Main Chapel. The cemetery was only recently recognized for its contribution to architecture: it established 'a new form of cemetery that has exerted a profound influence on cemetery design throughout the world'.[236] Rather against the prevailing spirit of the time, the designers chose a subtle approach as they 'started with the experience of the visitors – the concept of mourning and the feelings surrounding it'.[237] The designers sought to 'imbue the site with a sacred quality by using landscape as the essential point of departure for their architectural solution'.[238] There are numerous non-explicit references pervading the place, such as sudden clearings in a dense forest landscape; gradual transitions between different spaces of ritual, for instance the diminishing height of the steps leading up to the meditation grove that means visitors feel at ease as they reach the place of meditation; the slight kink in the middle of the benches in and around the three chapels of the Crematorium, intended to open the intimate space of the mourners and bring them closer towards each other. Since Asplund and Lewerentz had great concern for the psychological turmoil architectural design can inflict on mourners, the cemetery is designed to create the feeling of an uncanny familiarity with death. The suppressed architecture that merges with domesticated nature – the Woodland Chapel (1920) for example, as a synthesis of the temple and the primitive hut[239] – shelters the visitor from the intimidating nature surrounding it.[240] A sudden clearing

[235] Treib, 'The landscape of loved ones', p. 101.

[236] A quote from the UNESCO World Heritage List in Mauro Felicori and Annalisa Zanotti (eds.), *Cemeteries of Europe: A Historical Heritage to Appreciate and Restore* (Bologna: Comune di Bologna (SCENE Project), 2004), p. 141.

[237] The City of Stockholm- Varldsarvet Skogskyrkogården, 'Designed experience', available at http://skogskyrkogarden.stockholm.se/in-english/architecture/landscape/the-experience, last accessed 5 October 2017.

[238] Caroline Constant, *The Woodland Cemetery: Towards a Spiritual Landscape, Erik Gunnar Asplund and Sigurd Lewerentz, 1915-1961* (Stockholm: Byggförlaget, 1994), p. 1.

[239] The idea of the primitive hut has been an architectural trope since Vitruvius' classical treatise on architecture. See Ingrid D. Rowland and Thomas Noble Howe (eds.), *Vitruvius: 'Ten Books on Architecture'* (Cambridge: Cambridge University Press, 2017). It was reintroduced into architectural discourse by Marc-Antoine Laugier's *Essai sur l'architecture* (Paris: Chez Duchesne, 1753).

[240] Peter Blundell Jones, *Gunnar Asplund* (London: Phaidon Press, 2006), p. 64.

Figure 2.9 *Passages: Homage to Walter Benjamin* (1994), Portbou; Dani Karavan. Photo: Author

where the chapel is placed, made by cutting into the forest's untamed nature, brings to mind Boullée's description of the shadowy forest and a strong feeling of melancholy.

Relying on the same concept, Dani Karavan's *Passages*, a homage to Walter Benjamin, stands at the entrance to a cemetery on the cliffs of the Costa Brava. It was realized in 'an approach akin to Benjamin's own, connecting the traces of past pain, memory and exile with the possibility of a new and better future'.[241] Seeking to materialize the symbolical merging of Benjamin's life and death, Karavan conjured up Benjamin's theoretical work and the space of the cemetery where he is buried. The memorial punctuates the landscape by fragmentation and the use of industrial materials – COR-TEN – in order to achieve a strong contrast with the natural surroundings, a technique Karavan often employs in his works. The main space of the memorial consists of a long staircase which descends towards the sea (Figure 2.9). Reaching the water is, however, not

[241] 'Walter Benjamin in Portbou', at http://walterbenjaminportbou.cat/en/content/lobra, last accessed 7 November 2017.

possible because of a transparent barrier bearing the most explicit reference to Benjamin – his words inscribed on the glass:

> Schwerer ist es, das Gedächtnis der Namenlosen zu ehren als das der Berühmten. Dem Gedächtnis der Namenlosen ist die historische Konstruktion geweiht.[242]

One cannot enter the cemetery without passing the memorial, which then becomes its extended entrance. As such, it serves as a prime example of the enhancement of the sense of place. Its other features, such as a small staircase situated higher in the landscape, can be seen as 'stepping stones for pulling together the ideas necessary to consider the whole'.[243] Furthermore, by being submitted to the landscape and focused on the view, the memory that the memorial tries to capture is naturally susceptible to weather conditions, as the atmosphere – and thereby the meaning of the memorial – differs significantly, ranging from the view and sounds of a raging sea to the lulling melody of calm water movements. In this sense the memorial operates as a living structure, with its elements anchored in space as signposts of memory. In its formal and metaphorical meaning the memorial is highly evocative of Karavan's earlier installation for 'Documents 6' in Kassel, where he used elements of staircases to create a room for contemplation and remembrance.[244]

The addition of the memorial as an introductory space to the existing cemetery is relevant as an antidote to the contemporary tendency towards architecture without clear borders and thresholds. In memorial architecture this is noticeable in public memorials, such as the MMJE, that are conceptualized on the spatial merging with surroundings in order to guarantee an easy approach for the visitors. This, however, raises a set of issues concerning security, maintenance and the conveyance of meaning.

The equilibrium between nature and architecture achieved in Woodland Cemetery is abandoned in the fourth type of approach, in which verbal and symbolic language prevail in a landscape design. Here the meaning of the design is put straightforwardly in a didactic framework, to the point of 'describing the visitor's desired response',[245] an approach exemplified by

[242] Beneath the inscription, there are translations offered in four languages. The English reads: 'It is more difficult to honour the memory of the nameless than that of the renowned. Historical construction is devoted to the memory of the nameless.'

[243] Hornstein, 'Invisible topographies', p. 17.

[244] Fritz Jacobi, Mordechai Omer and Jule Reuter (eds.), *Dani Karavan Retrospective* (Tubingen and Berlin: Ernst Wasmuth Verlag, 2008), p. 172.

[245] Treib, 'The landscape of loved ones', p. 102.

the Forest Lawn complex. In a modified form we see this strategy gaining more ground in memorial landscapes such as Westerbork in the Netherlands and the Interment and Deportation memorial in Royallieu, in France. To answer contemporary demands geared by tourism and general fascination with memory, it seems only a logical step to incorporate nature's cycle of growth and decay in memorial architecture as a symbolic remedial action to balance the anthropocentric character of remembering and its ecological impact.

PART II

Case Studies

3 | Memorials to the Victims of Terrorism

More than a lump of clay in the hands of a technically capable artist is needed to produce a form which is emotionally moving.
Thomas H. Creighton[1]

Hace falta mucha fantasía para soportar la realidad.[2]

The Oklahoma memorial was dedicated in 2001. In the same year, terrorists attacked New York. In 2004, when the competition results for the 9/11 memorial were announced, there were fresh attacks in Madrid. Shortly afterwards, in 2005, further attacks in London and several other places shocked the world. And in 2017, when the city of Brussels revealed a memorial to commemorate victims of the recent terrorist attack on its airport, the UK faced yet another tragedy when a suicide bomber exploded in a Manchester concert hall. In Europe today, terrorist attacks are a reality; and they have been anticipated since the 1970s. One of the responses to these gruesome acts is to design memorials for the victims. In these cases, a memorial is one of many possible ways to express solidarity with the survivors and the bereaved. At the same time, they are much more than that.

Among the various kinds of memorials introduced in the previous chapters, memorial spaces designed in the aftermath of terrorist attacks highlight several issues that touch on the very core of what memorials are about. Unlike memorials intended to perpetuate a particular memory of things that happened in a more or less distant past, terrorism memorials are first-hand witnesses of the bereavement process. In terms of timing, they are closest to the traumatic event and to the first waves of spontaneous mourning. These memorials are often demonstrations of shock and grief. Moreover, they originate from the genuine need to act, or rather, counteract the senseless destruction, and therefore epitomize the collective struggle to overcome its consequences.

[1] Creighton, *The Architecture of Monuments*, p. 13.

[2] 'It takes a lot of imagination to endure reality' was the inscription on the inner membrane of the Atocha 11-M memorial.

Due to the nature and severity of such attacks, terrorism memorials are widely present in the media, and the world is promptly updated on new developments. Likewise, as photogenic counter-acts, these structures are televised and soon become recognizable. Consequently, they are infused with the opportunity to become attractions or targets of antagonistic reactions even before their actual materialization in real time and space.

This chapter will examine memorial spaces dealing with consequences of terrorist acts of a political and religious character to gain a better understanding of their formal language and underlying meaning. The investigation will start with an in-depth study of Madrid's 11-M memorial, which commemorates the victims of the 2004 terrorist attacks. After taking a closer look at the initiation phase, the design process and the materialization of the memorial, the chapter will continue with an overview of various memorials commemorating terrorist attacks, which are currently being planned and built, or have recently been inaugurated.

3.1 Materializing Trauma: The 11-M Memorial

Context and History

The 2004 Madrid train bombings, commonly referred to as '11-M', were coordinated attacks on the Cercanías commuter rail system in Madrid on the morning of 11 March 2004. Explosions at four stations killed 192 people, a third of whom were immigrants.[3] Approximately 1,857 people were wounded. Adding to the already traumatic character of the event, there was controversy about who executed the attacks.[4] 11-M came to

[3] Three bombs were exploded at Atocha Station. At El Pozo del Tío Raimundo Station, two bombs exploded in different carriages as the train departed the station. Another bomb exploded at Santa Eugenia Station, and at Calle Téllez, just 800 m from Atocha Station, four bombs exploded in different carriages of a single train.

[4] The suspicions of the press and the majority of Spaniards turned immediately to ETA, the Basque nationalist group, against which the retreating prime minister had preached a policy of force. But with the arrest of a group of Moroccan suspects on the eve of elections, the suspicions of the public redirected towards Al-Qaeda. Spain's two main newspapers took starkly opposing viewpoints when addressing the terrorist attacks of 11 March. *El Pais* (politically centre-left) argued there were no legitimate doubts about the Islamist theory, while for *El Mundo* (centre-right nationalist) the Islamist theory was nothing more than a police set-up. See Mathieu Miquel, 'March 11, 2004. The Madrid 3/11 bombings: was it really an attack by "Islamic Terrorists"?' *Global Research*, 28 November 2009, available at www.globalresearch.ca, last accessed 30 January 2015.

be considered the archetype of an 'independent local cell at work and the perpetrators depicted as self-recruited, leaderless terrorists'.[5] In the days following the attacks, numerous grassroots memorials appeared at the sites where the bombs had exploded. This outburst of public grief was enhanced by the fact that the attacks happened just three days before a general election in Spain.[6] Hence, next to the photographs of the victims and other objects expressing private grief, many messages were directed at events in the political arena. Massive protests and public mourning were explained as a reaction to corruption, with the aim of pre-empting any possible manipulation of the calamity by the political powers that be.[7]

After the first outburst of public mourning, a research project entitled 'the Archive of Mourning' launched with two goals: to archive and analyse the displays of mourning and thereby create a heritage collection of the materials deposited at the places of grieving; and secondly, to analyse the very process of mourning.[8] All the artefacts at the bombing sites were removed after three months to allow Spanish Railways (RENFE) to return to normal operation. In addition, its workers complained that the spontaneous memorials were too confrontational to be faced on a daily basis and asked for them to be removed. They argued for a permanent monument to the memory of the dead, to be built nearby,

[5] Fernando Reinares, 'The Madrid bombings and global jihadism', International Institute for Counter-Terrorism, 17 April 2010, available at www.ict.org.il. Originally published in *Survival*, 52.2 (2010), 83–104.

[6] The national government, ruled by the People's Party (Partido Popular), in the early moments following the attacks claimed that ETA were responsible. When evidence pointed to the possibility that an Islamic extremist group was behind the massacre, the ETA theory lost weight. If Islamic extremists were responsible, the attack could have been perceived by the electorate to be a consequence of the Spanish government's support for the invasion of Iraq. The opposition – the Spanish Socialist Workers Party (PSOE) led by Jose Luis Zapatero – received more votes than expected as a result of the government's handling of the train bombings.

[7] There are a few factors that should be considered in relation to these protests, such as the demonstrations that happened before the attacks, against the war in Iraq, and the Spanish government propaganda in favour of it. A second issue is the mourning of victims of the Spanish Civil War (1936–9) which was used as a tool of legitimization during Franco's dictatorship, by which the ones who died for the state were memorialized while the dead 'enemies' were subjects of forgetting. See Sánchez-Carretero and Ortiz, 'Grassroots memorials'.

[8] See Cristina Sánchez-Carretero, Antonio Cea, Paloma Díaz-Mas, Pilar Martínez and Carmen Ortiz, 'On blurred borders and interdisciplinary research teams: the case of the "Archive of Mourning"', *Forum: Qualitative Social Research Sozialforschung*, 12.3 (2011), available at www.qualitative-research.net, last accessed 23 May 2019.

so that they would 'be allowed to overcome this tragedy'.[9] As the collection of candles, dried flowers, messages and other objects started to become an obstacle, in June 2004 'cybershrines' known as Espacios de Palabras were installed at the entrances of the Atocha and El Pozo stations, so that people could leave messages of condolence in an electronic form until a permanent memorial could be built.[10] These 'video walls' attracted a wide audience of people interested in leaving messages of condolence, and were therefore recognized as powerful instruments of living memory, the meaning of which was shared and instantly understood.

Following the installation of these temporary shrines, many argued that permanent memorials might never achieve the same effect in engaging the public.[11] Referring to Picasso's *Guernica* and its powerful representation of the horrors of war, exhibited at the Queen Sofia Art Centre in Madrid, one British historian remarked that the 'video walls' at Atocha station were not Picasso – they appeared after the 'real Guernica' happened in Madrid on 11 March. They were instead perceived as appropriate modes of representation, in all their banality and lack of artistic grandeur. For, as one journalist argued, 'this war will be won or lost not in some grand showdown but in a trillion tiny everyday encounters.'[12] Joining these electronic efforts to encourage human interaction, on the first anniversary of the tragedy another memorial was inaugurated in the Parque del Retiro. Comprising 192 olive and cypress trees planted on an elevated mound symbolically surrounded by water, this was originally known as the Forest of the Departed (Bosque de los Ausentes). Later, however, out of respect for the survivors and the families of the victims, who argued that those killed in the attack will remain forever present in their hearts, it was renamed the Forest of Remembrance (Bosque del Recuerdo). The space

[9] Ibid., p. 109.

[10] Madrid Atocha (Estación de Madrid Atocha, also named Madrid Puerta de Atocha) is the largest railway station in Madrid. It is the primary station serving commuter trains (Cercanías). The name Atocha has become attached to the station because of the nearby basilica dedicated to Our Lady of Atocha. The present building, designed by Alberto de Palacio Elissagne in collaboration with Gustave Eiffel, was inaugurated in 1892 after a fire damaged the old Estación de Mediodía. In 1985 a project of remodelling of the station began following the design of Rafael Moneo.

[11] See Lisa Abend and Geoff Pingree, 'Spain's path to 3/11 memorial', *The Christian Science Monitor*, 14 July 2004, available at www.csmonitor.com/2004/0714/p07s01-woeu.html/(page)/2), last accessed 30 January 2015.

[12] Timothy Garton Ash, 'Our new Guernica', *The Guardian*, 10 March 2005, available at www.guardian.co.uk/world/2005/mar/10/spain.comment, last accessed 18 July 2013.

provides natural, meditative surroundings, with each tree a unique component recalling the individuality of each victim – a concept which may have inspired the memorial to the victims of yet another tragic terrorist attack, in London, just a few months after the inauguration of the Forest of Remembrance.[13]

Considering the importance of the events of 11 March 2004, their scale and the great public interest displayed in the spontaneous memorials, the idea of creating an official permanent memorial at Atocha station started to take shape. Originally, national and local governments each planned to dedicate separate memorials, but eventually it was decided to join all efforts in a single competition.[14] Two leading political parties were involved in the erection of the Atocha memorial, since the Ministry of Public Works and Transport was controlled by the Socialists (PSOE) and Madrid's City Council by the People's Party (PP). Consequently, families of the victims split into two factions, which ultimately restricted their participation in the design process, resulting in what has been designated as a case of a failed and flawed commemoration.[15] One of the new memorial's key purposes was to incorporate messages left at the spontaneous shrines at the bombing sites. Even with the decision to create a memorial to commemorate the 192 victims of 11-M, some still questioned its purpose, arguing that it should also commemorate hundreds of victims of previous terrorist attacks in Spain organized by ETA – a yearlong focus of Spain's war on terror.

Morphology

Following an open competition in November 2004, the task of creating the 11-M memorial was entrusted to a team of five young architects working under the name FAM Arquictetura y Urbanismo.[16] As a motto for the

[13] The attacks in London occurred on 7 July 2005, taking 52 lives. The memorial was inaugurated in 2009 in London's Hyde Park and consists of 52 individually cast columns standing at close distance.

[14] Explaining the decision, Minister of Development Magdalena Alvarez said: 'Initially we thought that we [the ministry] would put our monument inside the station, and the city government would erect theirs outside. But we realized that that didn't make sense, since our goals are the same, and the message is the same.' In Abend and Pingree, 'Spain's path'.

[15] Christina Flesher Fominaya, 'The Madrid 2004 bombing: understanding the puzzle of 11-M's flawed commemorative process', in Anna Lisa Tota and Trever Hagen (eds.), *Routledge International Handbook of Memory Studies* (London: Routledge, 2015), pp. 414–27.

[16] The competition was organized by the city council and the Ministry of Public Works (Ministerio de Fomento). Almost 300 proposals were presented for the competition. The

memorial, the team focused on the changing quality of light as a way to accentuate individual absences. The initial architectural idea was to create a sacred space for the bereaved. The memorial was imagined as a sort of oasis in the middle of the busy roundabout around Atocha station. Because of this, traffic noise was the first practical problem the design had to address. Despite the competition brief requesting designs for the roundabout space only, the winning team felt it impossible to confine their design solely to this portion of the location, and so decided to take a risk by suggesting that the main memorial space be situated beneath the boundary defined in the competition. In this way the idea of creating a serene and intimate space, contrasting with the noisy surroundings, became more achievable. The main guideline for this underground area was to achieve a quality of space similar to an 'underwater experience'.[17]

At the beginning of the design process, the team created multiple models carved out of blocks of ice to emphasize light as the focus of their overall concept. Despite this fragile and poetic idea of light as an immaterial component in the creation of space, however, the actual memorial had to be built from materials resistant to the aggressive surroundings. Yet at the same time they had to be translucent, to allow sunlight to penetrate the introverted space from ever-changing angles and so accentuate different victims' names inscribed on the walls of the memorial.[18] One of the initial ideas was to create an organic, blob-like structure which would bear the statements of public mourning. The messages from the public had to go through 'a political filter' – no texts about Al-Qaeda or ETA were permitted. After consulting engineering experts, however, the organic form was redesigned so as to be retained within a cylindrical architectural form, making it fully visible only from the interior space of the memorial. The fact that survivors were excluded from the design process was perceived as a mitigating factor by the designers, in the sense that they could continue to pursue their work without needing to meet compromises in their design concept.

The memorial was inaugurated on 11 March 2007 and, as imagined by the winning team, had two levels: the quiet underground space and a

winner, FAM (Fascinante Aroma a Manzana – 'Fascinating Smell of Apple'), was established in 2002. Members of the team were: Esaú Acosta, Mauro Gil-Fournier, Raquel Buj, Miguel Jeanicke and Pedro Colón de Carvajal.

17 Interview with Buj+Colon arquitectos (Pedro Colon de Carvajal and Raquel Buj), April 2011, Madrid.

18 In later stages, the names of the victims were replaced by the messages of condolence that had been left in the spontaneous outburst of public mourning.

Figure 3.1 11-M memorial (2007), Madrid; FAM Arquictetura y Urbanismo.
Photo: Author

prominent marker at street level (Figure 3.1). The underground part is accessible from Atocha station, where it is divided from the station hall by an uneven transparent facade, creating a hazy membrane between the two environments: the busy realm of the station and the silent, meditative room of the memorial. The entrance to the memorial is a large glass door, leading to a small dark vestibule with the victims' names printed in alphabetical order on an illuminated frosted glass panel. A second glass door leads into the main space, which can accommodate a maximum of 200 people at any one time (Figure 3.2). This memorial space is empty, except for a long bench positioned at the entrance. Echoing the idea of an 'underwater experience', the interior walls are designed as reflective dark blue surfaces, while the edges of the space are not easy to define. This was achieved by juxtaposing the walls of the central space and the glass facade towards the station hall in an angular position. The main source of daylight is a round central opening in the ceiling, which revealed messages of condolence in ETFE foil, translated into multiple languages (Figure 3.3).[19]

The transparent, organic form of the membrane allowed the outside part, the cylindrical tower, to be fully visible as the text swirls upward

[19] Ethylene tetrafluoroethylene or ETFE, a fluorine-based plastic, was designed to have a high corrosion resistance and strength over a wide temperature range. ETFE has a very high melting temperature, as well as excellent chemical, electrical and high energy radiation resistance properties. There were around 20,000 messages inscribed on the foil and all of them were selected by the design team from numerous messages left at the station during the spontaneous mourning.

Figure 3.2 11-M memorial (2007), Madrid; FAM Arquictetura y Urbanismo.
Photo: Author

Figure 3.3 11-M memorial (2007), Madrid; FAM Arquictetura y Urbanismo.
Photo: Author

towards the glass beams holding up the roof of the structure.[20] Also visible are the large lights installed at the edge of the opening and directed upwards to the roof of the cylinder. At night, the lights accentuate the

[20] See Hattie Hartman, 'Madrid memorial', *Architects Journal*, 10 January 2008, pp. 40–2.

cylinder: the effect at street level, with the light filtered through the glass bricks, is reminiscent of candlelight as the cylinder displays a soft light with a changing quality. Protruding from the roundabout, the 11-m high oval glass cylinder, symbolizing the date of the event, the eleventh of March, is made of curved glass bricks. Having no precedent, the tiles were glued in place using a translucent adhesive, causing small deviations which are still visible on the outside skin of the cylinder.

During the day, and depending on the angle of the sun, the organic form of the cylinder's inner membrane was slightly visible as rays of sunlight protruded through the glass brick facade. By the time of its inauguration, the memorial had attracted great interest due in part to the fact that the controlled environmental conditions needed within the construction site meant that it had to be completely concealed from the eyes of the public. That enclosure lent an air of mystery and suspense to the project; as one of the designers noted, 'it became the mysterious place everyone wanted to see – like a magician's hat.'[21]

Performance

The 11-M memorial demonstrated architectural experimentation in search of a beautiful effect. Its contemporary materialization, most prominent in the structure of the cylinder, testifies to this. At the same time, the objects and messages that continue to appear at the site allude to the memorial's fixed character. The translucent cylinder is prominently situated in front of the station and in the middle of the roundabout, but the ambiguity of its purpose is perhaps its most powerful feature – it remains mysterious. The abstract cylindrical shape might serve as a sign to indicate its hidden content: were it not for the collection of dried and fresh flowers, candles and other objects often placed at the cylinder's base, it could easily be interpreted as a somewhat odd part of the station's technical infrastructure.

Those objects are an indication of the apparent need to express personal respect for the memory of the victims, and to memorialize the tragic event at the exact place it occurred – even if that means risking one's own life by crossing the heavy traffic circling the cylinder. The initial outburst of public grief was memorialized in the apex of the memorial, the membrane, but it is not possible to add new messages of condolence. The space inside the

[21] Ibid., p. 42.

memorial is not intended as a place to leave objects of any kind, instead being maintained as a 'clean' and sacred place.

The memorial's original technical performance was largely dependent on good maintenance, one of the most significant aspects that was supposed to secure its future. The effects of a poor maintenance strategy were immediately visible. The inner alternating tangential flow (ATF) system supporting the membrane was designed to stabilize and improve over time, as sufficient, constant pressure levels are preserved by controlling air intake and extraction.[22] However, this tangible requirement has been difficult to meet in reality, since the entrance and exit doors supposed to ensure pressure stability have not been controlled properly and the equipment installed to maintain pressure levels has been operating only during the memorial's opening hours. The combination of these factors has resulted in active deterioration of the inner membrane and its collapse in 2015 even though the main entrance to the memorial is controlled by a doorkeeper, who allows only a certain number of visitors to enter the narrow access vestibule before the door into the main space is opened. With this in mind, the risk the architects took in relying on such a highly sophisticated system for the overall design to work properly seems a questionable choice. Because of it, the memorial's restoration became an issue only a few years after its dedication.

New adjustments, such as making the original entrance door the only access to the memorial, do have their advantages, in the sense that visitors, not being able to enter the space immediately, understand its importance more clearly. A doorkeeper regulating their flow introduces a notion of sanctity, of the memorial as a protected realm amidst a busy station hall. Upon entering the vestibule and while waiting for the first entrance door to be closed so that the second one can open, visitors are immediately presented with the names of the victims. Even though the relatives of the victims did not participate in the creation of the memorial, it was their wish that the names not be inscribed inside the cylinder but instead listed in the entrance foyer.[23] Visitors are thus forced to ponder them for a few seconds, and possibly realize the scale of the tragic event. Both physically and semantically, the entrance is a transitional space towards the space of absence waiting ahead. Once in that main space, the blurred reality of Atocha station, still visible through the blur facade on the right, seems even more distant.

[22] The ATF system is based on the technology of Alternating Tangential Flow, created by the action of a diaphragm moving upwards and downwards within a pump head, connected to a filter housing and attached to a standard bioreactor. The interest in the system is due to the surprising results that this simple technology offers.

[23] Hartman, 'Madrid memorial', p. 42.

At the entrance it is possible to obtain more information about 11-M from small leaflets which are placed discreetly on the adjacent bench. This is the only historical information provided anywhere in the memorial. Stripped of any educational or informative material, the memorial itself is a space of experience. The position and intensity of the daylight provided by the central opening, and the darkened corners of the 'blue' space, indeed create the intended feeling of an 'underwater experience'. Visitors are invited to move around the space at will, but the central opening is the focal point and acts as a magnet. Their attention is immediately drawn to the source of light, making them gaze skywards, where they were able to read sentences about peace, hope and sorrow. The effect is similar to that created inside the Neue Wache, where Tessenow's oculus becomes the focal point of a design in which the light defines the space. But rather than an enlarged sculpture of Käthe Kollwitz's *Mother with her Dead Son* standing in the beam of light, at the Atocha memorial visitors are invited to enter the domain of light themselves. They become part of an almost religious experience.

Since all its details augment the notion of a sacred space, the material performance of the memorial ought to be impeccable. In reality, it is not – and this represents a possible obstacle. Due to its rapid deterioration, whole segments of the cylinder's inner foil, while it was still fixed in its place, were damaged to the point that certain sections of text were no longer legible – this represented a great distraction in the overall experience. The subsequent collapse of the complete inner foil was a dramatic reminder that spaces of remembrance assign responsibility to a society as a whole. A memorial's physical condition is a sign of its significance. The failure to preserve the 11-M memorial in its original design painfully reminds on the contentious process of commemoration. On the other hand, even stripped of content and clearly lacking maintenance, the cylinder of light would still create a sacred atmosphere. Its meaning would be significantly changed, however. Without the words of human compassion, the memorial would be an empty underground space of absence, a space of death from which it is possible to see the light; but what would it mean were the words of hope and condolence to disappear from it? Even though southing, stripped of its essential component it would refer mainly to trauma and, arguably, the impossibility of maintaining hope in the face of the destruction of human life. It is here that the memorial demonstrated its resilience: messages of grief, compassion and hope did not disappear with the collapse. Instead, they were moved onto the blue walls of the memorial space. Echoing the psychological process of mourning and recovery, the memorial adopted to safeguard the idea of wound healing.

3.2 After Atocha

The 9/11 Memorial and the Berlin Wall Memorial

The tension arising from the need to commemorate a traumatic event, to effectively transmit the memory and to console the survivors, is well demonstrated in the commemoration of the terrorist attacks on New York on 11 September 2001. The aftermath of the attacks was coloured by an ongoing, contested debate about appropriate ways to commemorate them. Almost from the start, two distinct positions emerged: rebuilding the site or leaving it empty. Unsurprisingly, many architects advocated building new structures on the ashes of the old, while other voices urged for an immaterial 'phantom building' made of light.[24]

A version of this idea became reality only six months after the attacks. In an annual commemoration of the victims, a 'Tribute in Light', consisting of two vertical columns of light, was installed at the base of the demolished Twin Towers, piercing the sky on each anniversary of the attacks.[25] The temporary memorial was intended to 'reconstruct the void as opposed to reconstructing the buildings'.[26]

In 2011 the art exhibition 'September 11' was held by the Museum of Modern Art (MoMA) in New York to commemorate the tenth anniversary of the attacks.[27] This was a difficult task since, unlike architects, few artists had reacted to the tragedy. Of the many works chosen on the basis of their possible indirect reference to 9/11 (all of which were created before 2001),

[24] This was proposed by Robert Rosenblum, Professor of Art History at New York University, quoted in Deborah Solomon, 'Art/architecture; from the rubble, ideas for rebirth', *The New York Times*, 30 September 2001, www.nytimes.com/2001/09/30/arts/art-architecture-from-the-rubble-ideas-for-rebirth.html, last accessed 14 February 2018.

[25] The installation, a project of the Municipal Art Society, started in 2002 as a temporary installation and was initially called 'Towers of Light'. The relatives of the victims, however, found the name inappropriate since it emphasized the destruction of the buildings more than that of the victims. The designers were John Bennett and Gustavo Bonevardi of ProUn Space Studio in Manhattan, and artists Julian LaVerdiere and Paul Myoda who had had studios in the Twin Towers.

[26] David Dunlap, 'From 88 searchlights, an ethereal tribute', *The New York Times*, 4 March 2002, www.nytimes.com/2002/03/04/nyregion/from-88-searchlights-an-ethereal-tribute.html?src=pm&pagewanted=1, last accessed 14 February 2018. Little attention was given to the striking similarity of the 'phantom towers' to Albert Speer's Cathedral of Light at the Nuremberg Rallying Grounds. Even though proposals to commemorate victims with light installations that resembled Speer's project also existed in the immediate post-WWII period in Europe, such an installation would probably provoke severe criticism if ever employed for a commemoration project in Germany. See also Cohen, *Architecture in Uniform*, p. 417.

[27] MoMA PS1, 'September 11' exhibition, 11 September 2011–9 January 2012, available at http://momaps1.org/exhibitions/view/338, last accessed 14 February 2018.

Ellsworth Kelly's 2003 proposal to memorialize the site with a green patch of land, inspired by Indian burial mounds, was the only work to directly address the issue of memorialization. Kelly's collage drew attention to the much-needed space for the psychological process of mourning, which seemed all but forgotten in the rush to reconstruct and rebuild, a strategy supported by the numerous architects who delivered design proposals for the memorialization of 9/11. As though foreseen by Lebbeus Woods' thought on the burning towers of Sarajevo, the issue of architecture as associate to both destruction and the healing of the human spirit was the locus of interest after the 9/11 attacks.

When it was decided to realize a permanent memorial for 9/11, a long discussion ensued over the meaning and form the memorial was supposed to take.[28] Once the masterplan for the site was adopted, developed by Studio Daniel Libeskind,[29] an international competition – considered the largest in architectural history – was launched in 2003.[30] Two sets of concrete guidelines for participants, initially provided by the commissioner, were to a certain level modified by the competition jury, with the aim of securing more room for creative solutions by expanding the 'competition boundaries'.[31] Out of eight finalists, a concept design entitled 'Reflecting Absence' was selected, designed by architect Michael Arad and landscape architect Peter Walker. The winning entry was praised for succinctly capturing the motifs of loss in a memorial 'by allowing absence to speak for itself'.[32] Furthermore, the design was chosen for its simplicity and minimalist aesthetics: 'the voids themselves really seemed to be in keeping with a post-war vocabulary that attempted to articulate absence,

[28] The World Trade Center Site Memorial Competition was initiated by the Lower Manhattan Development Corporation (LMDC). By March 2003, a 'Memorial Mission Statement' was formulated by the Advisory Council, originally appointed by the Families Advisory Council. James E. Young, 'The stages of memory at Ground Zero', in Oren Baruch Stier and J. Shawn Landres (eds.), *Religion, Violence, Memory, and Place* (Bloomington, IN: Indiana University Press, 2006), pp. 214–35.

[29] In the specifications for the urban plan, provided by Libeskind's studio, a portion of the World Trade Center site was planned for the design of a World Trade Center Site Memorial (later renamed the National September 11 Memorial).

[30] The competition garnered 5,201 entries from 63 nations and 49 US states out of 13,800 registrants. For comparison, the competition for the Vietnam Veterans Memorial attracted 2,573 registrants and 1,421 final entries.

[31] Young, 'The stages of memory', p. 221. The jury feared that potential designers would perceive Libeskind's plan as an overall memorial in which they would have to insert their own design, hence to create a 'memorial within a memorial'. The expansion of the competition guidelines by the jury was positively received by the LMDC.

[32] Young, 'The stages of memory', p. 232. This quotation is taken from the jury statement issued on 13 January 2004.

Figure 3.4 'Reflecting Absence' design concept (2003).
© Michael Arad

which is a very difficult thing to do.'[33] The designers aimed to evoke 'a persistent absence, one that isn't erased by the passage of time'.[34]

In practice, the realization of the memorial met with numerous changes and difficulties. It was only after considerable adjustments were made to Arad's original design that the memorial was finally constructed, adjustments like moving boards with the names of the victims above ground level instead of beneath footprints of the destructed towers (Figure 3.4).

Arguing that the memorial needed to commemorate the event while remaining an active public space, the designers stressed the idea of using the memorial as a place for 'work and play' without certainty that a public memorial can be used only for 'good purposes' as promoted by the government and the chosen master plan.[35] Stressing the importance

[33] Sam Lubell, 'Inside the fury: an interview with James Young', *Architectural Record*, 192.2 (2004), 24. The reception to the memorial had been balancing between, on the one hand, a critique of its unoriginal appearance and large scale, and on the other, the perception of it as a much-needed space that would bring hope and normality to the haunted Ground Zero. See Rowan Moore, 'Ground Zero 9/11 memorial flows with mournful splendour', *The Guardian*, 15 August 2001, www.theguardian.com/artanddesign/2011/aug/15/ground-zero-memorial-september-9-11, last accessed 14 February 2018. Also, Richard Lacayo, 'Remains of the day: at the 9/11 museum, history is preserved in memories and debris', *Time*, 26 May 2014, 38–41.

[34] Blair Kamin, 'A first look at the national September 11 memorial: a tough work of abstract minimalism, softened by waterfalls and oak trees, seeks to meld remembrance and regeneration', *Chicago Tribune*, 14 August 2011, http://featuresblogs.chicagotribune.com/theskyline/2011/08/a-first-look-at-the-soon-to-open-national-september-11-memorial-a-tough-work-of-abstract-minimalism-.html, last accessed 14 February 2018.

[35] Michael Arad quoted in Harel Shapira, 'Reflecting absence: an interview with Michael Arad', *Public Books*, 20 August 2013, www.publicbooks.org/reflecting-absence-an-interviewwith-michael-arad/, last accessed 14 February 2018.

of the inclusion of the memorial into the public life of the city, Arad believed that:

> We have to be optimists and hope that people will use public space in a way that is affirmative and not destructive, but you would be naïve to think that it can't be co-opted and used in a way that will injure other people. It would show more than a little hubris on the part of any designer to say, I've designed a space that can only be used for good. But to deny public space altogether would be repressive.[36]

The memorial, dedicated on the tenth anniversary of the attacks, eventually became a fountain inserted in the footprints of the Twin Towers. The surrounding public space serves as an extension to the memorial as a carefully organized public park. Nearly 3,000 names are inscribed into the thick, bronze parapets of the fountains. The names are arranged in groups, depending on the location of the victims at the time of the attack. Furthermore, they are positioned according to the 'meaningful adjacency requests' that allowed relatives and colleagues to ask for particular individual names to be inscribed next to each other, depending on who they were with at the time of the attack. At night, the names perforated into the boards are illuminated from behind, allowing the light to pass through – memorialized out of 'the absence of the material'.[37]

The process of arranging the names provoked the most controversy, but for the designers this aspect was also the most rewarding, in the sense that in this way the memorial, as Arad has argued, 'brings individual human stories into an arrangement'.[38] The sunken basins of the memorial are visible from the underground museum, opened as part of the memorial site in 2014. The basins are coated in aluminium, arguably to designate the absence of the Twin Towers as a 'ghostly presence'.[39]

Attention to the individualization of the victims was also adopted in the design of the Pentagon memorial (2008) by KBAS studio, where each of the 184 victims is represented by a personalized cantilevered bench. The 9/11 memorial museum in New York, however, focuses on the

[36] Ibid.

[37] Michael Arad in 'Names of the 9/11 Memorial', *9/11 Memorial*, 3 June 2013, available at www.youtube.com/watch?v=mxFfaFepyA8, last accessed 14 February 2018.

[38] After a long discussion, in 2006 the decision was made to list the names in nine broad groups to reflect where the person was on the day of the attack. Hence the idea of the adjacency request was still applied, with hundreds of requests from families offering their personal reasons. Shapira, 'Reflecting absence.

[39] Kristiaan Versluys, *Out of the Blue: September 11 and the Novel* (New York: Columbia University Press, 2009), p. 133.

didactic aspects of remembering. It contains numerous artefacts, including the tower footprints, the slurry wall and the towers' still intact foundations, but also the unidentified remains of many victims, a topic that proved highly controversial.[40] Contrary to the ambivalence of the entrance pavilion – a deconstructivist structure that should serve as a 'bridge between two worlds',[41] the museum exhibition was designed with an overriding focus on the psychological aspects of mourning by acknowledging the loss and taking the role of a witness. It is 'meant to be a healing environment and a healing experience, and we each have the option to view certain artefacts or not view them'.[42] The architecture of the museum connects the artefacts, seeking to clearly distinguish the original from the added. Furthermore, the museum continues collaboration with the designers of the memorial: a new memorial entitled the 'Memorial Glade', dedicated to all those 'who are sick or have died from exposure to toxins in the aftermath of 9/11', is designed by Arad and Walker and supervised by the museum to ensure 'the site's aesthetic continuity and timeless sacredness'.[43]

The July 22 Memorial, Oslo and Utøya

Fighting against multiculturalism and its supporters (the Labor Party youth camp), and against a 'Muslim invasion', the right-wing extremist

40 The remains were removed to a repository in a subterranean space below the museum, which is a permanent medical facility where the process of identification is planned to be carried out, eventually returning the remains to the victim's families once they are identified. However, this concept provoked outrage among several families. See Stephen Farrel, 'In "ceremonial transfer," remains of 9/11 victims are moved to memorial', *The New York Times*, 10 May 2014, www.nytimes.com/2014/05/11/nyregion/remains-of-9-11-victims-are-transferred-to-trade-center-site.html, last accessed 14 February 2018.

41 This is a description offered by the designer of the pavilion, the Norwegian office Snøhetta, available at http://snohetta.com/project/19-national-september-11-memorial-museum-pavilion, last accessed 14 February 2018. The full description is: 'With its low, horizontal form and its uplifting geometry the Pavilion acts as a bridge between two worlds – between the Memorial and the museum, the above and below ground, the light and dark, between collective and individual experiences. Inclined, reflective and transparent surfaces encourage people to walk up close, touch and gaze into the building.'

42 Interview with Dr JoAnn Difede, director of the Program for Anxiety and Traumatic Stress Studies at New York-Presbyterian Hospital/Weill Cornell Medical Center. See Jessica Firger and Hannah Fraser-Chanpong, 'Visit to 9/11 museum may be cathartic for some; traumatic for others', *CBS News*, 15 May 2014, www.cbsnews.com/news/visit-to-911-museum-may-be-cathartic-for-some-too-traumatic-for-others, last accessed 14 February 2018.

43 '9/11 Memorial Glade', 9/11 Memorial & Museum, www.911memorial.org/memorial-glade, last accessed 24 May 2019.

Figure 3.5 'Memory Wound' design concept (2013).
© Jonas Dahlberg

Anders Breivik murdered 77 people – 8 in central Oslo government square and 69 in a killing spree on the island of Utøya on 22 July 2011. Following this gruesome political terrorist attack, several projects ensued as an attempt to commemorate the victims of the violent attack on political freedom and multiculturalism. In downtown Oslo, where a car bomb exploded, the July 22 Centre opened in 2015. Its main goals are to inform visitors about the event and to combat extremism by encouraging further research into its causes. The events of 22 July are presented chronologically, while the immediate reactions, such as public mourning, are also given a prominent place. The centre includes a separate room dedicated to the 77 people who lost their lives.

Meanwhile, creating a national memorial exclusively dedicated to the victims proved a highly contested process. In 2014 a winning proposal for Norway's national July 22 memorial, 'Memory Wound' by the Swedish artist Jonas Dahlberg, was made public.[44] Located at the Sørbråten peninsula on the mainland facing Utøya, the artist's envisioned design evoked a physical incision, a symbolic wound (Figure 3.5).

[44] For the chronology of the commissioning process see KORO – Public Art Norway, *Factsheet: Memorial Sites after 22 July, Minnesteder Etter 22 Juli*, https://koro.no/prosjekter/minnesteder-etter-22-juli/, last accessed 28 May 2019.

The literal cut into the landscape, with the names of the victims to be engraved on the flat vertical stone surface, was welcomed by the jury as radical and brave: 'the void that is created evokes the sense of sudden loss combined with the long-term missing and remembrance of those who perished.'[45] The design interprets the aspect of recovery from trauma so central to other memorials – among them the 9/11 memorial and the VVM – in a radically different manner. While most memorials allow visitors to touch the names of the victims, Dahlberg proposed taking away this possibility and introducing a gap separating the wall with names from the viewing gallery. Aiming to activate the site of memory by reinforcing the sense of loss, the artist believed that 'the cut is an acknowledgement of what is forever irreplaceable'.[46] Recognizing that the journey to the actual site is equally important, Dahlberg aimed to direct visitors coming to the island to be self-reflective, proposing the memorial as a transitional space of introduction, a private room for contemplation. The memorial was meant to hinder the sight towards Utøya and in that way allow it to succumb to a process of transformation by time and nature.[47]

The material from the excavated cut was planned to be transferred to Oslo and used to create slabs on which names of more than five million people listed as living in Norway by the National Registry on the day of the attacks would be engraved together with the 77 people murdered – the living of that day to be listed randomly and the murdered with a few centimetres of additional space around their name, the perpetrator's name left out. Eventually, the engraved slabs, after serving as a temporary memorial during the building activities in Oslo's government area, were envisioned to form a public memorial square, inviting visitors to explore and, perhaps, find their own name inscribed (Figure 3.6). Sharing a similar political message like Jochen Gerz's project *The Square of the European Promise* (discussed in Chapter 1), the square tackles the issue of personal and collective responsibility in relation to the commemorated event.

In an unexpected turn of events, however, the realization of the memorial was aborted, in large part due to opposition from the public. Utøya locals perceived the proposed design as intrusive, a 'rape of nature' and

[45] July 22 Memorial, jury's evaluation of Jonas Dahlberg's proposal, in 'Jonas Dahlberg to design July 22 Memorial Sites in Norway', *World Landscape Architecture*, https://worldlandscapearchitect.com/jonas-dahlberg-to-design-july-22-memorial-sites-in-norway/#.XO2ajIgzZPY, last accessed 28 May 2019.

[46] Jonas Dahlberg, '22 July Memorial Norway', www.jonasdahlberg.com/22-july-memorial-site-ut%C3%B8ya-kopia-copy-copy-2-kopia.html, last accessed 10 January 2019.

[47] Jonas Dahlberg Studio, *Notes on a Memorial*, short movie (unpublished, 2018).

Figure 3.6 Concept proposal for Oslo memorial (2017).
© Jonas Dahlberg

damaging to the 'mental health of those locals who suffered traumatic stress after participating in the rescue operations after convicted terrorist Anders Behring Breivik's shooting spree on the island'.[48] The fact that 'the cut' was only fully visible from one perspective displayed in the artist's impression and the participation of right-wing politicians in the protests was generally ignored. Attempts at reaching a compromise by moving 'Memory Wound' to another location (Utøykaia), proposed by the youth wing of Norway's Labour Party (AUF) and a support group for the families of Utøya victims, were met with contempt.

More recently, a subtler and environment-friendly approach that emphasizes aspects of 'healing' has come to the fore: the newly installed memorial at Utøya entitled '*Lysningen* – The Clearing' (2015), designed by the architectural team 3RW and made through a collective participation, including relatives of the victims. A 12 m-wide clearing overlooking the fjord was made among the island's pine trees, in which a suspended,

[48] 'Norway offers to scrap the controversial Utøya memorial', *The Local*, 15 September 2016, www.thelocal.no/20160915/norway-offers-to-scrap-controversial-utya-memorial-design, last accessed 14 February 2018.

Figure 3.7 '*Lysningen* – The Clearing' memorial (2015)', Utøya; 3RW architects. Photo: Martin Slottemo Lyngstad

4 m-diameter metal ring was installed with the names of the victims perforated into its surface. Not all the names are engraved at the same time, since relatives of several victims found it too confronting to have the names of their loved ones appear on the memorial (Figure 3.7).

Even though its title suggests notions of voided space and absence as signifiers of traumatic memory, the memorial was conceived as a structure subordinate to nature and the passing of time. Observing Utøya as a place where the beauty of nature echoes terror due to the attack as a severe break in normalcy, the designers argued:

> Within this catastrophic paradigm-shift, it is important to focus on the fact that Utøya still is a piece of unique Norwegian nature – this space, in and of itself, does not have any memories of the tragedy. The essence of nature is that it can, through transformation, slowly erase all traces of the tragic events that happened here. With the changing of the seasons, as the waves wash away the shore, new growth can begin.[49]

The notion of a clearing refers to the resilience of nature. The aspect of mutability through natural processes is reinforced by a careful selection of vegetation. It is further enhanced by the deliberate choice for a location without any site-specific history:

[49] '3RW wins the competition to design memorial on Utøya', 3RW, 2 December 2014, https://3rw.no/3rw-wins-the-competition-to-propose-memorial-on-utoya/, last accessed 14 February 2018.

> No lives were lost at the site of the memorial on that day, and none of the dramatic events took place here. We might talk about the memorial as a kind of void to be filled with the individual's needs to process grief, remember the lives that were lost and detach themselves from the drama that took place elsewhere on the island.[50]

The memorial also changes depending on weather conditions: humidity contributes to the condensation of water on the steel ring whereas winter frost blends it with natural surroundings.

The inclination towards psychological, emotional and memory detachment was also present in the process of creating the so-called Hegnhuset, or Safehouse – a memorial established at the small Utøya cafe where a group of the targeted youth hid from the terrorist. Here 13 teenagers were murdered while 19 others managed to escape death. It is an authentic place of both tragedy and hope. Nevertheless, members of the youth party who survived the attack wanted the building demolished, as it was a ghastly reminder to a past they wished to forget. With this in mind the first anniversary of the attack saw an architectural proposal that envisioned a small village with happy 'inhabitants' on the very top of the island as a symbol of unity and diversity.[51] There was no space for remembering and dwelling on trauma in this vision.

It was the families of the murdered, initially left out from the development of this plan, who argued for Utøya to be a place of remembrance and for the cafe to be a constituent part of their grieving process. After inviting scholars and experts in the field to discuss solutions for this opposition in interests, a compromise was found in an architectural solution that tries to balance erasing the past with keeping it alive.[52] One of the participating scholars was James Young, who was also a member of the committees responsible for creating some of the most publicly visible memorials, among them 9/11 and MMJE. Young stressed that 'perhaps never before had a national memorial process been so open to the experiences of others, and perhaps never before had such process built into itself the capacity for self-analysis and self-correction as it went forward.'[53] His experience

[50] Ibid.

[51] Fantastic Norway, official website, available at www.fantasticnorway.no, last accessed 14 February 2018.

[52] It was the so-called *July 22 and the Negotiation of Memory* project that initiated the transparent process of opinion and experience exchange between all the parties involved. See www.ntnu.edu/web/july22memory/july22memory, last accessed 14 February 2018.

[53] James E. Young, 'Utøya and Norway's July 22 memorial process: the memory of political terror', in James E. Young, *The Stages of Memory: Reflections on Memorial Art, Loss, and the*

Figure 3.8 Hegnhuset Memorial (2016), Utøya; Blakstad Haffner Architects. Photo: Are Carlsen

proved to be instrumental in laying out possible solutions for the predicament of making a memorial for this specific place, without having its rich history overshadowed by the recent episode of destruction. Recalling the Sandy Hook Elementary School shootings from 2012, where the survivors opted for the school's demolition to protect themselves from painful recollections, Young argued against the complete, undocumented demolition of the cafe, since leaving no trace of what existed on the site before the act of terror 'could even be construed as an extension of Breivik's crime, not its memorialization'.[54]

The commissioned designers developed a concept that envelopes preserved segments of the authentic building and shields it from outside, hence from those who don't want to be reminded of what happened. The facade consists of 495 wooden poles symbolizing those who survived the attack (Figure 3.8). Inside, in a different angle, a new structure envelopes around authentic parts of the cafe as a protective shield – its roof supported by 69 wooden pillars representing the victims. Between these two orders of pillars a cloistered passageway was created, similarly infused with symbolic meaning and creating a spatial experience that makes visitors feel, in the words of the project team, 'entrenched but seemingly free'.[55]

Spaces Between (Amherst, MA: Boston University of Massachusetts Press, 2016), pp. 185–210, p. 192.

54 Ibid., p. 198.

55 Project leader, Erlend Blakstad Haffner, and his team members, Ivana Barandovski, Branko Belačević, Petar Stelkić and Vladimir Cvejić, describing the Utøya memorial in Henrietta Thompson, 'Fitting tribute: Blakstad Haffner Architects unveil latest piece in Utøya's

Aligned with the Hegnhuset stands a new cluster of accompanying buildings that accommodate assorted facilities, such as an auditorium and a library. As one journalist describes it:

> The cafe building now stands like a piece of forensic evidence in this woodland vitrine, chopped and sliced in a process of architectural editing, so that only the rooms relevant to the events of that day are left standing.[56]

Interestingly, the process of designing the temporary memorial in Oslo's government quarter eventually became a collaborative affair involving all related stakeholders. As an outcome, the memorial that was created follows guidelines developed through an inclusive debate about memorial's materialization. In conclusion, preference was given to a landscape, non-obtrusive and 'passive' memorial that will communicate the 'seriousness of the event'.[57] The 3RW architects, commissioned to design it, blended the participants' observations into a poignant public space featuring four linden survivor-trees, a wall made out of the names of the victims, and a pavement materialized from recycled broken glass – a direct reference to the wreckage after the attack. Attuned to 'create something beautiful from this painful story', the designers hope that, by using broken glass as a symbolic connection to that day, the memorial will 'reprogram the broken glass, and perhaps create new positive memories of it'.[58]

Memorials to Terror: Paris, Brussels, Haarlemmermeer

After the attacks in Paris on the 13 November 2015, spontaneous expressions of public mourning were overwhelming. Numerous makeshift memorials appeared, public offerings were made, and a non-profit civilian organization called 'Generation Bataclan' was formed, with the aim of realizing a memorial to the victims:

rebuilding', *Wallpaper*, 22 August 2016, www.wallpaper.com/architecture/blakstad-haffner-architects-remembers-utoya-massacre-with-new-memorial-and-learning-centre-hegnhuset, last accessed 24 May 2019.

[56] Oliver Wainwright, '"We had to tell this dark story"... how Utøya is remembering the massacre', *The Guardian*, 5 October 2016, www.theguardian.com/artanddesign/2016/oct/05/utoya-massacre-memorial-norway-architects, last accessed 14 February 2018.

[57] 3RW Architects, 'Temporary Memorial for the 22 July in Oslo's government quarter', available at https://3rw.no/work/temporary-memorial-for-22-july-in-oslos-government-quarter/.

[58] Ibid.

> France has always commemorated victims of war and erected monuments to honor its fallen soldiers. However, only a simple memorial plaque is put to honor the memory of murdered civilians. We think that it is important to invoke and keep their memory alive. Following the tragic attacks in Paris and the outpouring of solidarity from around the world, it seems essential to work together to have a monument in Paris, selected and funded by the citizens, to commemorate the victims of these horrendous attacks. To erect a monument is to mark the gravity of what happened. Those who died on November 13 embodied our values and it is our duty, now more than ever, to keep these values alive.[59]

Having been offered a location on a traffic junction relatively close to where the attacks took place, the association initiated an open call for a memorial design. It received 54 proposals, out of which ten were selected to compete in a public vote. Most of the proposed designs advocate symbolic, spatial, sculptural memorials based on a sensory approach. They invite visitors to observe, and sit down to listen, contemplate and learn. One proposal, entitled 'Mémoire vivante', relies on historical examples such as Aldo Rossi's monument to Sandro Pertini in Milan, but in addition to a public amphitheatre it offers space for mourners to interact with the memorial beneath it. Others are inspired by the outpouring of spontaneous mourning, but instead of providing a place for it to continue they focus on symbolism and aesthetics. The proposal 'Mur de la liberté', for example, displays a photographic collage of the spontaneous grief and public offerings that occurred after the attacks, arguing that this outburst was the strongest representation of civil unity and solidarity against the madness of terrorist destruction of life.

On 17 July 2014, the crash of flight MH17 into a Ukrainian field while en route to Kuala Lumpur became one of the most traumatic events in the collective memory of the Netherlands. A location for a national memorial was chosen at a short distance from Amsterdam Airport Schiphol, from where the airplane took off. The forest monument is created in the Park Vijfhuizen, in the municipality of Haarlemmermeer, and is inspired by the black memorial ribbon used as a symbol in the aftermath of the crash. It consists of 298 trees, each planted for an individual passenger, assuming the shape of the ribbon from bird's-eye view. The forest ribbon was in part planted by the victim's relatives and is surrounded by a ring of sunflowers associated with the actual location where the plane crashed.

[59] Statement available at the Generation Bataclan website, www.generationbataclan.fr. Translation by the author.

Stichting Vliegramp MH17, the foundation representing the relatives of the victims, which was the driving force behind the realization of the memorial, explains the choice for a nature memorial as follows:

> A tree symbolizes 'hope' and 'future' in many cultures, a strong symbol. We not only want to honor the MH17 victims, but also want to create a place where everyone can keep their memories of the 298 passengers alive. Every victim's life will live on metaphorically through these memorial trees.[60]

Eleven types of trees were carefully selected to suit the climate conditions and to blossom throughout the year. Attention was also given to the location of the different trees so that they correlate with the seating of the passengers and the crew members of the flight. In the centre of the forest is an amphitheatre and a stainless-steel memorial consisting of two parts – a curved wall and a central circular sculpture. While the curved wall is designed to strengthen sounds and thereby 'let people go silent to bring respect for the victims and especially the relatives', the sculpture is reflective and hollow, so it 'gives memory' and its reflective materiality 'enlightens the sadness'.[61] In a floorplan projection, the memorial represents an eye 'that looks up to the heavens'.[62]

Unrelated to the official memorial organization, an independent architectural platform called 'matterbetter' organized a design competition to commemorate the tragic event on an imagined small island on the IJmeer, north of Amsterdam.[63] Seeking to find an answer to the question 'how we design hope', the platform selected 'Memorial in the Sky' as the winning design for its minimal architectural interference, while still managing to create a specific sublimity. The proposal imagined a processional route with lush nature and 298 chairs installed in the open to reference airplane seats. Opting for a design that can completely immerse visitors into its narrative, the designers used 'spatial empathy' to transport the visitor 'to a new spatial realm, floating between the clouds, the sun, the columns, and the trees, where they may walk, sit, play, dream, and remember with those lost in the sky aboard flight MH17' arguing that they 'begin this memorial with the creation of life'.[64]

[60] Quoted on Stichting National Monument MH17 website at www.monumentmh17.nl.

[61] Quoted from the website of Ronald A. Westerhuis at www.ronaldawesterhuis.com. [62] Ibid.

[63] See the announcement of winners on the matterbetter website at http://matterbetter.com/blog/article/32.

[64] William Smith and Hiroshi Kaneko, 'Memorial in the Sky', available at http://matterbetter.com/media/competitioners/files/f9e000eb-7e0d-49ca-8838-7a7c5bbcbbe6.pdf.

Figure 3.9 Brussels Memorial 22/03 (2017), Brussels; Bas Smets.
Photo: Author

In a more recent memorial, commemorating the victims of the Islamic State terrorist attacks in March 2016 at Zaventem and Maalbeek in Brussels, the notion of healing is also explored in two ways. In a forest close to Brussels, a circular memorial composed of 32 Belgian blue stones, traditionally used for tombstones, have been inserted amongst 32 carefully planted birch trees to symbolically recall each victim of the attacks (Figure 3.9). To arrive here, visitors need to cross the adjacent valley and a bridge over a stream. Designer Bas Smets explained the choice of trees and the memorial's position, arguing that birch trees symbolize life and that crossing the stream recalls crossing the Styx river from Greek mythology.[65] Smets aimed to delineate a double void created by the two circles – the first one of the trees and the second of the stone circle, as he explained: 'the trees cut out a circle in the sky, while the stones draw a ring on the floor. The memorial positions itself between the changing sky and the stable forest floor. It is mute, beyond words, offering a moment of peace.'[66]

At the airport where the attack happened, however, the anniversary was marked by the unveiling of the 'Flight in Mind' sculpture which stood in the departures hall. The sculpture suffered great damage and was restored, but the visible marks of the explosions of the 22 March attacks are

[65] See 'Herdenkingsmonument in Zoniënwoud voor de 32 slachtoffers van de aanslagen van 22 maart', *Nieuwsblad*, 21 March 2017, www.nieuwsblad.be.

[66] Bas Smets, 'BBS292 Brussels: Memorial 22/3' (unpublished text, 2016).

preserved as a tribute to the victims. Also, near the seat of the European Union a sculpture entitled *Wounded But Still Standing in Front of the Inconceivable* was installed in 2017 to officially commemorate all victims of terror attacks – a seemingly correct effort by the government to remain responsible and recognize the importance of loss.

3.3 Public Sentiment and Memorial Design

A question Thomas H. Creighton asked some 60 years ago is equally relevant today: 'In a time of existentialist belief and action, can we expect an architectural expression that will memorialize the past and point to the future?'[67] Survivors and communities want their loss to be recognized and memorialized, a desire usually displayed in the immediate outpouring of spontaneous mourning. Public mourning is a delicate issue and, in most cases, difficult to manage for official institutions due to their impact and, more practically, the stuff left in the public space. The memorials discussed above respond to the immediate post-traumatic period. As such, they are recognized as a part of the collective but also intimate mourning processes, since in most cases the designers felt personally affected by the attack. In Madrid, these offerings were archived and documented in projects preceding the official memorial. Once the 11-M was built, however, public mourning was in large part restricted. Conversely, at the Vietnam Veterans Memorial, visitors continue to leave objects that are collected on a daily basis and added to the growing collection of offerings. In this way, the memorial stays true to its reputation of a healing structure, by reaffirming the importance of public mourning as an ongoing phenomenon. In contrast, the 11-M did recognize the public sentiment, but chose to ossify it instead.

This was not done intentionally by the designers, who opted for a spiritual realm where people could contemplate the loss. To achieve this, they extended the official programme of demands, which initially only called for a public memorial at street-level. Even though some of the messages of public mourning were used in the design of the memorial, the public, and indeed public mourning, were excluded from the design process. The result was an architecturally inspiring piece of work that was highly contentious in terms of its function and meaning. In fact, the project

[67] Creighton, *The Architecture of Monuments*, p. 13.

seems to have become a victim of its own architectural supremacy, since unfulfilled demands for high quality maintenance has caused the memorial's deterioration. Perhaps more importantly, the memorial obstructed the appropriation of the space by the public, which became difficult – if not impossible.

In the case of the 9/11 memorial, on the other hand, public sentiment was included in the decision-making process when some of the crucial elements of the memorial were resolved, namely the inscription of the victims' names. The origin of the project was similar to that of the 11-M memorial, since outbursts of spontaneous mourning after the attacks inspired many to think about permanent ways to commemorate the victims. The designer Michael Arad was equally touched by the coming together of people in the public space after the attacks, which led him to think about the importance of public memorial space in society.

Unlike the construction process of the 11-M memorial, building the 9/11 memorial was much less straightforward and involved numerous alterations of the original proposal. Even though it is today a highly controlled public space, the very process of its making confirms how relevant the role of the architect is, as the mediator between public opinion and official bodies. Due to the transparent approach and highly public character of the process, the creation of the National 9/11 Memorial and Museum was an exemplary illustration of contemporary debates surrounding the work of memorialization, in which the question of architecture in the service of memory faces multilayered issues. One of the most prominent issues during this process centred on the role of architecture as an embodiment of what society prefers in terms of a memorial's morphology. For example, the final deliberations of the competition jury dismissed proposals that were focused solely on consoling memorialization, and therefore emphasized the beauty and sacredness of the space. Instead they looked for a design that would represent an equilibrium between, on the one hand, encouraging redemption and, on the other, demonstrating the destruction.[68]

[68] Next to 'Reflecting Absence', the second round included two other finalists: 'Garden of Lights' by Pierre David with Sean Corriel and Jessica Kmetović, and 'Passages of Light: The Memorial Cloud' by Giesela Baurmann, Sawad Brooks and Jonas Coersmeier. The first proposed planting over the tower footprints with meadows of wildflowers, whereas the second was designed as a highly engaging architectural scenography. The jury dismissed 'Garden of Lights' on the basis of its predominantly redemptive character, whereas 'Passages of Light' was not chosen precisely because of its architectural qualities, which seemed to overshadow and impede its commemorative purpose. See Young, 'The stages of memory', pp. 226–9.

In the end, this was also the goal in the creation of memorials for the 22 July attacks in Norway. While the importance of the authentic location remains relevant, the drama of the event is perceived as something that needs to be neutralized and hopefully removed from the memorial. In some ways resonating with the environmental shift in funerary design, where gravestones are being replaced with earth urns containing tree seeds, memorials are becoming more inspired by cycles of nature. The memorial to MH17 near Schiphol airport, for example, is designed as a living forest dedicated to the victims of this tragic flight, a concept already applied in the commemoration of the Madrid attacks in 2004. Importantly, the MH17 memorial was initiated by the relatives of the victims. Both the turn to nature and the inclusion of those directly affected by the event are significant impulses in understanding memorial design and its relation to the mourning process. Various competition proposals for the events discussed dealt with the topic of recovery through natural cycles, light and reflection while exploring the scenography and cinematic possibilities of space to create an interactive relationship. In this respect, memorials are indeed similar to cemeteries as sacrosanct spaces, heterotopias that in the words of Michel Foucault begin 'with this strange heterochrony, the loss of life, and with this quasi-eternity in which its permanent lot is dissolution and disappearance'.[69] Arguably, choices for unpretentious spatial design interventions are also a statement against giving prominent space to the unfortunate exercises of extreme radicalism and manufacture of fear.

Keeping in mind that public mourning is a continuous process, as underlined by our knowledge of psychology, it is essential that architecture provides space for spontaneous expressions of grief and acknowledges that individual and collective grief are not straightforward process. These take time. A memorial that fulfills its purpose as a public space is a memorial that is appropriated by its users. The process of creation needs to allow for this to happen on both an informal and an institutional level. Essentially, the core ideas of the 'Memory Wound' and 'The Clearing' are comparable, but their manifestations are radically different, as were their processes of creation: the making of 'The Clearing' and the temporary memorial in Oslo were interdisciplinary and allowed families and volunteers to take part and, in that way, render this space of remembrance meaningful in the face of recent tragedy. The 'Memory Wound', on the other hand, derived from a

[69] Michel Foucault, 'Of other spaces: utopias and heterotopias', trans. Jay Miskowiec, *Diacritics* 16.1 (1986), 22–7, p. 26. Originally published as 'Des espaces autres', *Architecture-Mouvement-Continué*, 5 (1984), 46–9.

less transparent process which, in the end, proved reason for its failure in spite of the ingenuity of the design solution. In this sense, the examples of Atocha, New York, the citizen's initiative in Paris and other similar examples of creating a memorial by organizing an open design competition and then inviting public voting seem most appropriate. A democratic path seems the only logical choice here. It certainly will open up a space of potential for innovation and creativity against violence and destruction. In reference to Adolf Loos and his conclusion that people 'hate art' but 'love buildings' we can recognize the contemporary preference for curative and hope-giving designs. The question is: what does this mean for the genre of memorial architecture in its service to preservation of memory? Will eschewing provocative solutions, as exemplified in the case of the 'Memory Wound', lead to production of memorial spaces, to paraphrase Erwin Panofsky, ending up as old maids?

4 | Memorial Museums

Today, our work is to transmit. That is the spirit of this memorial.
Transmission: there resides the future of remembering.

François Hollande[1]

Since the 1970s, the debate about transmitting memory to future generations through evocative architectural forms and metonymic devices has become more and more prominent. Hence, contemporary ways of transmitting memories and histories are versatile and continue to evolve. Memorial designs are increasingly moving towards more interactive, proactive and experimental spaces. As such, memorial design (focused explicitly on the spatial component) meets the museum – an institution for the conservation, documentation and contextualization of historical knowledge on a specific topic. The architectural logic of these museums normally aims to adjust to the topic and the location, to serve as an introduction to the existing site and thereby strengthen the visitor's experience. If the memorial museum is built elsewhere, hence not on an authentic site, the principle is the same, but with more freedom of expression. Arguably, it is a more challenging task. Already some of the earliest examples of this trend, such as the Kragujevac memorial museum, were designed to fortify historical events with their architecture and spatial disposition. As a result, didactic components are becoming more prominent in memorials, while memorial museums, on the other hand, aim towards spatial frameworks that are congruent with their contents and in this way come closer to memorial design. In this context, Pingusson's Memorial to the Deportation in Paris is a project where we can see the impulse towards an aesthetic that derives from moral imperative and historical knowledge, supported by museological content.

By now, memorial museums are established as a specific type of memorial architecture geared towards the transmission of memory to later

[1] The former French president François Hollande in his address at the memorial in Drancy on 21 September 2012. Scott Sayare, 'At Holocaust Center, Hollande confronts past', *The New York Times*, 22 September 2012, www.nytimes.com/2012/09/22/world/europe/at-drancy-holocaust-center-hollande-confronts-grim-chapter-for-france.html, last accessed 16 February 2018.

generations. Memorial museums such as *La Mémorial* in Caen or *Terror Hazza* in Budapest, to name but two, have become theatres, with abundant visual effects aimed at raising empathy in visitors. Technological possibilities create new forms of public cultural memory, that allows anyone to experience the past through mediated experience.[2] However, the effects of such sophisticated remembrance mechanisms escape precise analysis. The drama of the recreated environment will most likely have some effect on the visitor, but what is the purpose of creating the stage in the first place? By recreating the experience of soldiers in war, for instance, which we perceive as authentic – something which makes the border between past and present events relatively ambiguous, there is a considerable risk involved. While they might ensure the authenticity of their memorialized realities, such projects can easily produce more possibilities for elusion and manipulation, by using advanced means of representation in an uncontrolled way where authenticity is immersed in a profitable form of entertainment.

Similar questions can be raised with regard to the architectural qualities of memorial museums, particularly those built on authentic sites. Existing war memorials are often coupled with contemporary museums and vice versa. The most prominent are probably the various Holocaust memorial museums that continue to emerge across the globe. In the United States, building Holocaust museums has become an architectural trend, demonstrated by the many museums that were built in the last few decades. Most of these museums aimed at emotionally evocative architecture, and some adopted a post-modern language that alluded to concentration camp iconography, including barbed wire, crematorium chimneys, guard towers and so forth. These projects were characterized by an extensive use of brick and stripped metal, as materials associated with the industrialized destruction of lives during the war. As we noted in Chapter 2, such references were employed so liberally in some cases that Gavriel Rosenfeld has drawn comparisons with Disney Animation Studios. Others have been globally recognized, such as the USHMM in Washington, DC – a memorial museum that raised new questions about curatorial strategies and the representation of trauma. This museum is probably the most prominent example of the new genre – a typological hybrid of memorial and museum. The process of creating the museum entailed numerous difficulties, described elsewhere at length.[3] It also problematized the

2 Alison Landsberg, *Prosthetic Memory: The Transformation of American Remembrance in the Age of Mass Culture* (New York: Columbia University Press, 2004).

3 See Linenthal, *Preserving Memory*.

relation between ethical responsibility and beauty in architecture. The curatorial concept of the museum, together with an interior design unfolding in several structured, experiential, theatrical stages served as a role model for many future museums.

Concerned with 'how the mission, audience, educational strategies, and generational framing of memory change when a memorial has, as its main feature, a museum, or when a museum seeks to function as a memorial',[4] researchers have scrutinized many recently established memorial museums around the world, and they will continue to do so.[5] Selecting case studies across nations and contexts, authors engage with the goals and strategies of these institutions while trying to assess their public significance. While there is a profound body of work, an independent academic field in fact, dealing with Holocaust commemoration, the underlying fact is that the commemoration of the Second World War and the Holocaust was formative for the development of memorial museums. Museums and memorials dedicated to the Second World War served as a weapon against dehumanization, or better, an attempt at rehumanization.

To gain a clearer picture of what a memorial museum is today and how architects approach the task, this chapter will look at architectural solutions for two Holocaust museums that grapple with contemporary demands. A thorough analysis will zoom in on two congruent museum sites: the Dossin Barracks at Mechelen, Belgium, and the Cité de la Muette at Drancy, France. After comparing the case studies, the chapter will move on to discuss and analyse the projects along the lines of the theoretical framework established in the first two chapters, with special attention to the issues of design concepts and architectural space, and their implications for the transmission of memory.

4.1 Dossin Barracks

Context and History

In the 1940s, the General Dossin de Saint-Georges Barracks (1756) in Mechelen (Malines), Belgium, provided a convenient and strategic location for the occupying Nazi authorities to establish a transit camp for

[4] Paul Williams, *Memorial Museums: The Global Rush to Commemorate Atrocities* (Oxford and New York: Berg, 2007), p. 8.

[5] See also Amy Sodaro, *Exhibiting Atrocity: Memorial Museums and the Politics of Past Violence* (New Brunswick, NJ: Rutgers University Press, 2018).

Jewish deportees.[6] After the war, even though Belgium was one of the first countries to establish a national Holocaust memorial, the work of memory came slowly and belatedly.[7] This was due to the long-ignored fact that those deported from the Dossin Barracks were selected strictly on racial grounds. Another reason was that the Jewish community showed little interest in the former camp premises once they were vacated by the Belgian army in 1975. Even though the first memorial gathering was held in September 1956,[8] it was only after the Lischka Trial in 1979 in Cologne that awareness of the fate of Belgium's Jews began to increase, and with it the interest in the Dossin Barracks[9] – also known as the 'antechamber of death'.[10] After protests against its proposed demolition in the 1980s, organized by the Jewish community in Mechelen, the barracks was transformed into a luxury apartment complex and the inner courtyard was remodelled into a garden, with a parking lot underneath it. This modification of the building's purpose was perceived as a deliberate act of covering up the past.[11] At about the same time – in 1986, to be precise – a monument, consisting of six segments taken from the original railway line connecting Mechelen to Auschwitz, was installed at the entrance to the barracks as a symbol of the six million murdered Jews. Later a small plaque was added, commemorating the Sinti and Roma victims of the deportations.[12]

[6] Unlike Antwerp or Brussels, Mechelen had a relatively small Jewish community. From September 1944 to April 1946, the camp was used as an internment centre for *inciviques* (persons who collaborated with the Germans). The important transport connections passing the Dossin barracks, located halfway between Brussels and Antwerp, the high percentage of the Jewish population of Belgium that lived in this area, and its proximity to the infamous 'reception camp' (*Auffanglager*), Fort Breendok, made the Dossin barracks a suitable location.

[7] Martin Winstone, *The Holocaust Sites of Europe: An Historical Guide* (London and New York: I.B. Tauris, 2010), p. 36.

[8] Lieven Saerens, 'Van vergeten naar genegeerd: Dossin en Joodse herinnering', *Belgisch Tijdschrift voor Nieuwste Geschiedenis*, 42.2 (2012), 138–69, p. 142.

[9] In 1979 a Jewish committee 'Hulde Comité van de Joden' was established which denounced the lack of interest in memory-work in Belgium as 'moreel verval' ('moral corruption'). Saerens, 'Van vergeten', p. 152. See also Laurence Schram, 'The transit camp for Jews in Mechelen: the antechamber of death', *Online Encyclopedia of Mass Violence*, 6 February 2008, www.massviolence.org.

[10] Ugo Janssens, *Historische Gids voor België: Een boeiende kennismaking met ons verleden* (Antwerp: Standaard, 2002), pp. 148–9.

[11] The Dossin Barracks had been the legal property of the city of Mechelen since 1977. The building was remodelled to house luxury apartments in 1984. In 1989 the first inhabitants arrived. Saerens, 'Van vergeten', p. 156.

[12] The memorial plaque commemorating the deportation of 'Gypsies' was added to the facade of the Dossin Barracks on 3 June 1995. The memorialization of these ethnic minority groups

In 1996 the Jewish Museum of Deportation and Resistance (JMDR) opened to the public in the north-eastern section of the barracks.[13] Due to increasing interest, reflected in rising numbers of visitors, the shock of the Rwandan genocide in 1994 and also a shift in the overall political atmosphere in 2001, the idea of turning the JMDR into a prestigious Flemish Holocaust Museum was put forward by Patrick Dewael, then Prime Minister of Flanders.[14] This new museum was perceived as complementing Fort Breendonk, a memorial site not far from Mechelen which served as a prison camp during the Second World War. Accordingly, in 2004 a committee was established to consider the future museum's 'thematic delineation'. It was soon disbanded for various reasons, chief among which was the committee's persistence in focusing on the theme of human rights.[15] This was opposed by the Jewish community, which feared that the ambitious plan to address such a universal theme might lead to a simplification, and thus a banalization, of the local story. After some heated debate and the establishment of a new committee, it was finally decided that the new museum would house a permanent exhibition about the 'Belgian case', positioned in the wider historical framework of the Holocaust in Europe and human rights violations in other parts of the world.[16] In 2007 the government announced an international architectural competition, stressing that participating teams should be multidisciplinary since the particulars of the commission demanded that architecture, public space and museological content work in synthesis.[17] After selecting six finalists out of hundreds of entries, former Flemish Government architect Bob van Reeth, considered one of the most important post-war Belgian

was practically non-existent until the 1990s, due to the very limited number of remaining Sinti and Roma survivors of concentration camps.

13 The Union des Déportés Juifs de Belgique (Union of the Jewish Deportees of Belgium) and the Consistoire Central Israélite de Belgique (Jewish Central Consistory of Belgium) purchased part of the barracks and established the museum. The museum primarily targeted schoolchildren and educational institutes, which made up 80 per cent of the visitors.

14 See Saerens, 'Van vergeten', pp. 159–60.

15 The committee was directed by Professor Bruno de Wever and consisted of the members of the local academic community. The idea was to name the museum 'Transit Mechelen. Museum over Vervolging en Volkenmoord' and the theme of Holocaust would have been a part of the overall exhibition. Saerens, 'Van vergeten', p. 163–4.

16 The second committee was organized under the leadership of Professor Herman van Goethem. The final name of the new institution was the Kazerne Dossin: Memorial Museum and Documentation Centre on the Holocaust and Human Rights.

17 Brecht Blondeel, 'Kazerne Dossin, Memoriaal, Museum en Documentatiecentrum over Holocaust en Mensenrechten: Historiek, analyse en maquette' (unpublished master's thesis, University of Ghent, 2009), p. 16.

Figure 4.1 Kazerne Dossin Memorial Museum (2012), Mechelen; Bob van Reeth. Photo: Author

architects, and his team were selected as winners. The new museum, a dark grey, five-storey, monolithic building with openings only on the top floor of its facade and at the rear, was to be located opposite the Dossin Barracks, on the site of a former remand centre.[18]

Soon after the winning design was announced, local people launched a protest campaign under the slogan 'Museum Yes, Mausoleum No'. Another protesting body was RIM (Restoration and Integration Mechelen) which argued for preserving the former detention centre as a significant part of Mechelen's prison system and a showcase of a more humane approach to detaining prisoners.[19] They opposed both the planned demolition of the remand centre and the sombre look of the design slated to take its place. A compromise was reached only in the colour of the building, which, instead of a grey 'mausoleum' became a white monolith (Figure 4.1). The government backed the chosen design as a symbolic 'grave' for all

[18] The former detention house was also known as the IKA – Instituut voor Kunsten en Ambachten – and was housed in the premises in the 1960s. During the Second World War it was used by the Nazis as accommodation.

[19] 'Voor het behoud van het Arresthuis', *Vanonderuit Krant*, 8.33 (2009), 2.

those who had disappeared without a trace after the deportations from the barracks to Auschwitz.[20] The Kazerne Dossin: Memorial Museum and Documentation Centre on the Holocaust and Human Rights was finally opened in November 2012.

Morphology

The designer of the Kazerne Dossin museum had quite considerable room for manoeuvre, which resulted in him thinking specifically about the content of the building once the architectural space was realized. Its symbolic meanings are often hidden or discreet, such as the front windows being sealed with more than 25,000 bricks symbolizing the number of deportees from the former camp, or the twelve cast-iron columns in the lobby standing for the twelve tribes of Israel. Van Reeth consciously avoided explicit symbolism in order not to fall into the trap of becoming too literal and thereby 'anecdotal'.[21] One driving force behind the design for the Kazerne Dossin was the desire to create an edifice confronting a past that had been ignored for six decades. Consequently, it began with the idea of creating a provocative, unfriendly monument to protest that long period of neglect – or, in the architect's words, an 'embarrassment built in stone'. At the same time, the designer opted for a building that would not be too shocking or have too 'loud' an appearance. This was also the reason for changing its colour to white, as opposed to the original, darker colour, which is evocative of mourning and death.[22]

Van Reeth drew his inspiration partly from the Jewish religion, especially the notion of the synagogue as a place of learning and communion which has to be recognizable within the urban tissue, usually being taller than its surroundings, making it 'visible for everyone'.[23] Another relevant factor defining the museum's composition was the decision not to interfere with the original site, but to build adjacent to it, so respecting the modifications which had occurred to the barracks over the course of history – not

[20] Eric Stroobants, 'De Klok tikt voor Kazerne Dossin', *Gazet van Antwerpen*, 8 June 2012, www.gva.be/regio-mechelen/mechelen/de-klok-tikt-voor-kazerne-dossin.aspx, last accessed 14 February 2018.

[21] Bob van Reeth, 'Ik heb schaamte in stenen willen bouwen', *Campuskrant* (magazine of University of Leuven), 2 (2012), 8.

[22] Van Reeth argued that, referring to Avraham Burg, the white colour in his design is fitting to the existing context. As for the aggressive appearance in memorial architecture, the designer gives the Jewish Museum in Berlin as an example. See Bob van Reeth, 'Bouwen aan een eervolle plaats van herinnering', *de Nieuwe Maan*, May 2012, pp. 14–15, www.mechelen.be.

[23] Van Reeth quoted in Blondeel, 'Kazerne Dossin', p. 117.

Figure 4.2 Kazerne Dossin Memorial Museum (2012), view on Dossin Barracks; Bob van Reeth.
Photo: Christophe Ketels

least its present state as an apartment block. The same argument supported the demolition of the former remand centre. Otherwise destined to become a quasi-archaeological relic or a *nature morte* due to its previous use as a prison and a Nazi logistics centre, the architect decided the only way to do it justice was to integrate its remnants into a new building. This choice had to do with practicalities as well, since finding an alternative for the people living in the 'barracks' was perceived as much more demanding a task than working on the location of the former remand centre and the front section of the barracks' wings, which were government property.

The Kazerne Dossin Memorial Museum is four storeys high, but the only connection to the barracks itself is on the top floor, since the lower levels are orientated inwards to the permanent exhibition, and windows have only been inserted at the rear. The uppermost level is reserved for temporary exhibitions and, in contrast to the lower levels, is flooded with daylight as a wide panoramic view over Mechelen opens up on three sides. The barracks is visible from this level, but only partially – the view is restricted to the rear section of the building and the entrance where the documentation centre and the memorial are located. The inner courtyard cannot be seen (Figure 4.2).[24]

[24] Van Reeth argued that it would not 'feel right' to integrate into the memorial the modified inner court of the Kazerne or Hof van Habsburg, since it has been completely changed since the Second World War.

In fact, this level is designed as a 'decompression' space after the first three floors, bringing a contrast in light as a symbol of hope and future prospects.[25] On this level, a narrow terrace along three sides allows the visitor to step outside to gain a better view of the city and the barracks. Van Reeth described the building metaphorically as a 'hortus conclusus', an enclosed garden defined by its outer border, consisting here of the old 'execution wall' and its extension, which separates the museum from the busy Tinellaan road running alongside it and offers a peaceful place for reflection.[26] Respecting the former layout, the new border then becomes a gate to the museum's forecourt. The entrance to the museum is set to one side, neither symmetrically in the middle of the facade nor precisely opposite the entrance to the barracks, and is accentuated by fragments of the former remand centre incorporated into the front wall. The ground floor develops on the exact spot where the demolished building used to stand, providing another link to its former existence. The brickwork of the facade and the sealed, indented windows of the middle three floors are executed in a specific pattern, using the same number of bricks as there were deportees from the camp.

The square in front of the museum, reinforced by the position of the entrance, has been realized exactly as imagined in the original design: as a place for contemplation, furnished only with a long white bench and a few symbolic trees. The first impression of the interior is determined by the naturally lit foyer and the contrasting darkened space of the introductory exhibition, divided by twelve cast-iron columns. Perhaps the most dominant element in this space is the wall of photographs of victims, which extends downwards to the cafeteria. The wall itself is an autonomous element (Figure 4.3). The function of the underground level has been modified from the original design – instead of a parking lot, it is a cafe, which was originally planned to be on the top floor. The layouts of the three levels above are determined by the precise museological scenography of the permanent exhibition, with the only daylight coming from slit corner windows overlooking the car park and the old cloister behind the building.

25 Blondeel, 'Kazerne Dossin', p. 124.

26 The border is made up from the old wall belonging to the former detention house and its newly designed continuing part. The old wall served as an execution place during the Second World War. Blondeel points out (ibid., p. 31) that the competition regulations permitted perforations in the wall, as long as the character of the wall as a unity was kept intact. Future plans integrate the wall into a park which will be dedicated to human rights, while the present parking ground is planned to be situated in an underground garage space.

Figure 4.3 Kazerne Dossin Memorial Museum (2012), Mechelen; Bob van Reeth. Photo: Author

The entrance to the Dossin Barracks, where the JMDR was stationed in the past, also contains entrances to the documentation centre and the memorial. At the entrance to the memorial, a cloakroom and a plan of the exhibition spaces await the visitor. Once in the exhibition space, one is free to stroll through the memorial rooms, here called galleries, each of which has its own distinct content. In first galleries, entitled 'Vestiges of the past' and 'Traces', personal belongings are exhibited together with an artwork by Philip Aguirre y Otegui. The next two galleries are entitled 'Their names' and 'Their faces' and commemorate the victims of the deportations, displaying a wealth of personal data and information about the deportation trains. Originally, the windows were to be sealed and a mourning wall added, with perforations in which people could place offerings, referencing the Wailing Wall in Jerusalem. This element was removed from the final design, however, since that reference proved controversial.[27]

Performance

Due to the increasing number of schoolchildren visiting the Kazerne Dossin, a key target group for the new museum, the primary aim of the new building in Mechelen was to provide more spaces for education, or rather, multifunctional spaces.[28] Compared with similar institutions,

[27] Blondeel, 'Kazerne Dossin', p. 126.

[28] Interview with Marjan Verplancke, Head of Education, Kazerne Dossin: Memorial Museum and Documentation Centre on the Holocaust and Human Rights, 28 February 2014.

knowledge about the conditions at the Dossin Barracks is limited due to the fact that there were relatively few survivors.[29] Nevertheless, there are four valuable authentic photographs documenting the atmosphere in the former camp, while the register of the names of those deported is comprehensive and well-preserved.[30]

Moreover, the architectural solution had to address a few additional points, which made the purpose of the building slightly vague. What further complicated the situation was the fact that the survival of the former remand centre was in doubt.[31] Other points concerned the remains of the old wall against which prisoners were executed, the treatment of the inner courtyard of the barracks and the need to connect the site with the rest of the city, with a new square as a prominent location. To guide participants, the competition's organizing committee produced a thorough analysis of the location, accompanied by examples of conceived or completed design solutions dealing with similar issues, and also a number of possible urban-scale configurations for the future museum. The requirements for the new museum and its relationship with the Dossin Barracks and the city were put as follows:

> For a project with this theme, it is important to realize that there is a tension between the scientific and the emotional aspects. However, both of these have to form an organic whole. For the designers this becomes a task of delicate balancing where architecture can strengthen the museum's story and let it come to the fore without becoming the story itself. The architecture must not be determinative, but it should not be neutral: it has to support the importance of the Dossin Barracks and it has to encourage citizens of Mechelen to identify and interact with the site and its history.[32]

Finally, the pedagogical focus of the memorial was not to be placed exclusively on the Holocaust and the history of the Dossin Barracks in particular, but also on the methods and mechanisms which led to such scenarios of mass destruction of human life. This demand became an

[29] Only 1218 of those deported survived, which is about 5 per cent. Published accounts of life at Mechelen transit camp are rare. Most of the deportees spent only a few days in Mechelen on their way to Auschwitz-Birkenau. Judicial sources, such as written reports of witness interrogations and legal statements by the accused and their victims, tend to be the most complete sources of information on the history of the camp. See Schram, 'The transit camp'.

[30] Interview with Ward Adriaens, conservator at Kazerne Dossin, 28 February 2014.

[31] The competition criteria stated designers must give clear reasons if arguing for the demolition of the former detention house. Blondeel, 'Kazerne Dossin', p. 36.

[32] Rob Cuyvers quoted in Blondeel, 'Kazerne Dossin', p. 34 [author's translation of original Dutch].

aspect which, as the Mechelen museum claims, makes it unique among Holocaust memorial museums: it presents a psychological portrait of the perpetrator. This is exhibited most directly in the closing sequence of the permanent exhibition, where a long passage leads towards a large print of the Auschwitz gate, in which stand photographs of the perpetrators rather than images of the victims. Such strong scenography does indeed require a neutral architectural space, and it could be placed in other multifunctional spaces offered by the new museum. In relation to the competition brief, however, which stressed the importance of architecture as a medium that would strengthen the museum's story, the question is whether such neutrality fulfils that request.

The ambition to house an exhibition on human rights as a general topic concerning all society has overshadowed the local story, and because the viewpoint at the top of the building overlooks the city, the story becomes even more ambiguous. The one part of the design which is completely dedicated to the Dossin Barracks is the memorial situated in the barracks itself, but due to the lack of any physical connection with the museum, it presents itself as a separate entity and could easily be missed by visitors to the museum. Indeed, the memorial space, which has been criticized as cold and unemotional, is overshadowed by the new building, which is due in part to its unwillingness to interact with the original site.[33]

Once inside the memorial, one cannot escape the feeling of a well-executed and logically designed exhibition. This is augmented by the diagrams about the numbers of victims and the survivors. Each exhibition room has different content and offers new information, but the overall atmosphere remains sterile. The architecture of the memorial tells a story of the precision and vastness of the Nazi regime, and the consequences. Details of the number of victims from the Dossin Barracks, their stories told from speakers and their personal belongings forensically exhibited, the memorial offers a well-documented track of events (Figure 4.4). The only room with no textual highlight contains instead a sculptural work by Philip Aguirre y Otegui about the psychedelic atmosphere of the times, portraying a family hiding under a dining table. The memorial resists becoming personal in its presentation. Differing from the museum only in having a fixed layout rather than multifunctional spaces, the memorial remains a

[33] 'Kazerne Dossin: Gelijkvloers wordt herwerkt na klachten van te kille inrichting', *Joods Actueel*, 16 December 2013, available at http://joodsactueel.be/2013/12/16/kazerne-dossin-gelijkvloers-wordt-herwerkt-na-klachten-van-te-kille-inrichting, last accessed 14 February 2018.

Figure 4.4 Kazerne Dossin Memorial (2012), Mechelen; Bob van Reeth.
Photo: Author

space of documentation. In spite of its intention to provide families of the victims with 'a substitute for the missing grave',[34] and in spite of the fact that it is situated at the actual site, the memorial offers no space for private contemplation within its well-organized spatial sequences. Moreover, it refuses to reinforce the sense of place – as demonstrated by the blurring of the windows facing the inner courtyard of the Dossin Barracks. The memorial operates as an addition to the museum and the documentation centre, but its location is of little significance to the overall concept.

Finally, in some respects the new situation in Mechelen contradicts Van Reeth's eagerness to support the *genius loci*. Rather, it represents the architect's own doubts about what 'a place wants to become'.[35] The decision to demolish the former remand centre and to build a new layer of history, combined with the unwillingness to relate more explicitly to the Dossin Barracks and its courtyard, was perhaps taken too lightly. In this respect, the many years of discussion about the preservation of the former camp commander's house in Westerbork, or even the removal of authentic structures in Risiera di San Saba, are telling examples of how any trace of the history of a specific site can help reinforce the sense of place.

[34] See www.kazernedossin.eu.

[35] Inne Broos, *bOb van Reeth en de genius loci in Antwerpen*, Master thesis, Ghent University, 2001, available at http://lib.ugent.be/catalog/rug01:000789390, last accessed 30 January 2015.

4.2 Cité de la Muette

Context and History

Like the Kazerne Dossin, the museum in Drancy, a north-eastern suburb of Paris, was not built on the actual site, but adjacent to it. And, as in Mechelen, it is separated from the original location by a busy road junction. The memorial museum lies just opposite the Cité de la Muette, the building block constituting the former transit camp known to survivors as the 'Gateway to Hell' (Porte de l'Enfer) and 'place of fear' (lieu d'angoisse).[36] The site, however, morphed into a place with 'concentrationary armature' before the Nazi occupation of the Third Republic of France.[37] From an architectural point of view, La Muette is also interesting for its history, as one of the first projects in 1930s France to include high-rise 'American-style' skyscrapers.[38] The five sixteen-storey towers were destroyed in 1976, and today can only be seen on old postcards with the caption 'Skyscrapers of inner Parisian suburbia'. Only the housing block designed in a U-shape, framing the large inner courtyard that was the actual site of the Second World War deportation camp, survived the demolition.[39] Glimpses of this space and the atmosphere that prevailed there when the complex was in use as a transit camp were depicted by some of its internees, such as artist Jane Lévy. Recognized for its dual past as both a valuable architectural edifice and the biggest transit camp in France, the site was finally listed as a national monument in 2001. Its importance was confirmed in the famous

[36] Built as a collective living space in the 1930s but never finished, the large U-shaped form of La Muette was easily transformed into a place of surveillance and detention. The Cité de la Muette became an internment camp in 1941, and then in 1942 a regrouping camp for the Jews of France, in preparation for their deportation to the extermination camps. Between March 1942 and August 1944, approximately 63,000 Jews went through Drancy. On 25 May 2001, the social housing complex was listed as a historical monument.

[37] See Caroline Wiedmer, *The Claims of Memory: Representations of the Holocaust in Contemporary Germany and France* (Ithaca, NY and London: Cornell University Press, 1999), p. 61

[38] Designed by modernist architects Marcel Lods and Eugène Beaudouin, the structure was built on the principle of what was termed the 'vertical garden city'. The engineer Eugène Mopin developed the construction system and Jean Prouvé designed the system of metal forms used in the casting of the concrete elements. La Muette as the first 'grand ensemble' in France, together with another French example – Villeurbane, near Lyon – were important examples of high-rise social housing schemes in Europe that aimed at attractive, higher-density alternatives for traditional housing.

[39] La Muette consisted of three typological building elements arranged in four distinct ways: towers, *peignes* and *redan* blocks. *Peignes* or 'combs' are three- to four-storey slab buildings that used to connect the towers.

Figure 4.5 Shoah monument with the new memorial museum in the background, Drancy.
Photo: Author

1995 acknowledgement by then president Jacques Chirac, who spoke about France's complicity in the persecution of the Jews and other minorities during the Second World War. Memorialization of the former transit camp began in the 1970s when a symbolic sculpture by Shelomo Selinger, thick with Jewish symbolism, was placed on the site (1976). The monument consists of three granite blocks forming the Hebrew letter *shin*, positioned on a mound and accessible by a flight of stairs.[40] The three blocks are inscribed in angular letters with the one in French giving most statistical information (Figure 4.5).[41] One block contains only text in Yiddish and the absence of the translation 'enables the whole ensemble to resist its

[40] For the symbolic meaning of the memorial see Wiedmer, *The Claims of Memory*, pp. 57–69.

[41] The wagon was added in 1988, the same year that the Drancy Historical Conservatory was founded, and it served as an exhibition space. Its location is considered misleading since the transport of prisoners started from the adjacent bus station, not from the spot where the wagon is placed. It has been temporarily closed due to vandalism.

assimilation into the very French landscape that surrounds it'.[42] Other traces of memory include a rail wagon of a type used to transport prisoners, later added to the memorial, and the 'graffiti' drawn by inmates before being deported to the death camps. Unlike the memorial, which confronts contemporary residents with the harrowing past of the Cité de la Muette on a daily basis, due to its fragile state this graffiti is preserved in the Departmental Archives of Seine-Saint-Denis. Several institutions connected to the memory of La Muette as an internment camp already existed on the site, but a new centre for education and research was needed in order to facilitate the work of witnesses and associations and to reach out to a wider audience.[43]

The new memorial museum was initiated and financed by the Foundation for the Memory of the Shoah (Fondation pour la Mémoire de la Shoah; FMS), which insisted on building a museum adjacent to the location so that the Cité de la Muette housing block itself could stay a place of life, not one of 'embarrassment'.[44] The foundation entrusted the Shoah Memorial in Paris with the organization of an international competition in 2006, in which first prize was awarded to the Switzerland-based architectural firm Diener & Diener, known for their analytical approach. Despite many doubts about its financial and practical viability, and a fear of possible acts of vandalism, the memorial museum was built on land generously donated by the municipality of Drancy, and inaugurated by French president François Hollande in September 2012 (Figure 4.6).[45]

The museum in Drancy is perceived as a place of mediation between the public and the former site, with a focus on 'the central role of the Drancy camp in the exclusion of the Jews of France during the Second World War and in the implementation of the "Final Solution" by the Nazis in France,

[42] Wiedmer, *The Claims of Memory*, p. 68.

[43] Several associations are located there, including the Drancy Historical Conservatory of Drancy and the Auschwitz Memory Fund Association (AFMA). *Rapport d'activité 2012*, l'action de la Fondation pour la Mémoire de la Shoah, 2012, p. 10.

[44] Lawyer and historian Serge Klarsfeld, author of the *Mémorial de la deportation des Juifs de France* (1978), declared for this place of memory, 'Il fallait que la Cité de la Muette demeure un lieu de vie, et ne pas gêner les gens'. Nicolas Weill, 'Drancy, mémoires à vif', *Le Monde*, 13 September 2012, available at www.lemonde.fr/culture/article/2012/09/13/drancy-memoires-a-vif_1759966_3246.html, last accessed 13 February 2018.

[45] President François Hollande was personally involved and linked the government to three events that were extremely important for the Foundation for the Memory of the Shoah: the commemoration of the seventieth anniversary of the Vél d'Hiv Roundup, the inauguration of the Shoah Memorial at Drancy, and the inauguration of the Camp des Milles Memorial Site near Aix-en-Provence.

Figure 4.6 Memorial museum at Drancy (2012), Diener & Diener architects.
Photo: Author

with the complicity of the Vichy government'.[46] This mission statement produced a clear programme of requirements for the competition, further aided by the decision to use a location adjacent to La Muette and to refrain from interfering with its present purpose as a housing block.

Morphology

The museum in Drancy is conceived as a transparent vertical structure opening towards the public and the site of the Cité de la Muette, so that the 'work of memory' is not hidden but visible to everyone. Consistent in their rational approach towards architectural spaces, Diener & Diener focused on the particularities of the programme imposed by the commissioning body and how they needed to be related to its subject. The building is recognized as an example of 'sober and dignified architecture', respectful to the site and its urban environment.[47] The architect drew inspiration from the museum's proximity to the original site of the camp, aiming to strengthen the relationship between La Muette and the new building by creating an open structure which would communicate with the

[46] Memorial de la Shoah-Musee, Centre de documentation, www.memorialdelashoah.org.
[47] See www.memorialdelashoah.org.

surroundings without falling into the trap of becoming a monument to the existing monument. Instead the aim was that the relationship between these two sites becomes the subject itself.[48] In fact, the building's monumentality is perceived through its utility as an aid in the work of memory – or rather, as a form of remembering itself.[49] Understanding memory as an active process achieved by an ever-recurring effort, the building was conceived as a 'composite memory', with each floor offering a different way of remembering.[50] Naturally, designing a building that is 'transparent' so the public can explore and engage with the work of memory within, when at the same time it is supposed to operate as an administrative building, proved a challenging task.

The museum in Drancy occupies the corner of a block of houses divided from La Muette by the busy Avenue Jean Jaurès. The building looks compact and has five levels, with a foyer at ground level, conference halls at underground level, a documentation centre and archives on the first level, pedagogical spaces on the second and, finally, the permanent exhibition on the uppermost level.[51] The reinforced concrete facade appears staggered, oriented towards the original site via large windows and with a 20cm extrusion at each level. Contrasting with the transparency of the windows, the indented entrance is in reflective glass so that the Cité de la Muette reflects on its surface (Figure 4.7). The entrance door is an integral part of the cladded facade, distinguishable only by the text naming the museum; there is usually also a security guard standing in front of it. The interior of the museum gives the impression of a well-organized administrative building with plenty of daylight, in a rather neutral setting. An introduction to the Shoah is given in the underground space, where visitors also find the cloakroom and toilets. Unlike the permanent exhibition on the top floor, which is highly engaging scenographically, the rest of the building's interior is 'anonymous' and has a rather calm atmosphere.[52]

With its fully glazed front, the top floor effectively opens onto the site. An architectural model of the former deportation camp is placed next to

[48] Pascale Joffroy, 'Le mémorial de la Shoah à Drancy, un bâtiment qui regarde', *D'Architectures*, 214 (2012), 86–91.

[49] Roger Diener, 'Shoah Memorial Drancy', in Roger Diener and Joseph Abram, *Diener & Diener*, trans. Sarah Robertson (London: Phaidon Press, 2011), pp. 262–4.

[50] Ibid., p. 264.

[51] A permanent exhibition, designed by Patrick Rotman and Dephine Gleize, retraces the history and function of the camp as well as the daily lives of those interned there.

[52] Diener & Diener, *Memorial de la Shoah-Drancy-Paris*, press release, 2012.

Figure 4.7 Memorial museum at Drancy (2012), Diener & Diener architects.
Photo: Author

Figure 4.8 Memorial museum at Drancy (2012), Diener & Diener architects.
Photo: Author

the window overlooking La Muette (Figure 4.8). From here it is possible to see the existing memorial and part of the U-shaped block. The model allows comparison between the site today and how it looked when it was a transit camp.

Performance

The main goal for both memorial museums in Mechelen and Drancy remains the transmission of memory to younger generations through education and research. This mission is clearly defined in the case of Drancy, the purpose of which is 'to raise awareness among young people as to the causes of this tragedy: the abandonment of human rights, Nazism and its ideology, the political organization it created, anti-Semitism, hatred, violence, murder'.[53] At the same time, a new structure is dedicated to all those who did not return once they had been deported from these camps.

In a more linear process than the one in Mechelen, demands for the new museum in Drancy were put forward more clearly, set in the framework of preserving the memory of the local story and the connection with the site. Unlike the design process in Kazerne Dossin where the designer had considerable room for manoeuvre, the competition call for Drancy offered a well-defined set of demands for the building.

Both architectural teams were multidisciplinary and could cover various aspects related to the complex set of requirements in projects of this scale and importance. Of course, the lead architects determined the overall design. Bob van Reeth pointed out that he had undertaken a thorough study of Jewish history and cultural specificities which offered a rich source of information for his creative process and eventually delivered a project laden with symbolic meaning related to Jewish tradition. Roger Diener, on the other hand, approached his task with a sense of his responsibility towards his own Jewish background – but in his design, he chose to fully respect the demands set out in the competition brief. The completed designs are certainly similar in two respects: both prominently occupy their locations, with a few floors rising above the ground; both also communicate at a visual level with the original sites.

The new museums in Drancy and Mechelen share the strategic decision to deal with the history of a former deportation camp through a building adjacent to the site itself and therefore invest strongly in the visual connection. Nonetheless, they differ significantly both in how they fulfil their purpose and in the effect they produce. Consequently, although they are imagined to act as 'transmitters of memory', in practice they work differently. The Memorial Museum in Drancy is certainly a good institution for research since the greater part of the building is devoted to a library and various educational functions. In Mechelen, by contrast, the spaces

[53] *Rapport d'activité 2012.*

designated for educational purposes are rather small and seem likely to be sufficiently enlarged to satisfy current demand.

The difference in perceptions of how to continue the memorialization of these places is clearly manifested in their respective architecture. Roger Diener's sense of responsibility towards his own Jewish background, together with the clear demands formulated by the FMS, have delivered an operational office building, whereas Van Reeth's pursuit of the *genius loci* and insistence on highlighting the 'embarrassment' of the decades-long neglect of the local story have produced a dominant edifice which possibly overshadows the historical site itself. The project in Mechelen is more ambitious regarding its connection to the city because the project was supposed to deliver an attractive public space. Moreover, the museum aspires to an image that will be recognized internationally, and this is quite legible in its overall theme.[54]

In terms of public space and interaction with its surroundings, the white monolith, with its asymmetrical entrance and blocked windows, strikes an uncanny note which makes it an intriguing gesture in the public space. The edifice in Drancy has rather the opposite effect. Even though it was imagined as a transparent architecture, the building refuses to interact with the public space. This is due simply to the large reflective glass surface at street level which, together with the strict security check awaiting visitors at the entrance, creates the impression of a controlled and uninviting place. Despite the poetic inspiration behind this reflective glass – the new building mirroring the site whose story it tells, thereby creating a potential for encounters between the visitor and the site's history[55] – in reality works simply as a mirror for passers-by to glimpse their reflections.

By contrast, the public space in front of the museum in Mechelen is augmented by the materialization of its pavement which, together with the building itself, creates a transitional public area prior to entering the museum. In this sense, there is some indication of a connection to the original barracks. Nevertheless, it can still be argued that any significant link is lacking due to the busy road passing between the two buildings and disturbing their physical relationship.[56] The view which opens up on the

[54] Before creating the permanent exhibition, the committee visited the Imperial War Museum in London as an example of a world-known museum on the general topic of war.

[55] See *La memoiré composée*, press release (2012), Diener & Diener.

[56] The initial plan was to redirect traffic around the site so that the road passing between the Dossin Barracks and the new museum would not divide the site. Few of the competition entries chosen in the first round developed their concepts around the square which would have been created between the two buildings as a space of mediation.

fourth floor is not sufficient if one does not know where the actual site is; another building in the immediate surroundings could easily be mistaken for it, such as the old cloister next door. In Drancy, this connection is firmly established on the top floor with a permanent exhibition dedicated solely to this specific location. The exhibition ends with a large model of the former transit camp as it once was, positioned directly in front of a large window opening out onto the actual site. This gesture underlines the relationship between the museum and the site, making its purpose instantly clear: the site continues to exist and change as a living block while 'the memory remains in the museum'.[57]

4.3 Perilous Landscapes

In recent decades, the creation of a museum or information point emerges as a common solution for 'perilous landscapes'. These buildings also serve as a transition towards the actual memorial grounds, for example in Dachau, Bergen–Belsen or Westerbork. In Bergen–Belsen, a new documentation centre introduces the visitor to historical facts and integrates the landscape into the exhibition space only at the end of the route, by opening a large panoramic window towards the historical site. Bergen–Belsen's lack of traces of its macabre past in the present landscape calls for a supporting framework of a considerate and perhaps more provocative design as some argued that any mild solutions, with a few commemorative monuments dotting a site otherwise subordinated to nature, represents the 'visual expression of Germany's ambivalence in dealing with its past'.[58] The example of many memorial sites being upgraded with contemporary architectural edifices, however, testifies to a different perspective on this burdensome heritage.

In any event, the oversensitivity of these sites puts all possible intervention under harsh scrutiny. For instance, commemoration work at the Mittelbau-Dora memorial site is open to some memory-work experimentation in the area of the former forced labor camp due to its specific situation, it being where the largest part of the vast underground working tunnel is preserved. Unlike the situation in Westerbork, where the only

[57] Interview with Annaïg Lefeuvre, Coordinator of Educational Services at Drancy memorial site, 25 July 2013.

[58] Joachim Wolschke-Bulmahn, 'The landscape design of the Bergen-Belsen concentration camp memorial', in Wolschke-Bulmahn (ed.), *Places of Commemoration*, pp. 269–300, 300.

remaining architecture is the house of the former camp's commander, in Mittelbau-Dora, there is less interest in the part of the site that belonged to the SS. Instead the focus is placed on the area of the camp that belonged to the inmates together with the fully preserved crematorium building, surrounded by the ashes of the numerous victims. All interventions are clearly distinguished by colour and material while the decisions about maintaining or adjusting the appearance of the site to the fast-growing flora are left to the memorial committee. Professionals working on the commemoration of the remains can make decisions concerning maintenance and design without seeking permission from the government, such as cutting down a certain number of trees. The performed actions are discussed with other professionals who decide whether these commemorative efforts are legible and if the memorial management team can pursue them in the future.[59] Some of the spatial interventions pursued as a part of commemoration work use natural changes of the site to create a context for active remembrance work together with younger generations.

At the same time, currently on the rise is the negative critique of Holocaust memorial projects as attempts that have failed society.[60] Its main arguments derive from the very specificity of the Holocaust as an 'absolute evil' and 'death of reason' that produced our predicament in designing aesthetic representations of it – a return to the Adornian dilemma. Critics more often than not see Holocaust commemoration as a cultivation of indifference precisely due to its specificity. A good example is Berlin's Holocaust Memorial; known for its ability to provoke discussion, as shown in the first chapter, it has been scrutinized for depicting 'an inaccurate vision of Nazism'.[61]

The memorial continues to inspire reactions and art projects such as Yolocaust that aim to scrutinize a society in which people take flattering selfies against a reminder that six million people were systematically dehumanized and destroyed. Hence the hypothesis that the memorial's form and scale will resist reproduction through camera snapshots and

[59] Interview with Torsten Hess, scientific assistant at Stiftung Gedenkstätten Buchenwald und Mittelbau-Dora (Buchenwald and Mittelbau-Dora Memorials Foundation), 27 July 2011.

[60] Jonathan Jones, 'War memorials have failed – we have forgotten the chaos of fascism', *The Guardian*, 9 December 2016, www.theguardian.com/artanddesign/jonathanjonesblog/2016/dec/09/war-memorials-have-failed-peter-eisenman-holocaust, last accessed 23 February 2017. See also Tanya Gold, 'Smile for the Auschwitz selfie: why Holocaust memorials have failed', *New Statesman*, 13 March 2017, www.newstatesman.com/culture/2017/03/smile-auschwitz-selfie-why-holocaust-memorials-have-failed, last accessed 23 March 2017.

[61] Jones, 'War memorials'.

thereby reinforce active participation, as imagined by the commissioners, is proven wrong. While the goal remains obvious – to shame and, hopefully, educate the public by exposing them in a viral internet circuit (once it is out there, there is no return) – one issue remains neglected: the responsibility of the memorial itself, and with that the responsibility of its makers. After all, it has been designed and interpolated in Berlin's public space as an inviting field of opportunities for bodily engagement – now a brand in its own right. The more relevant question here is whether the 'shaming' selfies were taken before or after visiting the documentation centre beneath the memorial. As a late addition in the revised plan for the memorial, the documentation centre was obviously not considered in the memorial's inception. Dani Karavan's Memorial to the Sinti and Roma victims of National Socialism, adjacent to the MMJE, offers a stark contrast. For one, it presents the visitor with historical facts first. Even though Karavan's initial models do not display any trace of the surrounding fence, the memorial is separated from the rest of the park by a milk-glass fence on which a historical timeline is inscribed.[62] Unlike the monumental field of concrete blocks that invite public participation through effortless transition, this memorial aims at structured involvement: first knowledge and then an emotional space. Regardless of the many differences that make these two memorials incommensurable, their respective designers had to make choices about how their designs communicate with the public. These two closely related memorials also show that lessons can be learned from practice and implemented in the process of the memorial-making.

In regard to the relationship between the curatorial focus and design, Holocaust memorial museums on non-authentic sites seem to adopt a more general view. The Los Angeles Museum of the Holocaust (2010), by Belzberg Architects, confirms this trend. The museum was designed along organic principles and embedded into the city's landscape, diverging from the popular narrative approach.[63] It was sited underground so that it became an organic feature of the park. The readiness to seemingly

[62] See Jacobi, Omer and Reuter (eds.), *Dani Karavan*, pp. 240–1.

[63] For instance, the Holocaust Memorial Center in Michigan or the Holocaust Museum and Education Center in Illinois, designed in 2009 by Stanley Tigerman. The latter displays an overtly religious underlining, again deploying the notion of *zimzum* together with a distinct use of dark grey and white colour. The grey is used to represent the moment of *shevirat ha-kelim* (when the light produced as a consequence of the *zimzum* act destroyed the vessels containing it and gave rise to the evil in the world), whereas the white part represents the task of *tikkun olam* as a reference to repairing the damage through education and remembrance. See Rosenfeld, *Building after Auschwitz*, p. 279.

undermine the outer appearance can be explained by the museum's curatorial orientation towards a wider thematic inclusion. Next to exhibiting and documenting the Holocaust, the museum considers other genocides and human rights violations in the world. Even though this is by now a common practice in Holocaust museums, this museum was criticized for departing from the main topic towards more general and, consequently, more schematic representations.[64] In terms of design, the memorial museum also hints at the resurfacing need for context-related spaces to counteract the arrogance of the aggressive, trauma-evoking architecture. This opens up yet another question to be considered here, and that is the omnipresent focus on selective representation of only traumatic historical narratives. For example, in a manifesto written by Belgian historians, a clear reference is made to the memorial museum in Mechelen in the following argument:

> History is not the new catechism of multiculturalism, a panacea to combat the far right and xenophobia, to promote democracy, European views or world solidarity. An exclusively negative memory, consisting of the enumeration of the Great Tragedies of history, contributes little to the formation of critical reflection. It may even create a feeling of moral complacency: an untroubled present is then indeed contrasted with a past rife with violence and brutality.[65]

What both museums in Mechelen and Drancy clearly manifest is that the living memory of these atrocities is ending, and that our perception of the past is immanently influenced by the present. The sense of place that the original sites carry has the potential to establish a relationship between past and present, and it needs to be rediscovered or reinforced. However, it is also necessary to distinguish between the character of a place, as determined by its architectural language, and the sense of place as a layered process, the integration of which is achieved through interaction between people and the place. If these two aspects are not balanced, or if the first

[64] For instance, Edward Rothstein criticizes the memorial's general approach, which de-emphasizes the story of the Holocaust instead of getting more individual stories and information that would make the memory more tangible for future generations. Edward Rothstein, 'Museum review: bearing witness beyond witnesses', *The New York Times*, 24 March 2011, www.nytimes.com/2011/03/24/arts/design/holocaust-museum-in-los-angeles-makes-hard-choices-review.html, last accessed 24 May 2019.

[65] Author's translation from the original Dutch. *Geschiedenis is meer dan herinneren* (*History is more than remembering*) authored by 151 Belgian historians and published in *De Standaard Online* on 25 January 2006, available at www.familiekunde-brussel.be/pdf/misc/geschiedenis_is_meer_dan_herinneren.pdf, last accessed 24 May 2019.

excludes the second, the new architecture creates its own separate entity, directly influencing the process of transmitting the memory of a particular narrative. In addition to the complex issues raised by the musealization of the Holocaust on matters of authenticity and identity, one danger is that the image of a new museum can become more recognizable than the story which initiated its creation. Heeding the more recent debate about 'down-sizing' art museums versus broadening contents and collections, it is inviting for these institutions to rethink their strategies to avoid generic solutions.

At the aesthetic level the sensitive field of symbolic references which are abundant in Mechelen's museum possibly adds another layer to the design. But they are more likely to remain hidden or become the subject of a private intellectual quest to find them. For example, the fragments of the demolished building incorporated into the facade, reminiscent of Aldo Rossi's funerary designs discussed in Chapter 2, together with the bricked-up windows, take on the symbolic function of tombstones for those who never returned. In this respect, the museum in Drancy is certainly more straightforward in its connection with the original site and is immediately legible.

Unlike the Memorial to the Deportation in Paris and its seeming non-presence within the urban tissue – which was perceived as a great quality in the 1960s – the museums studied in this chapter are prominent edifices, particularly the Kazerne Dossin museum. There are several reasons for this, among them the demands of tourism and political gain. But it also indicates an evolving process of memorialization which, in the case of the Dossin Barracks, has escalated into a gigantic monument to the pre-existing memorial, whereas in Drancy the 1970s-era memorial space at the site and its administrative connection to the Paris memorial have produced a piece of background architecture. In the perspective of their relationship to the site, and regardless their dominant presences, one memorial has become a neutral observer of the place whilst the other has itself established a new order. In the aspect of utility, both museums are protected and carefully curated castles for the well-maintained establishment of Holocaust memory that, hopefully, will open up to the contemporary culture of participation and not fulfil the concern of being 'marginal reflections of a tragic past'.[66]

66 Milton, 'Perilous landscapes', p. 266.

5 War Memorials

War nods off to sleep, but keeps one eye always open.

Jean Cayrol[1]

This is the time for drawing angels.

John Hejduk[2]

C'est un site unique par le mélange des amis et des ennemis d'hier.

Yves le Maner[3]

In 2014 the centenary of the outbreak of the First World War inspired numerous commemorative events across the globe. Citizens from many countries commemorated fallen soldiers. Even in Sarajevo, where the memory of the First World War often seems distant and overshadowed by more recent conflicts, a grand performance by the Vienna Philharmonic Orchestra was held, in the country where, according to many accounts, the conflict began. There are similarities between twenty-first-century commemorative ceremonies and those of 80 or 90 years ago and yet, with the death of the last of those soldiers who survived the war, the complex pattern of First World War commemoration has inevitably changed. A whole evolution of memorial techniques of the war happened since the incident in 1977 when on the Remembrance Sunday in the United Kingdom, the red paper poppies that the members of the Royal Marines Guard Band wore 'had run and bled onto their white uniforms' because of rain.[4] The natural sequence of post-memory of generations that remember by modes and means available in the environment after

[1] *Nuit et Brouillard*, film, directed by Alain Resnais. France: Argos Films, 1955.

[2] K. Michael Hays, *Sanctuaries: The Last Works of John Hejduk* (New York: Whitney Museum of American Art, 2003), p. 1.

[3] Nicolas Chauty, 'L'anneau de la mémoire se dévoile, unique au monde', *La Voix du Nord*, 10 October 2014, p. 5.

[4] Robert Cooper, 'World War One: poppy legacy in Burneside firm James Cropper's Hands', BBC News, 11 November 2014, avaliable at www.bbc.com/news/uk-england-cumbria-29749204.

those who witness cultural or collective trauma relies on both old and new practices.[5] There is the same focus on family history and family loss as there was 100 years ago, but now commemorative projects promote other ends: tourism, education and regional redevelopment plans, particularly in areas blighted by the decline and disappearance of extractive industries like coal mining and textile manufacturing. Building new First World War memorials and museums and preserving the war's material and architectural heritage constitute a significant part of this process.

In Belgium, cultural activities were divided in two parts. One devolved to Flanders in the west, the other to Wallonia in the east. In a 2015 publication the government of Flanders stated that the purpose of commemorating the war through many projects:

> is to increase Flanders' visibility on the international level and generate an enduring association with the theme of world peace . . . [and also] to create among present and future generations in Flanders an awareness of the significance of tolerance, intercultural dialogue and international understanding . . . [since this is the only way] that we can foster an open and tolerant society, come to terms with our past and draw lessons from it for the future.[6]

These Flemish memory activists built on the work of earlier groups acting in the 1930s.[7] Forty years later, in the 1970s, a new regional impulse towards commemorating the First World War emerged in Flanders and in northern France. Its tone was distinctively European and pacifist.

This chapter will examine two projects planned for the centenary of the war in France and Belgium. By focusing on a project located at Notre Dame de Lorette in France and on the Remembrance Park 14–18 in Belgium, the analysis will focus on how contemporary designers and architects approach the challenge of linking today's citizens to yesterday's catastrophe.

[5] For postmemory see Marianne Hirsch, *The Generation of Postmemory: Writing and Visual Culture after the Holocaust* (New York: Columbia University Press, 2012).

[6] Pierre Ruyffelaere in *The Great War Centenary (2014–2018)* (Brussels: Government of Flanders Project Office, 2015), p. 5, available at www.fdfa.be/sites/default/files/atoms/files/2015_The_Great_War_Centenary_0.pdf, last accessed 27 May 2019.

[7] Maarten Van Alstein, *The Great War Remembered: Commemoration and Peace in Flanders Fields* (Brussels: Flemish Peace Institute, 2011), p. 14.

5.1 The 'Ring of Memory' International Memorial

Context and History

While the interest in the centenary of the First World War was global in character, most commemorative projects themselves remained focused on national losses and a national narrative. This unwritten rule was broken only in France, where the first regional and international memorial to the war was built. It is situated adjacent to the military cemetery of Ablain-Saint-Nazaire, dating from 1924, also known as Notre Dame de Lorette. The cemetery is located on a hill, a major strategic point during the war, around which more than half a million people died and nearly 300 villages were destroyed. Soldiers of many nationalities participated in the fighting in the region of Nord-Pas-de-Calais, which due to the severe devastation earned the name 'Hell in the North'. Among many destroyed villages and cities, Arras, like Reims and Verdun, was designated a martyr city. The cemetery occupies 27 hectares and contains 19,000 individual graves and the remains of 22,970 unidentified bodies, making it the largest necropolis in France. Two main buildings dominate the cemetery: a lantern tower designed in 1925 by French architect Louis-Marie Cordonnier and a basilica erected in 1937 inspired by the longstanding reputation of the location as a site of religious pilgrimage.[8]

To mark the centenary of the First World War, the Nord-Pas-de-Calais Regional Council and the Lens-Liévin Metropolitan District decided to redevelop this long-standing site of memory. The plan included improving the access road to the cemetery, starting at the bottom of the ridge in the commune of Souchez, and creating a museum memorial annex to the soldiers killed in the region of Artois and Flanders during the war, regardless of their nationality. The redevelopment plans were part of a state-supported regional programme entitled 'Trails of Memory in Nord-Pas-de-Calais' and dedicated to the commemoration of the First World War.[9] The programme consists of four trails intended to

[8] The lantern is 52m high, with a viewing gallery at the top, and radiates light up to a distance of 70km. The base of the tower houses an ossuary-crypt with the remains of 6,000 soldiers and a chapel of rest containing 32 coffins, including the unknown soldiers mentioned above. The tower also contains coil and ashes from the concentration camps of the Second World War. From the eighteenth century onwards 'Notre Dame de Lorette' or 'Our Lady of Lorette' refers to a small private chapel that used to stand on the location in 1794.

[9] The international memorial at Notre Dame de Lorette is supported by the Ministere délégué aux Anciens Combattants and is erected on land given to the Nord-Pas-de-Calais Region by the Ministry of Defence.

reconstruct significant routes and connect key points from the conflict.[10] The site, along with the Menin Gate, the Wellington Quarry and several others, is part of the trail that follows the former front line. The memorials closest to Notre Dame de Lorette are the Canadian National Memorial at Vimy, the German Military Cemetery at Maison-Blanche in Neuville-Saint-Vaast, and the British cemetery at Cabaret Rouge in Souchez. The latter can actually be seen from the hill of Notre Dame de Lorette and from the memorial itself.

The memorial was envisioned as a unique project, situated adjacent to the existing cemetery that commemorates 600,000 dead soldiers. The associated museum is dedicated to the history of the war, with an emphasis on the Nord-Pas-de-Calais region, and is located at the foot of the hill. A small-scale architectural competition launched in 2011 resulted in two proposals being chosen: Pierre-Louis Faloci's design for the museum and Philippe Prost's design for the memorial.[11] The museum, officially called Lens' 14–18 – Centre d'Histoire Guerre et Paix, aims to provide an atmosphere of silence and meditation and has a rather heavy appearance due to the materials employed: black steel, brute concrete, dark granite and dark wood (Figure 5.1). In addition to the museum's exhibition, organized in seven thematically distinct areas that aim to explain the chronology of the war, it also contains a commemorative room for the dead named in the 'Ring of Memory' ('L'Anneau de la Mémoire').

Although many doubts were raised during construction about whether such a structure was needed in the first place, particularly in an area abundant in graveyards and memorials dedicated to the war, the Ring of Memory drew considerable interest from its very inception. Its inauguration in November 2014 was widely reported in the Western media, with most critics sharing the view that it represents a valuable asset in the landscape of war memorialization listing together, as it does, the names of all fallen combatants by name but without nationality. One commentator added the memorial 'nicely combine[s] the informality, the order, and the darkness of those British, French and German cemeteries. Without cliché or ponderous symbolism, it thoughtfully opens a different

[10] 'Chemins de mémoire en Nord-Pas-de-Calais', or 'Trails of Memory', consists of four routes named respectively: 'The Allies' logistics base on the Channel coast'; 'The Front'; 'Post-war reconstruction'; and 'The war of movement and the first German occupation'. See www.remembrancetrails-northernfrance.com, last accessed 9 January 2015.

[11] See Pierre-Louis Faloci, 'The architect's point of view', Struthof: Site of the former Natzweiler concentration camp, available at www.struthof.fr/en/the-european-centre/the-creation-of-the-cerd/the-architects-point-of-view, last accessed 7 June 2015.

Figure 5.1 War and Peace History Centre Lens' 14–18 (2015), Souchez; Pierre-Louis Faloci.
Photo: Author

perspective on the war.'[12] In 2016 the project received the European Award for Urban Public Space as one of the most valuable architectural projects in France in recent years. Here is the language of that award:

> The International Memorial of Notre-Dame-de-Lorette is a monument imbued with pacifism. Its oval shape set over the landscape brings old enemies together in a fraternal, unitary embrace. Inside the gallery, the alphabetical order of their names proclaims the same brotherhood, while the focusing of views towards the empty central space is an invitation to reflect on the folly of so many deaths. Finally, the precariousness suggested by the cantilevered section is a reminder of the fragility of European peace. The 'Ring of Memory' returns from the past loaded with wise warnings for the present and future.[13]

Morphology

Architect Philippe Prost and his design team strove to give expression to the notion of peace and memory for all those who died fighting for their country in this region. These fallen soldiers are now reunited in what the

[12] Rowan Moore, 'Notre Dame de Lorette international memorial review: a different perspective', *The Guardian*, 2 November 2014, available at www.theguardian.com/artanddesign/2014/nov/02/notre-dame-de-lorette-international-memorial-review, last accessed 9 May 2017.

[13] *'Ring of Memory': International Memorial of Notre-Dame-de-Lorette, Ablain-Saint-Nazaire (France), 2014: SPECIAL MENTION 2016*, www.publicspace.org/works/-/project/j222-ring-of-memory-international-memorial-of-notre-dame-de-lorette, last accessed 27 May 2019.

Figure 5.2 'Ring of Memory' (2014), Souchez; Philippe Prost.
Photo: Author

designers called 'posthumous fraternity'.[14] This idea is clearly visualized in the initial sketches, which depict human figures holding hands and forming a circle. This form seemed logical to the designers, since they considered it the most representative of unity and eternity. The circular form also refers to the idea of eternity being outside distinctions of nationality, rank and religion.

The circle has a dual character, derived from the strong separation of outside from inside and public from semi-public. The 'public' side consists of a facade constructed from 122 segments of special industrial concrete in dark grey, which, according to the designers, is the colour of war. The facade is mostly closed, except for a few openings. In complete contrast, the interior is a light space opening towards the sky. This enclosed 'semi-public' space is made from 500 reflective, stainless metal sheets, faceted in such a way that they resemble the pages of a book (Figure 5.2). In a custom-designed typeface, 579,606 names are engraved lightly into

[14] Philippe Prost, 'Mémorial international de Notre-Dame-de-Lorette. Construction d'un mémorial aux soldats tombés dans le Nord-Pas de Calais au cours de la Première guerre mondiale' (September 2014). A plaque at the entrance to the memorial reads: 'This memorial was erected in a peaceful Europe in memory of a terrible tragedy which devastated a generation of young men, who for the most part could read and write.'

these copper-toned panels.[15] To make it easier for visitors to find a name, they are listed in alphabetical order with a large capital letter indicating the start of the list for that letter. Hailing from 40 countries, including former colonies, the names are presented without rank or nationality.[16] Space has been created after each letter to make it possible to add more names in the future as human remains keep being discovered in the area. During the design process, the names were perceived as an augmentation of the idea of unity. Arranged in alphabetical order, they progress across the surface of the memorial to evoke the symbolic notion of an endless human chain of brotherhood.

Another defining feature of the memorial is the horizontality of the composition, which was deliberately chosen to contrast with the taller buildings of the existing cemetery, notably the lantern. Since the memorial is spatially juxtaposed with the lantern, visible on the ground plan, the decision to contrast the two seems sensible. Accordingly, the section of the memorial facing the lantern is anchored to the ground. In fact, two-thirds of the memorial's perimeter is fixed to the ground and one third designed as an overhang. This reaffirms the notion of duality which pervades the design. Perceiving the memorial as 'a weightless space between heaven and earth', the anchored part was meant to create a sense of balance whilst the overhang suggests the fragility of peace (Figure 5.3).[17] The tension between the earthly and the divine, between peace and horror, is clearly visible in the memorial's materialization which augments that duality. In 2015 an explanation for the project's nomination for one of the most prestigious architectural awards, EUMiesAward, emphasized the innovative use of ultra-high-performance fibre and reinforced concrete as construction materials as an effective way to 'resist the passage of time' and guarantee 'transmission to future generations'.[18]

The overhang accounts for 56 of the 328 m of the complete perimeter, with several openings that offer a panoramic view over the Artois valley where a number of heavy battles were fought during the First World War.

[15] Graphic designer Pierre di Sciullo created a skinny font that would be suitable for listing numerous names.

[16] There are 241,214 British soldiers named on the monument (the highest number for any country), 173,876 Germans and 106,012 French soldiers. The list begins with Aa Tet, a soldier from French Indochina. Certain names repeat in great numbers, for example there are 30 men named William Williams and 72 called Karl Schmidt.

[17] Author's translation of the original French: 'En s'élançant à l'assaut de l'horizon, le Mémorial crée un espace en apesanteur, entre ciel et terre.'

[18] Notre Dame de Lorette International Memorial, EUMiesAward, available at http://miesarch.com/work/562, last accessed 9 May 2017.

Figure 5.3 'Ring of Memory' (2014), Souchez; Philippe Prost.
Photo: Author

It is possible to enter the memorial at two points. The main access point is located opposite the entrance to the old cemetery, but it is also possible to enter beneath the overhang. Both entrances symbolically recall battlefield trenches. The official entrance slopes downwards in the form of a passage-way with the word 'peace' inscribed in different languages on perforated metal plaques (Figure 5.4). The 'unofficial' entrance under the overhang climbs towards the centre of the circle.

The interior of the memorial is lit by a custom-designed 'great lamp', 'La Grande Veilleuse', installed at the bottom of the panels. This creates a dynamic effect by being programmed to move along the lists of names and to project stronger light on a few panels in sequence. To emphasize the central lawn sloping towards the overhang, attention has been paid to the flora at the memorial, designed by David Besson-Girard, with poppies, blewits and forget-me-nots.

Performance

From the Lens' 14 – 18 museum, the road to the memorial climbs the hill upon which the cemetery and memorial are situated and is lined with several freestanding panels depicting the faces of soldiers and their war-time surroundings (Figure 5.5). Juxtaposed with the present landscape, these panels offer a good impression of the devastation the area suffered in the conflict. They also serve as an introduction to the memorial at the top of the hill.

Figure 5.4 'Ring of Memory' (2014), Souchez; Philippe Prost.
Photo: Author

Figure 5.5 Ascending road towards the 'Ring of Memory' (2014), Souchez.
Photo: Author

For the visitor approaching on foot, a footpath starting on the left-hand side of the road leads towards the overhang of the new memorial. This route cannot be taken by motor vehicles. The first impressions of visiting motorists are influenced by an existing sculptural monument standing in front of the official entrance to the cemetery and memorial. Continuing towards the cemetery, the uncanny dark structure which initially seems to function as a background to the existing monument now reveals its curving form. The dark facade of the circular memorial seems to protrude from the ground, and does indeed contrast with the older buildings and the cemetery across the road. The curving facade leads to the entrance of the memorial. Descending the sloping path, a glimpse of the interior attracts the visitor.

The widely used kinaesthetic method of descending underground, as previously discussed in relation to cemeteries, is a common feature of First World War memorials. It is used to communicate the notion of trench warfare; it is also to be found at Tyne Cot cemetery, for instance. The Ring of Memory asserts this idea quite literally by using terracotta in the entrance passageway to refer to the colour of earth. In this way, the transition of entering the ring is made explicit and affective.

The design inevitably invites comparison with the Vietnam Veterans War Memorial. Firstly, both rely on alphabetical lists of the fallen. In their claim to textuality, then, both are structures of memory and death. Secondly, they share similar choices of materials: dark and heavy to represent war; reflective architecture to facilitate self-reflection. Thirdly, both are anchored into the ground and assume a visitor-embracing spatial design.

At the same time, however, these two memorials differ significantly in their configuration of architectural space. Even their use of lists of the dead have different purposes. Where Lin's memorial nurtures emotion with the names of men who are still part of the living memory of that particular war, the Notre Dame de Lorette memorial deals with a memory devoid of living witnesses. Perhaps it was this passage of time that enabled the possibility of memorializing enemies in the same shared space. This is certainly one feature which makes this memorial distinct from any other.

The architecture augments this. In its horizontality and dark exterior appearance, the memorial stands in complete visual contrast to the existing cemetery. Observed from the latter, it seems almost invisible, an unobtrusive backdrop.[19] Nonetheless, the circular form remains a strong presence, particularly if approached from the overhang. In its sheer scale, the memorial recalls French revolutionary architects and their quest for the architecture of the sublime. Here again, not unlike many other memorial spaces, a sense of thrill is created by the overhang, the danger of which is contrasted with the pleasure caused by the sublimity of the inner ring and

[19] On verticality and horizontality in commemorative architecture see Winter, *War beyond Words*, pp. 143–71.

the landscape. The same principle, for example, can be found in the entrance of Risiera di San Sabba.

The memorial's purpose complements the cemetery as part of the established route of memory, and visitors seem to pay equal attention to both old and new memorials. By serving as a sort of exploded catalogue of the names of all these soldiers, who presumably died nearby, the memorial recalls Chris Burden's *The Other Vietnam Memorial* – although only in the sense that it catalogues the names of 'the others'. In Burden's memorial these 'others' are known and unknown civilians, whereas in Prost's design they are combatants. The question of whether to incorporate the names of civilian victims from the many villages destroyed during the First World War into existing memorials thus remains an open one, and that is likely to be the case for some time.

Notwithstanding the potentially difficult issue of including civilian names, Prost's memorial is a poetic space which does indeed accentuate ideas of brotherhood and humanity by the simple gesture of bringing together the names of enemies. On a sunny day, the space is even more poignant as rays of sunshine reflect on the 'golden pages'. The space evokes Frank Lloyd Wright's inscription on the Blue Sky Mausoleum: 'A burial facing the open sky, the whole could not fail of noble effect.' At the same time, the memorial demonstrates the scale of the tragedy. This is pressed home by several plates which bear just one surname. This specific detail calls to mind the uniformity of numbers defining the New England Holocaust memorial in Boston.

After visiting the memorial and cemetery, one leaves by the same road. The photographic impressions of the devastated landscape inevitably resonate more strongly now that one realizes the scale of loss. Once again, the distinctive features which constitute the spatial elements of a cemetery burial ritual, as discussed in Chapter 2, are clearly distinguishable. For example, the path of initiation or way of approach to the memorial becomes the path of realization when leaving it. In the process of recalling and understanding this particular memory, the memorial serves as an experiential room with a transitional character.

5.2 Remembrance Park 14–18

Context and History

The commemoration in the province of West Flanders focused on the so-called 'frontzone' or Flanders Fields – an area approximately 60 kilometres long and ten kilometres wide, and specific in the context of the fracture of

Belgian commemorative practices. In 2002 the government of West Flanders decided to coordinate its tourist, cultural and educational war commemoration efforts in a provincial network 'Oorlog en Vrede in de Westhoek' ('War and Peace in the Westhoek'), fully devoted to 'learning from the War' and arguing that 'the story of the war' needs to be 'adjusted to a justified remembrance and an obvious peace message'.[20]

For the centenary of First World War, the Belgium Government planned several national commemorative events with international scope, and recognized that it is fitting that Belgium will 'play a central role in the centenary commemorations' due to its important role in the conflict.[21] With the promotion of peace as the main focus of the project, various events were planned on both local and international levels.

The same logic governed the Flemish Government's 100 Year Great War (2014–18) initiative. Its objectives were to commemorate the centenary in an appropriate and serene manner; to bring Flanders international visibility through reinforcement of the 'peace theme' or 'vredesthema'; and to make the present and future generations in Flanders aware of issues such as tolerance, intercultural dialogue and international understanding, with a view to creating an open and tolerant society with an active international orientation. Special attention was devoted to remembrance tourism at heritage sites. The overarching objective was to preserve and maintain the heritage of the First World War. In the national context, the project was met with scepticism, particularly by Belgian historians who fear scientific historiography being marginalized for the sake of fashionable tendencies in contemporary memory culture. These concerns were underlined in a 2011 report on First World War commemoration in Flanders published by the Flemish Peace Institute:

> Due to the institutional framework and the financing structures, this is now inevitably an unequivocal Flemish project. This not only creates tensions with the Belgian historical reality of 1914–1918. It could also lead to poor forms of remembrance education. The Flemish project '2014–18' could indeed easily become guided by ideological and political objectives. The danger exists that concrete projects and initiatives will be used intentionally to strengthen Flemish identity. This will reveal itself in the selection of projects and initiatives that will be financed. This is a

[20] https://brussels-express.eu/agenda/commemorations-of-the-100th-anniversary-of-first-world-wars-armistice/, last accessed 27 May 2019.

[21] www.be14-18.be/en.

problem because this will mean that the past will be manipulated (explicitly) to use it for contemporary political objectives.[22]

Notwithstanding this, in order to 'embed the Great War's heritage in a sustainable and permanent manner', the Flemish Government developed a four-track strategy.[23] As part of the third development track referred to as 'management', a design assignment entitled Remembrance Park 2014–2018 (Herinneringspark 2014–2018) was envisioned to 'evoke and commemorate the immense drama of the "Bloody Fields of Flanders"'.[24] Its aim was to clarify a vision of an integrated and comprehensive cultural tourism project in the region of the Westhoek. The open call brief specifically underlined that the project is imagined as

(1) a source of modern-day remembrance: adding its 'own' distinctive layer and providing a lasting, international anchoring point for remembrance and commemoration of the First World War in Flanders;
(2) an explanation: the aim is to inform visitors through experience and perceptions, in an educational way in multimedia form, about what happened 100 years ago in the Westhoek;
(3) a link: the project is based on clear identification and its own profile, linking the various physically and spatially graded 'destinations' of the tourist circuit. The story line will be written by outlining characteristic points of perception (including the references), with unity in the way the material is dealt with, its shape and form, signposting, and so on.

The project, however, was conceived already in 2008 when an open call was published on the initiative of then Flemish Government architect Marcel Smets. Out of 72 submissions, the commissioner – the Flemish Government in consultation with the government architect – selected five

[22] Report of panel discussion 3, 'Lessen uit het verleden?', Study day '100 jaar Groote Oorlog. Erfgoed, herdenking en herinnering', Brussels, 16 June 2011, quoted in English in Van Alstein, *The Great War Remembered*, p. 27.

[23] The first track concerns research into the architectural, landscape and archaeological heritage of the First World War to establish a scientific basis. The second deals with the traditional protection and spatial integration of a selection of war heritage. The third track comprises a management vision in terms of the restoration, maintenance and opening up of war heritage. The fourth, finally, underscores the importance of war heritage by pursuing UNESCO World Heritage recognition for the most important relics. See *The Great War Centenary (2014–2018)*, available at www.fdfa.be/sites/default/files/atoms/files/2015_The_Great_War_Centenary_0.pdf.

[24] See the project description, available at www.vlaamsbouwmeester.be/nl/nieuws/open-oproep-herinneringspark-2014-2018-op-kruissnelheid, last accessed 27 May 2019.

multidisciplinary teams to translate the commission task into an intelligent and integrated design proposal. Each team delivered proposals within the directives focused on the First World War landscape as the unifying factor of the 'war narrative' and crucial for understanding this historical episode today.

After a jury, under the direction of the Flemish Master Builder at the time, viewed these submissions in 2011, a concept design developed by a Dutch–Belgian design team, a temporary association of offices and professionals known as TV Park 14–18, was selected for its seeming simplicity and profound approach to strengthening important landscape sites and their connections in space. The team was led by Jeroen Geurst of Geurst & Schulze architects based in The Hague, and Lodewijk Baljon, landscape architects from Amsterdam, and was assisted by scenographer Terenja van Dijk from Antwerp, urban planner Jan de Graaf, also from The Hague, anthropologist Johan Meire from Halle and urban planning professor Pieter Uyttenhove of Ghent University.[25] The initiator of the association, Geurst was at the time deeply involved with research of Lutyens' First World War cemeteries and in fact promoted the idea of an architectural commemorative project even before the official call for the design of the Remembrance Park.[26]

The proposal included Belgian, British and German war territories with both the front zone and the areas behind the former front line. While the area of no-man's land constituted the backbone of the project, the concept design abounded in a variety of possible solutions for improving the existing situation in order to enhance the experience of both the war's architectural heritage and the landscape. In a following stage of the development of the concept, the province of West Flanders and municipalities of the districts of Nieuwpoort, Diksmuide, Ypres, Zonnebeke and Heuvelland were closely involved in the drafting of the Remembrance Park 2014–18 masterplan.

Morphology

A central argument for selecting the winning concept design was that the proposal was realistic since it offered a deep insight into the planning context and the existing infrastructure, and it treated each location

[25] The other finalists were (1) PROAP / D-RECTA, (2) TV NERO / Denis Dujardin, (3) STOSS Inc., (4) SumResearch / A2D Architects / Haley Sharpe Design / TWBA. See www.vlaamsbouwmeester.be/nl/nieuws/open-oproep-herinneringspark-2014-2018-op-kruissnelheid.

[26] Interview with Jeroen Geurst, 5 July 2017.

(the plan includes approximately 40 sites in Flanders) with a specifically tailored design solution. It was agreed by the Flanders Foreign Affairs Department that the proposal was in line with the expectations of all parties involved.

Treating the existing landscape as a 'spatially layered phenomenon',[27] the concept for the Remembrance Park was refined into three existing morphological elements: the central no-man's land, the front line, and focal points such as towers and existing monuments. Essentially, the proposal is a landscape design with a goal set to emphasize the importance of landscape during the war and to highlight a network of existing relics and sites, currently unrelated or only vaguely connected. This was done within a general framework based on a subtle and respectful approach to the ambiguity of the existing landscape, considered as the enduring and authentic material witness of war. Therefore, major scenic sites were given greater prominence and new network connections were carefully embedded in the existing context.

The design team posited that to add something contrasting in terms of structure to the existing narrative would be to work against the process of remembering through physical space. Thus, abjuring bold interventions, designers looked at existing cemeteries but also at various contemporary land art projects. Cemeteries were appreciated for their significance during the war and in its aftermath as the most tangible site of omnipresent and overwhelming mourning. Their existence in the present context was assigned a role of 'green churches in the landscape and the landscape as a cathedral of remembrance with the sky as a dome' – a direct reference to Lutyens' 1917 letter to his wife in which he described the post-war landscape as a 'milky way' created by numerous cemeteries.[28] At the same time, the team proposed to 'clean all the elements that disturb gaining of knowledge, empathy and reflection'. Remarking that the existing situation does not contribute to a meaningful representation, since the importance of many relicts and memorial sites are lessened by 'messy and frugal' representation, the design team was set to have each location 'improved' through a specifically tailored scenography.[29]

After mapping the given situation with all the locations included, a general plan emerged resembling a sky map with constellations. Thus the 'constellation' was derived from the existing network of locations

[27] TV Park 14–18, concept plan 'Herrineringspark 2014–2018' for the 'Open Oproep 1601 D', 24 February 2010, p. 12.

[28] Interview with Geurst. [29] TV Park 14–18, concept plan, p. 32.

Figure 5.6 'Remembrance Park 2014–18' design concept (2012).
© BALJON landscape architects and Geurst & Schulze architects

(including intangible artefacts of war referred to as a 'constellation of relics') and locations that have been added by the design team. Striving towards a unifying spatial coherence, they numbered the distinctive nodes within this spatial constellation according to their altitude, thus emphasizing the invaluable strategic significance of hills in warfare. These also coincide with existing war relics, for example bunkers, craters or trenches but also cemeteries and existing monuments. The clearest signalization of a particular node point is the so called 'information box' where one can learn about the historical significance of the site. Depending on the specificities of each location, a scale of design intervention varies from simple rearrangement and addition of pathways to significantly more intricate spatial undertakings (Figure 5.6). The goal always remained to generate a unifying landscape with a scenography that creates possibilities for better understanding and a clearer perception of the war in relation to the landscape. Nodes on the map also stand for places where scenography reaches an apex in influencing the visitor by reinforcing the experience through didactic and spatial stimuli.

The notion of scenography was set forth as an essential component in the proposal's determination to reinforce the area with as little intervention as possible to provide a scenic and informative experience for visitors. Modest interventions in the area, such as strengthening of key landscape structures, opening up of sight lines, construction of paths, establishment of uniform signage and introduction of didactic content are all aimed at providing a better understanding of the war and the importance of landscape in the front region. One design goal was to create a scenography that would cogently respond to a specific historical situation in a non-obtrusive and stimulating way. For example, attention was also paid to transitory sequences in preparing a visitor for a graveyard experience. Aiming to bring to the fore the authenticity of the memorial landscape, scenographic means such as vistas, panoramas and routes were developed to accentuate particularities of the area and assorted remains – still embedded in the landscape. As examples of successful scenography, Woodland and Larchwood cemeteries were considered. In addition, two arguments were brought forth: (1) that the scenography is directed towards 'new forms of rituals and remembrance' and (2) that future scenarios such as sustainable developments, agriculture and new infrastructure can be integrated into the present war scenery.[30] One of the ways of developing 'new forms and rituals' is to allow visitors to decide their own route, which differs strongly from the current arrangement in which tourists are more or less directed to visit the site according to a schedule. In practice, the visiting experience to a specific location is imagined in the following sequences:

- On arrival upon parking, distanced from the relics, visitors are offered condensed information about the site.
- No-man's land is marked with an observation post at which an embedded smartphone code gains further information for those who use it.
- In most scenarios, the visit continues via carefully designed pathways and along a relict (including cemetery and monuments), viewpoint, or a panorama photograph.
- At the end, a place for contemplation and reflection is provided (Figure 5.7).

This order clarifies how a scenography that is at the same time withdrawn and present derives from the principle of giving precisely the right dose of information and experience. Locations are interconnected, as visualized on the concept map, and each of several linear connections represent a thematic journey that visitors are able to take and tailor to their preference.[31] Hence, visitors can decide whether to follow, for example, a path that narrates a story, indicates morphological features of the landscape or retraces the former front lines.

[30] Ibid., p. 36.

[31] Possible themes are: the still war with inundation, front lines, no man's land, 'moving war' with the Battle of Passchendaele, the battle scene, the Spring Offensive and its end, the hinterland medical care, camps and cemeteries. TV Park 14–18, concept plan, p. 44.

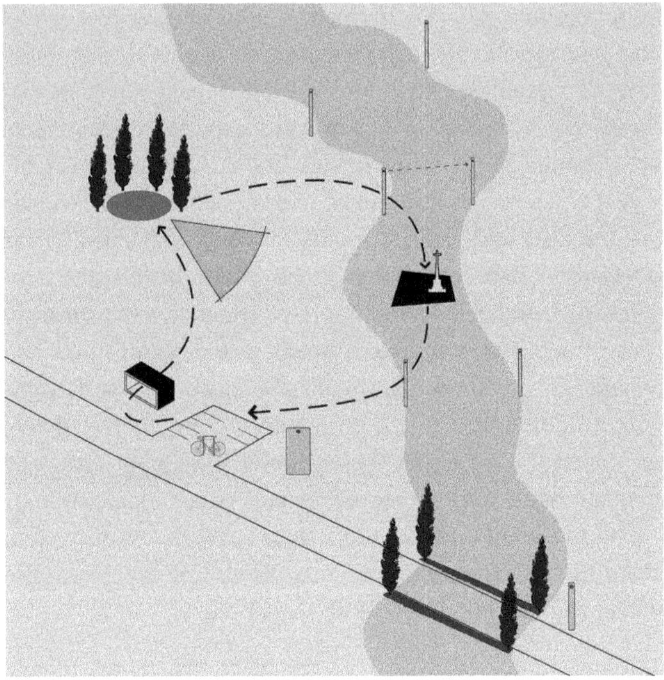

Figure 5.7 'Remembrance Park 2014–18' design concept (2012).
© BALJON landscape architects and Geurst & Schulze architects

To make the proposed connections legible, three strategic landscape interventions were planned: forestation, water retention and lane plantings with Italian poplars. These were designed in an integrated way with the existing situation and landscape preservation. For example, poplar alleys are angularly positioned to follow demarcations of former front lines and to accentuate the positions of graveyards, but they stop at no-man's land. In this way, they indicate the difference in landscape and thereby the infrastructure of war. In addition, sustainable urbanization demands were to be met by a strategy that imagined improved conditions for the natural development of the site.

After the selection procedure and with the collaboration of the involved municipalities, a masterplan appeared in 2012. Here the principal strategy was developed in detail with design solutions for every site. In the textual explanation, a clear distinction was underlined between the existing First World War remembrance parks in the region and the Remembrance Park in terms of size and specificity of the area. While other parks such as Verdun, Vimy and Chemin des Dames contain well-preserved landscapes and concentrated commemorative structures, the Remembrance Park is different in both its scale and in the profound architectural reconstruction that took place here. In fact, an often-encountered comment is that reconstruction in the area was performed so well as to render the new buildings more historical than they actually were.[32] The issue was addressed with a design strategy to make these interventions clearly visible in the structure of the area by marking the reconstructed infrastructure and with changes that occurred in the course of time, for example disappeared channel slots, as well with the addition of relevant orientation points in the panorama to aid orientation in the space.

As announced, the designers treated some locations with minimalistic intervention, for example clearing the overgrown flora to open up the view towards the landscape. In this way, the existing commemorative structures are intended to be integrated with the contemporary situation and not solely isolated as historical objects. Next to the existing four viewpoints, eleven additional viewpoints were added, accompanied with a panoramic photograph, panorama-table and a sitting place. A smaller number of observation towers was also added next to the existing ones. Windmills too were strategic observation posts during the war with only a few originals still standing today. The proposal used their positions to place viewpoints overgrown with creeper plants to symbolically refer to the cessation of combat on 11 November 1918. Additional vertical signs such as pylons are inserted to serve as orientation points, but also to mark roads leading to Passchendaele where, in 1917, front lines changed in a 'war of senseless movements'.[33] Other elements of the design such as parking facilities, signalization and information content are presented in rigorous detail, often with a prospective proposition for possible future developments. With an eye for local materials and existing forms, public furniture is designed to correspond with its environment and is thus proposed as minimalistic, but contemporary and utilitarian. In their materialization and aesthetics, architectural features of the design reference Lutyens' abstracted classicism, and at the same time refer to contemporary elements. For example, information boards are plain white stone 'tablets' marked by a red poppy.

[32] Interview with Lodewijk Baljon, 28 March 2017, Amsterdam. One of the TV Park team members, Prof. Dr. Uyttenhove, has conducted research at Labo S – the urbanism laboratory at Ghent University – on the current policy on the heritage of the reconstruction architecture and urbanism.

[33] TV Park 14–18, 'Masterplan Herinneringspark 2014–18', Vlaamse Overheid, Onroerend Erfgoed, January 2012, p. 39.

Figure 5.8 'Remembrance Park 2014–18' design concept (2012).
© BALJON landscape architects and Geurst & Schulze architects

The level of detail of each location design varies from final worked-out proposal to conceptual suggestion. While some locations are highly detailed, others are treated conceptually as design suggestions for future developments. For example, a crater known as the 'Pool of Peace' (*de Spanbroekmolenkrater*) at Heuvelland is represented as a detailed proposal with landscape solutions set to improve the visibility and connections and offer a place for reflection, whereas locations at Kemmelberg and Scherpenberg in the same area are treated with landscape design suggestions believed to improve the quality of the experience (Figure 5.8).

The area of Diksmuide, characterized by its open polder landscape with a demarcated inundation zone, contains a combination of several detailed proposals as well as conceptual ones. Here the location of the Yser tower monument, for example, is freed from parking and tourist buses to create more 'breathing space' for the monument and the adjacent crypt to be experienced. Next to this, walkways are designed in such a way as to refer to the war symbolically and in literary terms. The existing memorials are coupled with a minimalist landscape memorial, in reference to the VVM. Along the partially submerged border of the site, indicated by double lines of ash tree plantings, runs a wall containing the names of 47,500 Belgian dead. Here one is led into a secluded realm where it is possible to focus on the names and be aware of the very soil in which these men rest. The contested history of the Yser tower was not taken into the account. The site was even considered to be of marginal importance for the overall plan.

One site of specific interest was the location of the unfinished structure of the A19 highway. The construction of the highway was stopped due not only to the proximity of existing cemeteries and discovery of the earthly remains of soldiers and equipment that had been discovered in the process, but also in response to protests – which had started after a BBC documentary on Ypres and the First World War – opposing any further destruction

Figure 5.9 'Remembrance Park 2014–18' design concept (2012).
© BALJON landscape architects and Geurst & Schulze architects

of the area for the purposes of new infrastructure or development. One of the lead designers of the team argued that this site should be part of the focus of the centenary commemoration as a symbolic manifestation of the power of remembrance – a place where the heritage of war (both visible and hidden) literally overpowers forces that neglect it (Figure 5.9).[34]

The very entrance to the Remembrance Park – the Ganzepoot area with its famous King Albert monument – also received special attention due to its strategic position in the region. Looking back at the historical photographs and the significance of the location during the war, we can see the design adhered to the strategy of clearing up the overgrown areas, introducing connecting roads and improving traffic infrastructure to gain clearance and visibility of the architectural heritage and the landscape. In addition, a new visitor centre was planned to offer in-depth information and improve the visitor experience.

Performance

Approaching the open call with a strategic conceptual plan, rather than a definitive masterplan, proves an invaluable way to address the complex task of commemorating the First World War. In fact, the five shortlisted proposals adopted this strategy to a certain extent. All proposals addressed the existing landscape as a palimpsest with a contemporary intervention representing an added layer to its intricate structure. Similarly, the proposals explored ways to provide visitors with diverse possibilities to experience the landscape and the architectural heritage. A careful balancing would be struck between orchestrated spatial directives and space without many obvious constrictions where the personal preferences of the visitor came first. This approach is supported by expert studies that argue for an

[34] Interview with Geurst.

inclusive commemoration where 'visitors are encouraged to "read" and interpret the heritage to understand what message is conveyed by a monument or memorial.'[35]

One of the five finalists, the PROAP group, relied strongly on free spatial arrangements without instructive design interventions. They argued that time is the 'sculptor of the landscape', and proposed no prefixed pathways whatsoever, but observed the landscape exactly as it is, introducing mainly artistic interventions to enable the visitor to develop an intimate connection with the historical meaning of the place.[36] The proposal is based on emphasizing the historical distance from the First World War, and the subsequent oblivion, through rebuilding – stressing the use and impact of time. Rather than integrating or superimposing a new layer onto the existing landscape to make the past visible again, the design instead aims to add new meaning using 'art as an efficient tool for creating emotional attachment to the physical space'.[37] Hence, the predetermined scenography and the didactic aspect are in the background – if they exist at all. This logic, in fact, echoes some of the efforts of artists preoccupied with the problematic nature of representing war a century ago, such as Brâncuşi, who designed a memorial in the Romanian city of Târgu-Jiu.[38] Brâncuși grappled with the complexity of post-war commemoration in a tripartite ensemble: the Endless Column (a 30-metre-high column of zinc and brass-clad cast-iron modules threaded onto a steel spine), the Gate of the Kiss, and the Table of Silence. The three parts of the memorial create a 2km-long processional path that commemorates Romanian soldiers who died defending Târgu-Jiu against German forces in 1916. Stretching from the adjacent River Jiu, situated at the edge of the town and along which the young men died in their valiant defense, the abstracted composition demarcates a sacred place that suggests the journey from this life to the next. Similarly, PROAP's proposal advocates sensory-enhancing insertions that are abstractly inviting with the purpose of offering an incentive for personal connection with the space. Hence meaning derives primarily from the visitor experience and personal associations made.

35 Van Alstein, *The Great War Remembered*, p. 69.

36 See 'Herinneringspark', PROAP, www.proap.pt/project/herinneringspark-1, last accessed 27 May 2019.

37 Ibid.

38 The project was commissioned by the Women's League of Gorj to commemorate a decisive battle for Romanian independence that was fought in the town, defending a bridge across the River Jiu.

Such an approach – refusing to be determined or create any kind of top-down structural scenography – calls us to pause and rethink the ways the First World War is commonly commemorated, particularly the idea of relying solely on design to make clear the time distance between the reality of the war and the reality of here and now. Here the TV Park's winning project, which also explored various possibilities but in a significantly more structured way, might benefit from the qualities of PROAP's design proposal that derive from its strong focus on cognitive aspects and its determination to remain open to various interpretations of history. On the other hand, this somewhat idealistic contemplation of remembrance can easily fail the test of practice in which visitors need clear directions and, at times, clearly defined holding environments.

The Park 14–18 design concept similarly argued that the proposed design interventions, together with commemorative activities, are set to explore the commemorative potential of the landscape as an inescapable environmental reminder – earth as a place where we keep our dead but also as a 'humus', the raw material for regeneration and new life.[39] The Park 14–18 team adopted a research-oriented approach that relied on scientific sources, archival research, fieldwork and interviews with stakeholders. With the bold ambition of making the war tangible and visible in the landscape, they were determined to do this with respect for the heritage, or rather, in the framework of existing networks of relicts and commemoration sites. By focusing on authenticity, one of the goals was to put Flanders Fields on the international map of war tourism.

At the same time, designers acknowledge the fact that visitors will not only reflect on the hundred-year-old history but on contemporary developments too. With the grounded hypothesis that contemporary visitors in most cases have a variety of programmes on their agenda, such as a visit to the beach or a culinary experience, designers embrace the context in its fragmentary structure, arguing that visitors experience 'a fragment of the whole Remembrance park as only a part of the Western Front, which is again only a part of the whole war area'.[40]

To offer a tangible demonstration of their vision, the team focused on 35,000 unknown soldiers whose remains are still unidentified a century after the end of the war. They suggested four types of events to be integrated with the visiting ritual. (1) In Palingbeek a circular place is imagined where visitors can be directly involved with the earth – literally

[39] TV Park 14–18, 'Masterplan', p. 204. [40] Ibid., p. 25. Translation by the author.

digging out samples of earth to take back home. (2) There would be an open-air theatre integrated with the unfinished part of the A19 highway that would invite reflection through musical performance and a view of the landscape. (3) There would also be symbolic kite workshops for children – organized in temporary tents on locations where hospital tents used to stand during the war and marking the centenary of the 'Derde Slag' at Ypres – that would commemorate the unknown dead by

> symbolically freeing them out of the earth and letting them raise into the air in a moment of remembrance that at the same time demonstrates the scale of the death toll of the war and the significance of each individual missing person, but that also creates a moment of beauty and hope.[41]

(4) Finally, they also imagined a musical event performed by German and Belgian musicians on positions that once represented the closest juncture of the front lines to symbolically 'bridge through their music the emptiness of no-man's land'.[42] These imagined activities demonstrate the holistic approach that was likely due to the interdisciplinary character of the team. Members of the team familiar with the context through research and practice indicated the importance of human interaction with earth, for example, in experiencing its sense of place.

The implementation of the masterplan, however, ran into difficulties due to the change in the governmental office and financial autonomy assigned to the municipalities involved. With the project now separated from its initiating organization the next logical step became complicated – assigning supervision to the designers of the project. In the current arrangement, each municipality can decide whether and how to implement the design proposal. So far, only random and partial interventions have taken place, for example in Diksmuide where the area around the Yser tower monument has been remodelled and a new entrance building added. Also, the Westfront Nieuwpoort visitor centre has been added under the King Albert monument containing a gigantic animated Yser-panorama screen. Hill 60, one of the most important relic landscapes in the Ypres Salient, is an example where most of the elements of the masterplan have been implemented, but without any reference to the plan. Instead, design improvements executed in 2015 have been attributed to another architectural office, commissioned by the province and the Commonwealth War Graves. In addition, materialization was pursued in a way that was absolutely avoided in the master design – namely COR-TEN steel. In a

[41] Ibid., p. 205. [42] Ibid.

comparison to the solution offered in the masterplan, the implanted interventions only partially improve the visibility of war landscape and visitor experience.

5.3 Contemporary Commemoration

Fields of battlefield memorials and cemeteries with uniform gravestones powerfully translate the mechanized destruction of men into a palpable reality. However, the palpability of this reality fades with time. There are multiple official efforts today to preserve and perpetuate memory-work for the sake of future generations, just as participating nation-states did a century earlier. Building memorials and finding the most effective ways to memorialize remain relevant ever since Kollwitz's *The Grieving Parents*, Lutyens' Cenotaph and Brâncuşi's Târgu-Jiu memorials – designs emblematic of a transition from glorifying sculptural representation to a mournful lament in which the figure of the heroic soldier is reduced to an abstract form.

In Sarajevo, a three-metre-tall cubic stone installed in front of the city's History Museum bears the inscription: 'Under this stone lies a monument to the victims of War and the Cold War.' Installed as a part of a multidisciplinary initiative entitled De/construction of Monuments and set to rethink the notion of a modern monument,[43] the monument opens a window for inquiry. What is the context? Who are the victims? Is the stone only a sign that indicates the 'real' invisible monument or is it a monument itself? Is there a monument under the stone? In a similar logic, the landscape here is the signifier of the invisible, uncommunicable and vanished war. And here is the point: today we no longer see only the tragedy of war but also its highly nuanced repercussions which reveal curious scars. The landscape itself is a demonstration of this transformative process, as one participant in the commemorative project argued:

> Yet oddly enough, the war was actually also beneficial to nature. Bomb craters, for instance, became beautiful ponds which today provide an ideal habitat for the northern crested newt. The bunkers that once offered

[43] The objective of the initiative was the 'demystification and demythologization of the past, deconstruction of transitional realities in post-socialist, particularly post-Yugoslav countries'. See Dunja Blažević, 'New Monument', Sarajevo Center for Contemporary Art, available at http://scca.ba/scca-projects/deconstruction-of-monument/new-monument, last accessed 27 May 2019.

> protection to soldiers are now excellent shelters for bats. In other places as well, nature has shown its resilience and new life has sprouted from the destruction. We want to keep taking care of this new nature, hence our slogan for the coming years of commemoration: Taking care of Flanders Fields.[44]

Taking care, however, becomes a debatable concept when one is aware of the gruesome death inflicted upon millions of people and the thousands of bodies literally embedded in the contemporary landscape. Similarly, the Ring of Memory at Notre Dame de Lorette is a memorial of names, a burial beneath the open sky, borne by the lasting symbolism of a circular form. Nevertheless, there is a significant difference here from some earlier examples of this form: a small fraction of the circle is not rooted in the ground but suspended in the air as a symbol of the fragility of peace. But this also symbolizes the fragility of memory, countered by the persistence of the societal aspirations to build permanent forms which memorialize. Hypothetically, if the suspended fraction of the Ring of Memory were to break off, the once closed circle could extend its form into an infinite spiral: the persistent need to memorialize. This tension is inherent in memorials and is often clearly depicted in the architectural space; in some cases, this relationship is augmented by physical deterioration, as is the case at the Atocha memorial (discussed in Chapter 3). This memorial demonstrates the fragility of human memory, but the changing appearance caused by the deterioration of its textual component – stripping the space to its mere architectural form, an empty tomb of memory – confirms humankind's ubiquitous craving for sacredness, sanctity and values that are lasting.

If a century ago cemeteries and classical monuments were built to deal with unprecedented destruction, today we need structures attuned to the present that will help us understand existing memorials from our perception of temporality. Likewise, if reconstruction and erasure of the traces of war was a way for farmers, fisherman and citizens to continue living, today we need to understand this too – the reconstruction of destroyed architecture was a way to move forward. Erasing traces of war was a part of remembrance. During a hundred-year span, the process of erasure continued through tourism, agriculture and contemporary infrastructural development. Invariably, remembrance and oblivion continue their intricate relationship. Risks that run parallel to these efforts also need to be considered with every commemorative project. For example, boosting

44 Marleen Evenpoel in *The Great War Centenary (2014–2018)*, p. 34, available at www.fdfa.be/sites/default/files/atoms/files/2015_The_Great_War_Centenary_0.pdf.

tourism through providing infrastructure that allows access to the existing war heritage can potentially endanger sensitive sites such as cemeteries in their originally prescribed capacities. Thus, the legitimate question is whether war heritage (particularly in the Westhoek region) can facilitate new demands in a sustainable way – an answer to which can probably only be given in the future and through in-depth research. Yet, tourism has become a prominent partner and stakeholder in today's revalorization and commoditization of war memories and is clearly one of 'the main vectors in the mutation of former war landscapes to landscaped parks of memories, tourist routes along the front line, museums and places for memorial events', while modelling of emotional tourist experiences has even led to war maps being redesigned for visitors' purposes.[45]

Next to recognizing that tourism has become a driving force in preserving war heritage, what the two case studies above make apparent is that our changing perception on commemoration and the particular history of the First World War requires us to search for memorial spaces contemporary with our own time. Existing memorials and monuments no longer suffice if the intention is to keep the place of commemoration present on tourist maps. Internationalization and regional fragmentation frame the new context. The Ring of Memory and the Remembrance Park are both focused on multiple participating nationalities. This is particularly relevant when one recalls that soldiers from no fewer than 50 modern-day nations were involved in military operations in the Westhoek region. As the war recedes in time and remembrance projects develop within a framework of the European context, we think of tools to make this past tangible again, as these projects demonstrate. New layers are added and imagined as organic evolutions from the memory-work of earlier generations.

For their architectural and landscape qualities, both projects are demonstrations of well-balanced memorial spaces, reminders of the maturity society has reached in its memorialization of the war. This is manifest in the way that national prejudices are overcome to commemorate all participants in the war, something only previously done in the abstract. In this

[45] Myriam Jansen-Verbeke and Wanda George, 'Memoryscapes of the Great War (1914–1918): a paradigm shift in tourism research on war heritage', *Via Tourism Review: International Journal, Multilingual and Interdisciplinary*, 2.8 (2015), available at http://viatourismreview.com/2015/11/varia-art4, last accessed 1 July 2017. Authors point to the important role war museums play in the spatial clustering of touristic visits: the Imperial War Museum is the most frequently visited, followed by the Flanders Field Museum, Historial de la Grande Guerre in Péronne, Memorial Museum Passchendaele 1917, Musée du Chemin des Dames in Oulches-la-Vallée-Foulon and the new Musée de la Grande Guerre in Meaux.

respect, several unique projects took place within the Flanders Fields programme such as the 'GoneWest' four-year artistic initiative with the goal of creating a complete list of all war victims who died in Flanders, civilian and soldier. As part of the project, 600,000 participants moulded clay sculptures representing each of the victims, installed in no-man's land between the front lines surrounding Ypres.[46]

At the same time, even though these projects do not convey any explicit national symbolism, but rather emphasize the trauma of war and the mourning of veterans and surviving relatives, a number of questions remain unanswered. For example, as the memorial that unites all the participants in one common story, has the Ring of Memory simultaneously obliterated the complexity of historiography and multiplicity of stories that have been marginalized for decades, such as the multicultural and colonial aspects of the war? By creating an uplifting memorial space that unites all men in their tragic end, does the memorial serve as a contemporary extension of the immediate post-war national efforts to commemorate their deaths as patriotic sacrifice? Similarly, the apparent unity in the Flemish commemoration project seems to have actually been more nuanced and deeply embedded in local politics as different provinces expressed their own preferences and ideas about how the war should be commemorated.[47]

The architectural craftsmanship needed to carry projects to their conclusion provided supporting design solutions that were the outcome of an interdisciplinary collaboration. The lead designer of the Park 14–18 team even argues that the design would have been less informed and probably less engaging architecturally without the insight and profound contributions of the other team members to the overall discussion when devising the plan.[48] Reconsidering the notion of a park as a spatial formation of storylines that in fact form the given landscape was one of the valuable examples of such cross-disciplinary work.[49] This is promising and useful for future projects in this field.

In a brochure that offers a detailed plan of activities for the centenary, the impetus behind the commemoration project comes into sharper focus through the inclusion of personal views of people involved in the project.

[46] See *Flanders Fields: A Place to Remember* (Brussels: VisitFlanders, Flemish Government, 2015), pp. 28–9, available at www.visitflanders.com

[47] Interview with Geurst. [48] Ibid.

[49] Interview with Prof. Dr. Uyttenhove, 29 June 2017. Uyttenhove refers to routes soldiers and others used during the war, for example trenches, evacuation routes, hospitals and so forth – all of them perpendicular to the front zone.

Reflecting on one particular commemorative initiative, *The Flanders Fields Post* – an English-language one-off newspaper distributed exactly a hundred years after the outbreak of the war – one participant argued:

> We knew from the very start that this could well be the last time we will be able to 'reanimate' the commemoration of the First World War on such a large scale and make people truly realise the sense and nonsense of it. Who knows how long it will take before we remember this episode like we remember the Battle of Waterloo? There are no direct witnesses left and soon our emotional connection to this story may start to fade, as may our natural curiosity about how this war could ever take place and what impact it has on today's society. What we can learn from it today. It is almost an existential question.[50]

While these seem like reasonable concerns, there is no ground to assume that these projects represent one last opportunity to remember and rethink the consequences of the war. On the contrary, these efforts confirm the continued curiosity and emotional connections of family memory that keep remembrance and the European project alive.

Finally, we need to consider the specificity of Flanders, a semi-autonomous region of Belgium, and the complexity and sensitivity of the commemoration in the national context. While Belgian soldiers died here fighting for Belgium, today's Flemish memory activists insist otherwise. Instead, the Flemish dead are now remembered in terms of their sacrifice for the Flemish cause and the formation of Flemish national consciousness.[51] What further complicates the work of remembrance here is the fact that organizations that in the 1920s promoted a peace pilgrimage to Diksmuide, during the Second World War collaborated with the German occupiers. After the 1970s, remembrance focused on private experience and personal stories, an approach also adopted by the In Flanders Fields Museum (IFFM) which opened in 1998 in Ypres – a museum that 'transcends outdated national narratives of allies and enemies', but which works independently of Flemish politics and politicians.[52] Hence 'the problematic morality of war is brought to the foreground precisely by presenting war as

[50] Lea Winkeler in *The Great War Centenary (2014–2018)*, pp. 32–3, available at www.fdfa.be/sites/default/files/atoms/files/2015_The_Great_War_Centenary_0.pdf.

[51] For the historical and political context of Belgium during the First World War, see Sophie De Schaepdrijver, *De Groote Oorlog* (Amsterdam: Atlas, 1999); Jo Tollebeek et al. (eds.), *België, een parcours van herinnering: II. Plaatsen van tweedracht, crisis en nostalgie* (Amsterdam: Bert Bakker, 2008); Karen Shelby, *Flemish Nationalism and the Great War: The Politics of Memory, Visual Culture and Commemoration* (Basingstoke and New York: Palgrave Macmillan, 2014).

[52] Van Alstein, *The Great War Remembered*, p. 16.

a human reality.'[53] Still, there are a few points of concern as the Flemish project remains susceptible to nationalistic aspirations that also strongly rely on the commemoration of the war. What's more, the valorization of war memory landscapes as heritage risks compartmentalization, by which the war is removed from current political aspirations. In addition, the vigorous promotion of a 'war–peace' relationship seems less evident then believed.[54]

[53] Maarten Van Alstein, *From Ypres to Brussels? Europe, Peace, and the Commemoration of WWI* (Brussels: Flemish Peace Institute, 2014), p. 2, available at http://eu.boell.org/sites/default/files/uploads/2014/06/from_ypres_to_brussels.pdf, last accessed 23 August 2017.

[54] Jansen-Verbeke and George, 'Memoryscapes of the Great War'.

Conclusion

In its essence, architecture is a noble concept. Architectural creations are distinguished by their purposefulness. Residential buildings, public buildings or sacred buildings are all designed to fit their call within numerous written and unwritten rules of the profession. Principally, architects design spaces that answer multiple demands. Their success is measured through everyday use and the influence they will have on subsequent production of the built environment. The architecture we live in and encounter is beneficial for us in ways we are only just beginning to understand. Apart from serving a pure utilitarian function, the creation of spaces and forms that are appealing, elevating and impressive has been at the heart of architectural endeavour since ancient times. The concept of the sublime, for example, has continued to fascinate architects, and projects that deal with death and the destruction of life are intrinsic to architecture.

This concept of an architectural project is challenged in the field of memorial architecture – a paradoxical realm where transience meets the permanent. Memorial architecture makes time understandable and history palpable. Here designers have a platform to reflect on the unfathomable concept of memory, identity and human tragedies. Alongside all of this, memorials testify that our demand to know the past goes hand in hand with an expectation that the future will probably be unlike anything we commemorate. As a medium for externalization of memory, memorial spaces are anchored in the past, dedicated to the present and directed towards the future. They aim to support the process of remembering which is Janus-faced as every recollection entails exposure to memories, both hurtful and curative. As materializations of specific memories and histories, memorials share this quality of memory, which brings us to the first question: can contemporary architecture offer meaningful memorial spaces for society and the bereaved?

A rare example where architecture can be purposely created to oppress, harm or destroy is that of memorial spaces. As we have seen in a number of examples, if a traumatic memory needs to be addressed, in most cases designers instinctively incline towards an oppressive aesthetic. Notwithstanding the fact that the importance of reviving, empowering and recovering from traumatic experiences through memorial spaces still needs to be better understood, we can certainly recognize a contemporary tendency towards this aspect in commemorative architecture. Hence, just like memory, architectural spaces can be aggressive and soothing at the same time. Exploring the space between the two opposites is precisely where we can find the potential for the future. For example, Lin's Vietnam Veterans Memorial is a careful balancing act between witnessing trauma and its memorialization in a permanent form that is at once intrusive and organically embedded into the surroundings. This balancing act is crucial to its architectural value. Both official invitations and private efforts in finding architectural solutions to commemorating tragic events have produced a rich spectrum of design concepts with valuable examples that tackle traditional ways of commemorating in general and ways of dealing with difficult pasts in particular. We can certainly learn from the twentieth century's processes of memorial-making and existing knowledge on the psychology of mourning. Indeed, the number of examples discussed demonstrated that buildings and dreams of buildings can survive the impermanence of political and historical constructions. As we have seen, by looking into the rich history of the memorial design genre, we can contemplate and assess how we create war memorials appropriate to our own time of post-national era violence and terrorism.

The commemoration of the First World War was a watershed period. It set the course for the further development of memorial architecture, with numerous memorials and cemeteries built during and after the war. In the face of the enormous loss of human life, designers had to come up with solutions that would address the scale of death, coloured by millions of missing. Commemorative efforts found their expressions in the Tomb of the Unknown Soldier and in battlefield cemeteries, where rows of grave markers evoke the harrowingly sublime. British cemeteries, for instance, organized by the Imperial War Graves Commission, introduced features that strongly influenced future memorial design. These include the alphabetical listing of names of the missing – engraved on the walls of galleries that usually serve as introductory spaces to the actual burial grounds – and Sir Edwin Lutyens' *Stone of Remembrance*. The notion of descending into the ground was also a common characteristic, particularly in artistic depictions of death on the battlefields.

While the commemoration of the First World War focused on military cemeteries and on an aesthetics that was appropriate for soldiers of different nationalities, as well as on monuments that referenced traditional language as a way of making sense of the war, the Second World War presented profound changes and questions about the very meaning of monuments and memorials. Alongside commemorative forms that continued practice from the first war, such as dedicating a tomb to the 'unknown soldier', it was the search for appropriate forms to commemorate civilian victims that yielded innovative architectural solutions. After the trials of Nazi officials brought to light gruesome facts regarding the concentration camps, memorial architecture faced the task of addressing the overwhelming heritage the numbing violence against civilians imposed on our society. To grapple with the impossible, designers developed architecture based on the notion of alienation, and concepts such as negative, voided and wounded space emerged. At the same time, interest in psychological implications and individual responses to memorial spaces started to gain prominence. As a result, there was considerable focus on the interactivity, didactic and curative components of space.

The acceptance of both the Genocide Convention and the Universal Declaration of Human Rights in 1948 gave to memorial projects a transnational normative and educational thrust they had not had before. After the 1970s, memorial museums – Holocaust memorial museums in particular – started proliferating in number, and many memorials incorporated educational content while visitor centres were added to the sites of former concentration camps. In later years many First World War memorials and cemeteries were coupled with information centres: for example, Tyne Cot cemetery, the American cemetery in Normandy, Thiepval and, more recently, the Notre Dame de Lorette cemetery with both the Ring of Memory memorial and the memorial museum. In fact, adding architectural content to existing memorials and memorial cemeteries for the purposes of providing more information in order to offer a deeper insight into, and multiple perspectives of, the events commemorated can now be considered common practice. As the examples explored in this book demonstrate, the traditional monument as a sculptural work, essentially fixed and didactic, over the last century slowly gave way to the new spatial concept – the memorial: an architectural concept focused on participant's experience; to fulfil its purpose (transmit a particular memory or history through supporting experience), the memorial uses designed space and only partially incorporates the didactic (or the traditional sculptural work).

The assumed contemporary obsession with built memorial projects has different contributing factors, but in large part is connected to an upsurge in interest in memory studies in various disciplines, as well as the fact that we live in a victim-oriented society in which the survivors want their experiences and memories to be represented. Memorials, naturally, attract most attention since they are physical, and are meant to be lasting manifestations of memory-work in public. In order to stay relevant, memorialization needs to go through a difficult process of introspection and a re-examination of the context. The logic of counter-monuments, as defined by Young, is a demonstration of this process. In architectural terms, reinvention relates to our perception of space and the issue of 'invisibility' of forms we are accustomed to. This can be translated into other segments of the relationship between people and their built environment: the longer we live in a certain space, the less we see it as it becomes an integral part of our lives. Often, one needs a stranger's inquiry or reflection to make us look at a space or building again. Also, the traditionally unchanging essential qualities of monuments and memorials need to compete with the acceleration of communicational modes and methods. Counter-memorials attempted to be these innovative strangers in memorial architecture, determined to ask us why and how. There have been and still are many counter-memorials in this sense of the term that do the same without being recognized or categorized as a movement, but rather as single attempts to contribute to the evolution of our memorial space. To paraphrase Musil, I would say that there is nothing as present as a memorial when it comes to learning through interaction with space. Encountering, experiencing and learning through memorial spaces incites change that can manifest in an active engagement, as numerous examples have shown and continue to show us. What is more, the great potential of the digital medium and cutting-edge technology can become a great asset to architecture in the task of mediating the past by immersing visitors on many levels. Perhaps, literally, invisibility can be explored and used as a commemorative technique with architecture as a background or even immaterial mnemonic concept.

The more we understand human psychology and the natural world, the stronger the tendency among designers is to create spaces that are beneficial to both. Generally speaking, contemporary designers are looking back at historical examples of vernacular architecture. They are more engaged with context and use biomimicry to design buildings that respond to our ever-changing perceptions and growing knowledge. The same is true for contemporary memorial spaces – a better understanding of the psychology of mourning will inevitably influence their future development.

Indeed, contemporary memorials tend to be experiential, heuristic spaces informed by human progress and open for exploration. They aim to facilitate several functions, the most prominent of which include: creating a material framework for mourners and survivors; affirming collective and individual identities; and offering information and deeper insight into the story they are telling in order to forestall inhumanity. Visiting them has been a continued practice throughout the last hundred years – a confirmation to their relevance and evolution of the symbiotic relationship between spaces of memory and their users. To go back to the questions I asked in the very beginning of this book – whether memorial spaces foster forgiveness of the crimes and help in the recovery from trauma remains a subject of exploration, but there certainly is an indication that they do. What we can state with confidence is that in the face of incomprehensible tragedies, memorials (and the whole endeavour of creating them) provide us with an essential framework to at least address the subject. Having said that does not alter the fact that any acquisition of knowledge and process of recovery from trauma can only begin when there is a shared public interest in doing so. Memorials can only be useful to those who want to engage. What they can do is to be open to the public and inspire curiosity and participation through a synthesis of content and form.

Like cemeteries, then, memorials are spaces of transition between two realms, one of the present, the other belonging to a particular moment in the past. If concerned with the process of mourning and coming to terms with loss, memorials correspond with the 'rites of passage' in funerary practices, namely separation, segregation and integration. As was elaborated in Chapter 2, translated into architectural forms, these stages manifest themselves in three relevant sequential elements: entrance, path and room. The successful implementation of this architectural sequence can enhance the sense of place and create a strong holding environment not only for mourning but also for informing and educating the general public. However, here one has to think about experiencing public spaces for contemplation in memorials – depending on their popularity, other people's presence is unavoidable in public memorials. As a solution, many of these spaces are controlled by a gatekeeper, for instance the 11-M memorial in Madrid, but also the 'Holocaust Tower' in the Jewish Museum in Berlin. To provide the necessary private space, memorials often need to introduce planned constraints.

The process of creating a memorial varies according to the specificities of the social context. However, there are certain common stages we can identify. They include initiation, the design process, realization and effect. The initiation phase is defined by a commissioning body that needs to articulate the purpose of the memorial and lay down a set of requirements. In large part, the purpose of a memorial is defined by the intended visitor group. Depending on whether it is dedicated solely to facilitating the mourning process, or also to educating future generations, or whether it has a touristic purpose as well, the scope of the memorial or museum can be established, and pertinent questions can be answered, for example whether to include didactic content and, if so, to what extent. In order to address these matters in a comprehensive way, the assessing team can only benefit from a multidisciplinary approach: including experts from various relevant disciplines and also, if possible, families of the victims, survivors or other groups affected by the commemorated event. If a memorial is planned to be built in a dense urban context, commissioners certainly need to think about what changes will occur in the civic space – for example, those living on a location planned to be occupied by a memorial need to be considered. This is of great importance if the memorial is planned to contain names or remains of the victims. Involving these groups can be beneficial in two ways: (1) the commissioning body can gain a better understanding of the context and (2) the participants become contributors to the design. Such collaboration enhances the appropriation of the memorial space by users once it is built. Consequently, the process can prove to be a long and contested affair. In fact, this is so in most cases. The considerable time it takes to complete a memorial is recognized as important, even necessary. It becomes a platform for survivors where they can address their loss which, at the same time, is recognized by others. Numerous examples confirm this argument, as memorials in Oslo and on Utøya in Norway demonstrate.

Once built, memorials are exposed to contestation as subjects that invite public intervention. In some cases, this is welcomed regardless of the form the public expression takes. In most cases, however, any kind of antagonistic reaction is likely to be counter-productive. For this reason, the initiation phase and design process are ideally transparent and all-embracing. If the requirements are not presented clearly and in elaborate detail, particularly for more complex projects, it is likely that the parties involved in the creation of the memorial will face obstacles that are difficult to overcome later in the process or with the end result, as the example of the Kazerne Dossin museum in Mechelen and *a posteriori* adjustment of space demonstrate.

Designers can have a crucial impact already in the first stage of the memorial creation by voicing their view and proposing solutions that were not envisioned by the commissioner. Even at the level of an open call for a memorial design (which means that the process of creating a memorial is close to its finish line), the designers can have impact. For example, the architects of 11-M rightly recognized that the official requirements neglected the need for a space for quiet reflection. Instead of producing a single monument to mark the place, they therefore introduced the underground space as well, and thus successfully changed the project specification. This inevitably raises questions about architectural craftsmanship and the designer's sensitivity towards the context, since these qualities can help overcome impediments and help to create meaningful structures. The ability of the architect to recognize essential aspects and then translate them into a built form is demonstrated in the flexibility of the memorial to integrate possible future modifications which, if needed, can improve its quality and reinforce its purpose for future generations.

For a memorial to be effective, and hence to fulfil its purpose, there needs to exist an understanding of both the physical and historical properties of the location and the expectations and requirements of its future users. Of course, this is not the case where the purpose of the memorial is to obliterate memory and the history of the place or to modify it by leaving out crucial information, giving precedence to emotions over facts – a recognizable strategy in what has been called 'Post-truth politics'. Hence, understanding the interpretive grid of the local community is essential for a designer. As we have seen from the examples of terrorism memorials, it is not the spectatorship but the participation that creates meaning. To a certain extent, all the examples discussed demonstrate that top-down approaches to creating memorials that do not involve directly related groups face obstacles, unbridgeable at times. Even the most ingenious design concepts need to be explained and communicated before they are geared into production. After all, it is the process of making memorials that demonstrates how much we have learned and moved away from the political systems that led to the tragedies that we are today trying to commemorate.

The financial framework defines the outcome of the architectural project. Paying for a building or site of memory (even if it means no further change in the future political endeavours of the investor) is a historical act that matters in the present and thus creates possibilities in futures we are not able to foresee. Consequently, the influence of the sponsor often overrules other parties involved, including the designer. To achieve a balanced dialogue and effective cooperation with higher chances of creating quality, a transparent process is needed, and particularly so when designing official memorials and monuments. This means independent research, creating space for professionalism and expertise. On the other hand, the financial aspect does not define the essence of the architectural creation. Regardless of the financial constraints and investments, if an architectural space achieves what it is intended to do, it succeeds. If an architectural space offers more, it empowers. It is the relationship of people and space that is fundamental in all architectural concepts (also if dedicated with a specific political agenda; valuable architectural projects can be indications of progress). Even after the context that formed them is gone, their material and symbolic power endures and is recognized and appropriated by later generations for different purposes, sometimes to generate new sets of meanings. An exemplary demonstration of this can be found in those Yugoslavian memorials that have since been rediscovered for both their symbolic importance and design qualities.

In situations where memorials are planned to continue an already existing work of memory, the issue of designing within a context remains equally relevant. In Mechelen, the architect decided not to relate to the barracks and to demolish the building which used to stand on the site, only to reintegrate segments of it into the new design. Such decisions are of immense significance and should not be entrusted solely to the designer but need to include experts to avoid the possibility that the design will be alienated from its context and thereby become generic. There is a justified danger that this could be the future for many contemporary memorials which fail to deal with the particularities of their context. A memorial disconnected from the place in which it is situated risks social unsustainability and thereby endangers the preservation of the history of the site.

This is particularly significant when the emotional strength of sentiment about a particular facet of history has subsided, but the conscious responsibility to preserve a site remains intact. This matter is further complicated by the question of tourism. Since the early twentieth century, tourism has changed our understanding of memorial spaces and particularly so with hugely famous examples that have stirred global interest and placed memorial projects in the spotlight. In the lucrative business of memory tourism, memorial institutions (and in particular memorial museums) see tourists as the main target group and their main public. This has a direct impact on memorial spaces, which must balance the infrastructure needed to accommodate large numbers of visitors and the legitimacy of its own existence. Except in Atocha and Drancy, where the architecture carries its purpose straightforwardly, all the other case studies examined in this book integrate tourism prominently and are purposely designed to become part of the world's memory network. In the competition for attractiveness, promises of authenticity and uniqueness are put forward in design concepts.

The label of uniqueness can be attached to the Ring of Memory too as the first memorial to include fallen soldiers of different nationalities alphabetically ordered in one place. The originality of this approach naturally makes the memorial more appealing, regardless of how visitors may feel personally about it. The fact that these memorials are frequently thought of as 'unique' does not necessarily highlight the strength of their architectural design, but it can affect their relevance in the work of memory if the quest to attract tourists overshadows the task of preserving memory. In this light, a memorial space is inevitably an emotional space, and it is therefore essential that architecture provides spaces for spontaneous expressions of grief – a need underlined by our knowledge of the psychological aspects of mourning. Whether tourists engage superficially or search for an authentic experience, planning a visit to a memorial constitutes a sort of pilgrimage with preparation and interaction being part of the overall experience.

Finally, we should not forget that for any memorial to be realized there needs to be an already existing political will and agency dedicated to giving form to this statement: violence happened, and we need to know about it. Memorials are spaces of learning that expose visitors to new experiences. For mourners, the reverse process takes place. In memorial spaces dedicated to subjects they know all too well, they may feel their loss differently through re-encountering their grief in a space that recognizes its presence in their lives. Names of the victims are not a unity reduced to numbers, but embodiments of individual absences we aim to preserve. Initially built to prolong human memory and to educate future generations, memorials provide spaces which have become a constituent part of the mourning process and serve as a counterpoint, a way to establish normality and decency in places and sites marked by atrocity. In this respect, designers have a lot to learn from participatory design techniques, social interactions and grassroot mourning practices in public space. How memorial spaces respond to the diversity of visitors in terms of their engagement and how this in return enters the historical narrative (and the personal narratives of survivors and families of victims) invite closer examination. Understanding how even an accidental visitor, for example, interacts with a memorial space can prove instructive for future memorial-making endeavours directed towards sustainable design. Hence, the mechanisms that render memorial spaces visible and enable them to touch visitors with different levels of commitment are questions which invite future research.

The effect a built memorial can have rests primarily on its anchorage in the specificity of a place and its context, as recognized and crafted by the architect in communication with all those who can make the process of creation and its outcome meaningful. The task they set before us is to explore the positive potentials of these forms to reassert solidarity and compassion over domination of a belief that atrocities are not built into human nature, but happen when we collectively let them happen. Bearing all of this in mind, in all of its complexity and transformative potential, the unique genre of public memorial architecture is first and foremost a collective process and therefore a demonstration of human progress. Memorials challenge us to think critically about war and violence. That is the first step towards lessening the lethal hold destruction has had on our lives and those of our contemporaries in our times. This first step may not realize its purpose, but without it, violence has the last word. And that we must resist.

Bibliography

Abend, Lisa and Geoff Pingree, 'Spain's path to 3/11 memorial', *The Christian Science Monitor*, 14 July 2004, available at www.csmonitor.com/2004/0714/p07s01-woeu.html/(page)/2).

Abousnnouga, Gill and David Machin (eds.), *The Language of War Monuments* (London and New York: Bloomsbury Publishing, 2013).

Adams, Paul, Steven Hoelscher and Karen Till (eds.), *Textures of Place: Rethinking Humanist Geographies* (Minneapolis, MN: University of Minnesota, 2001).

Adorno, Theodor, 'On commitment', in Ronald Taylor (ed. and trans.), *Aesthetics and Politics: The Key Texts of the Classic Debate within German Marxism* (London and New York: Verso books, 1977), pp. 177–95.

'Trying to understand *Endgame*', in Brian O'Connor (ed.), *The Adorno Reader* (Oxford: Blackwell Publishers, 2000), pp. 319–52.

Aldrich, Robert, *Vestiges of the Colonial Empire in France: Monuments, Museums and Colonial Memories* (New York: Palgrave Macmillan, 2004).

Alexander, Jeffrey C., 'On the social construction of moral universals. The "Holocaust" from war crime to trauma drama', *European Journal of Social Theory* 5 (2001), 5–85.

Ambasz, Emilio, 'Pro-Memoria Garden (1978)', available at http://emilioambaszandassociates.com/portfolio/Pro-Memoria-Garden.

Amir, Tula, 'Life saver: typology of commemoration in Israel-architecture and society', in *The Israeli Pavilion*, curator Tula Amir, the 10th International Exhibition of Architecture, Venice Biennial, September–November 2006, pp. 12–17.

Amsellem, Patrick, 'Remembering the past, constructing the future. The memorial to the deportation in Paris and experimental commemoration after the Second World War' (unpublished PhD thesis, New York University, 2007).

Andrés, Estefane, 'Materiality and politics in Chile's Museum of Memory and Human Rights', *Thresholds*, 41 (2013), 158–71.

Arendt, Hannah, *The Human Condition: A Study of the Central Dilemma Facing Modern Man*, 2nd edn (Chicago, IL: University of Chicago Press, 1998).

Ariès, Philippe, *Western Attitudes towards Death: From the Middle Ages to the Present*, trans. Patricia M. Ranum (Baltimore, MD: Johns Hopkins University Press, 1974).

Ashplant, T. G., Graham Dawson and Michael Roper, (eds.), *The Politics of War Memory and Commemoration*, Routledge Studies in Memory & Narrative (London and New York: Routledge, 2000).

Assmann, Aleida, *Der lange Schatten der Vergangenheit – Erinnerungskultur und Geschichtspolitik* (Munich: C. H. Beck Publishers, 2006).

Assmann, Jan, *Das Kulturelle Gedächtnis: Schrift, Erinnerung und politische Identität in frühen Hochkulturen* (Munich: Beck, 1992).

Astbury, Jon, 'As good as grief gets', *The Architectural Review*, 1436.240 (November 2016), 37–8.

Audoin-Rouzeau, Stéphane and Annette Becker, *14–18: Understanding the Great War* (New York: Farrar, Straus and Giroux, 2014).

Azara, Pedro, 'The house and the dead: on modern tombs', in Mónica Gili (ed.), *The Last House* (Barcelona: Editorial Gustavo Gili, 1999), pp. 24–39.

Bartov, Omer, *Murder in Our Midst: The Holocaust, Industrial Killing and Representation* (New York and Oxford: Oxford University Press, 1996).

Bašić, Nikola, 'A monument to Kornati firefighters', *Pogledaj.to*, 27 November 2010, http://pogledaj.to/drugestvari/nikola-basic-a-monument-to-kornati-firefighters.

Bauman, Zygmunt, *Mortality, Immortality and Other Life Strategies* (Stanford, CA: Stanford University Press, 1992).

Ben-Ze'ev, Efrat, Ruth Ginio and Jay Winter (eds.), *Shadows of War: A Social History of Silence in the Twentieth Century* (Cambridge: Cambridge University Press, 2010).

Bevan, Robert, *The Destruction of Memory: Architecture at War* (London: Reaktion Books, 2006).

Blair, Carole, V. William Balthrop and Neil Michel, 'The arguments of the tombs of the unknown: relationality and national legitimation', *Argumentation*, 25 (2011), 449–69.

Blažević, Dunja, 'New Monument', Sarajevo Center for Contemporary Art, available at http://scca.ba/scca-projects/deconstruction-of-monument/new-monument.

Blocker, Jane, *Seeing Witness: Visuality and the Ethics of Testimony* (Minneapolis, MN: University of Minnesota Press, 2009).

Blondeel, Brecht, 'Kazerne Dossin, Memoriaal, Museum en Documentatiecentrum over Holocaust en Mensenrechten: Historiek, analyse en maquette' (unpublished master's thesis, University of Ghent, 2009).

Boelen, Paul A. and Holly G. Prigerson, 'Commentary on the inclusion of persistent complex bereavement-related disorder in DSM-5', *Death Studies*, 36.9 (2012), 771–94.

Bohm-Duchen, Monica (ed.), *After Auschwitz: Responses to the Holocaust in Contemporary Art* (London: Royal Festival Hall, 1995).

Boime, Albert, *The Unveiling of the National Icons: A Plea for Patriotic Iconoclasm in a Nationalist Era* (Cambridge: Cambridge University Press, 1998).

Bollerey, Franziska, 'Modesty versus monumentality: the quieter way of speaking about Holocaust in Europe', *Ezelsoren: Bulletin of the Institute of History of Art, Architecture and Urbanism, IHAAU*, 1.2 (2008), pp. 25–43.

Borsi, Franco, *The Monumental Era: European Architecture and Design 1929–1939* (London: Lund Humphries, 1987).

Brands, Gunnar, 'From WWI cemeteries to the Nazi "fortresses of the dead"', in Joachim Wolschke-Bulmahn (ed.), *Places of Commemoration: Search for Identity and Landscape Design* (Washington, DC: Dumbarton Oaks Research Library and Collection, 2001), pp. 215–56.

Brett, Sebastian, Louis Bickford, Liz Ševčenko and Marcela Rios, *Memorialization and Democracy: State Policy and Civic Action* (New York: International Coalition of Sites of Conscience, 2007).

Broos, Inne, 'bOb van Reeth en de genius loci in Antwerpen' (unpublished master's thesis, Ghent University, 2001), available at http://lib.ugent.be/catalog/rug01:000789390.

Bryan-Wilson, Julia, 'Building a marker of nuclear warning', in Robert S. Nelson and Margaret Olin (eds.), *Monuments and Memory, Made and Unmade* (Chicago, IL: Chicago University Press, 2003), pp. 183–205.

Burke, Edmund, 'A philosophical enquiry into the origin of our ideas of the sublime and beautiful', in Paul Langford, T. O. McLoughlin and James T. Boulton (eds.), *The Writings and Speeches of Edmund Burke: Volume I: The Early Writings* (New York: Oxford University Press, 1997), pp. 185–321.

Burstow, Robert, 'The limits of modernist art as a "weapon of the Cold War": reassessing the unknown patron of the Monument to the Unknown Political Prisoner', *The Oxford Art Journal*, 20.1 (January 1997), 68–80.

Butler, Judith, *Frames of War: When Is Life Grievable?* (London: Verso, 2009).

Carden-Coyne, Ana, *Reconstructing the Body: Classicism, Modernism and the First World War* (New York: Oxford University Press, 2009).

Carman, John and Patricia Carman, *Bloody Meadows: Investigating Landscapes of Battle* (Stroud: Sutton Publishing Limited, 2006).

Carrier, Peter, *Holocaust Monuments and National Memory in France and Germany since 1989. The Origins and Political Function of the Vél'd'Hiv' in Paris and the Holocaust Monument in Berlin* (New York and Oxford: Berghahn Books, 2005).

Caruth, Cathy, *Unclaimed Experience: Trauma, Narrative and History* (Baltimore, MD: Johns Hopkins University Press, 1996).

(ed.), *Trauma: Exploration of Memory* (Baltimore, MD: Johns Hopkins University Press, 1995).

Casey, Edward, *Remembering: A Phenomenological Study* (Bloomington, IN: Indiana University Press, 1987).

Chauty, Nicolas, 'L'anneau de la mémoire se dévoile, unique au monde', *La Voix du Nord*, 10 October 2014, p. 5.

Choay, Françoise, *The Invention of the Historic Monument* (Cambridge: Cambridge University Press, 2001).

Cohen, Jean-Louis, *Architecture in Uniform. Designing and Building for the Second World War*, Canadian Centre for Architecture (New Haven, CT and London: Yale University Press, 2011).

Colvin, Howard, *Architecture and the Afterlife* (New Haven, CT and London: Yale University Press, 1991).

Confino, Alon, 'From Psychohistory to Memory Studies: or how some Germans became Jews and some Jews became Nazis', in Roger Frie (ed.), *History Flows through Us. Germany, the Holocaust, and the Importance of Empathy* (London and New York: Routledge, 2018), pp. 17–30.

Connerton, Paul, 'Seven types of forgetting', in Paul Connnerton, *The Spirit of Mourning: History, Memory and the Body* (Cambridge: Cambridge University Press, 2011), pp. 33–50.

Connolly, Kate, 'Closed books and stilled lives', *The Guardian*, 26 October 2000, www.theguardian.com/world/2000/oct/26/kateconnolly.

Constant, Caroline, *The Woodland Cemetery: Towards a Spiritual Landscape, Erik Gunnar Asplund and Sigurd Lewerentz, 1915–1961* (Stockholm: Byggförlaget, 1994).

Cooke, Philip, *The Legacy of the Italian Revolution* (London: Palgrave Macmillan, 2011).

Cooper, Robert, 'World War One: poppy legacy in Burneside firm James Cropper's Hands', BBC News, 11 November 2014, avaliable at www.bbc.com/news/uk-england-cumbria-29749204.

Craps, Stef, 'Beyond Eurocentrism: trauma theory in the global age', in Gert Buelens, Sam Durrant and Robert Eaglestone (eds.), *The Future of Trauma Theory: Contemporary Literary and Cultural Criticism* (London: Routledge, 2014), pp. 45–62.

Creighton, Thomas H., *The Architecture of Monuments. The Franklin Delano Roosevelt Memorial Competition* (New York: Reinhold Publishing Corporation, 1962).

Curtis, William J. R., 'Abstraction and representation: the memorial complex at Kampor on the island of Rab (1952–3) by Edvard Ravnikar', in Aleš Vodopivec and Rok Žnidaršić (eds.), *Edvard Ravnikar: Architect and Teacher* (Wien: Springer, 2010), pp. 33–50.

Čusto, Amra, 'Bosnia-Herzegovina and the cultural memory of Bleiburg', *Croatian Political Science Review*, 55:2 (2018), 111–30.

Dal Co, Francesco and Giuseppe Mazzariol (eds.), *Carlo Scarpa: The Complete Works*, trans. Richard Sadler (New York: Rizzoli; Milan: Electa Editrice, 1985).

Dannatt, Adrian, *United States Holocaust Memorial Museum: James Ingo Freed* (London: Phaidon Press, 1995).

Danto, Arthur C., *The State of the Art* (New York: Prentice Hall Press, 1987).

Das, Veena, 'Language and body: transactions in the construction of pain', in Nancy Scheper-Hughes and Philippe I. Bourgois (eds.), *Violence in War and Peace: An Anthology* (Oxford: Blackwell Publishing, 2004), pp. 327–33.

De Certeau, Michel, *The Practice of Everyday Life* (Berkeley, CA: University of California Press, 2011).

De Coulanges, Numa Denis Fustel, *The Ancient City: A Study of the Religion, Laws, and Institutions of Greece and Rome* (New York: Dover Publications, 2006). Originally published in 1874.

De Keijser, Jos, 'Gecompliceerde rouw. Diagnostiek en behandeling', *Tijdschrift voor Psychotherapie*, 30 (2004), 60–9.

De Schaepdrijver, Sophie, *De Groote Oorlog* (Amsterdam: Atlas, 1999).

Den Boer, Pim, 'Loci memoriae-Lieux de mémoire', in Astrid Erll, Ansgar Nünning and Sara B. Young (eds.), *A Companion to Cultural Memory Studies* (Berlin and New York: De Gruyter, 2010), pp. 19–25.

Derrida, Jacques, *Archive Fever: A Freudian Impression*, trans. Eric Prenowitz (Chicago, IL: University of Chicago Press, 1995).

Di Carlo, Tina, 'Aldo Rossi: cemetery of San Cataldo, Modena, Italy', in Matilda McQuaid (ed.) *Envisioning Architecture: Drawings from the Museum of Modern Art* (New York: Museum of Modern Art, 2002), pp. 160–1.

'Bernard Tschumi. The Manhattan Transcripts Project, episode 1: The Park, New York City, New York', in Matilda McQuaid (ed.), *Envisioning Architecture: Drawings from the Museum of Modern Art* (New York: Museum of Modern Art, 2002), p. 204.

Diener, Roger, 'Shoah Memorial Drancy', in Roger Diener and Joseph Abram, *Diener & Diener*, trans. Sarah Robertson (London: Phaidon Press, 2011), pp. 262–4.

Diner, Dan, *Beyond the Conceivable: Studies on Germany, Nazism, and the Holocaust* (Berkeley, CA: University of California Press, 2000).

Dolff-Bonekämper, Gabi, 'The Berlin Wall: an archaeological site in progress', in John Schofield, William Gray Johnson and Colleen M. Beck (eds.), *Matériel Culture: The Archaeology of Twentieth-Century Conflict* (London: Routledge, 2002), pp. 236–48.

Domansky, Elisabeth, '"Kristallnacht", the Holocaust and German unity: the meaning of November 9 as an anniversary in Germany', *History & Memory*, 4.1 (1992), 60–94.

Doss, Erika, *Memorial Mania: Public Feeling in America* (Chicago, IL: University of Chicago Press, 2010).

Dunlap, David, 'From 88 searchlights, an ethereal tribute', *The New York Times*, 4 March 2002, www.nytimes.com/2002/03/04/nyregion/from-88-searchlights-an-ethereal-tribute.html?src=pm&pagewanted=1.

Dyer, Geoff, *The Missing of the Somme* (London: Phoenix Press, 2001).

Eggener, Keith, *Cemeteries* (New York: W.W. Norton & Company, 2010).

Ellsworth, Elizabeth, *Places of Learning: Media, Architecture, Pedagogy* (New York: Routledge Taylor & Francis Group, 2005).

Etlin, Richard A., *Symbolic Space: French Enlightenment Architecture and Its Legacy* (Chicago, IL and London: University of Chicago Press, 1994).

'In the face of death: calming the mind, mining the soul', in Claudia Denk, John Ziesemer and International Council on Monuments and Sites (eds.), *Der bürgerliche Tod: städtische Bestattungskultur von der Aufklärung bis zum frühen 20. Jahrhundert = Urban Burial Culture from the Enlightenment to the Early 20th Century; Internationale Fachtagung des Deutschen Nationalkomitees von ICOMOS in Zusammenarbeit mit dem Bayerischen Nationalmuseum, München, 11–13 November 2005*, ICOMOS: Journals of the German National Committee no. 44 (Regensburg: Schnell & Steiner, 2007), pp. 35–45.

'Architecture and the sublime', in Timothy M. Costelloe (ed.), *The Sublime: From Antiquity to the Present* (Cambridge: Cambridge University Press, 2012), pp. 230–74.

Faloci, Pierre-Louis, 'The architect's point of view', Struthof: Site of the former Natzweiler concentration camp, available at www.struthof.fr/en/the-european-centre/the-creation-of-the-cerd/the-architects-point-of-view.

Farrel, Stephen, 'In "ceremonial transfer," remains of 9/11 victims are moved to memorial', *The New York Times*, 10 May 2014, www.nytimes.com/2014/05/11/nyregion/remains-of-9-11-victims-are-transferred-to-trade-center-site.html.

Felicori, Mauro and Annalisa Zanotti (eds.), *Cemeteries of Europe: A Historical Heritage to Appreciate and Restore* (Bologna: Comune di Bologna (SCENE Project), 2004).

Fer, Briony, *On Abstract Art* (London and New Haven, CT: Yale University Press, 1997).

Feversham, Polly and Leo Schmidt, *Die Berliner Mauer heute: Denkmalwert und Umgang/The Berlin Wall Today: Cultural Significance and Conservation Issues* (Berlin: Verlag für Bauwesen HUSS-MEDIEN GmbH, 1999).

Firger, Jessica and Hannah Fraser-Chanpong, 'Visit to 9/11 museum may be cathartic for some; traumatic for others', *CBS News*, 15 May 2014, www.cbsnews.com/news/visit-to-911-museum-may-be-cathartic-for-some-too-traumatic-for-others.

Fominaya, Christina Flesher, 'The Madrid 2004 bombing: understanding the puzzle of 11-M's flawed commemorative process', in Anna Lisa Tota and Trever Hagen (eds.), *Routledge International Handbook of Memory Studies* (London: Routledge, 2015), pp. 414–27.

Forster, Kurt W., 'Monument/memory and the mortality of architecture', in K. Michael Hays (ed.), *Oppositions Reader: Selected Readings from a Journal for Ideas and Criticism in Architecture, 1973–1984* (New York: Princeton Architectural Press, 1998), pp. 18–35.

Forty, Adrian and Susan Kuchler (eds.), *The Art of Forgetting* (Oxford: Berg, 2001).

Foss, Sonja K., 'Ambiguity as persuasion: the Vietnam Veterans Memorial', *Communication Quarterly*, 34.3 (1986), 326–40.

Foucault, Michel, *Language, Counter-Memory, Practice: Selected Essays and Interviews* (Ithaca, NY: Cornell University Press, 1977).

'Of other spaces: utopias and heterotopias', trans. Jay Miskowiec, *Diacritics* 16.1 (1986), 22–7. Originally published as 'Des espaces autres', *Architecture-Mouvement-Continué*, 5 (1984), 46–9.

Frearson, Amy, 'Sam Jacob erects Adolf Loos-designed mausoleum in Highgate Cemetery', *Dezeen*, 14 September 2016, www.dezeen.com/2016/09/14/sam-jacob-adolf-loos-mausoleum-tomb-highgate-cemetery-london-architecture-foundation.

Freud, Sigmund, 'Mourning and Melancholia', in *The Standard Edition of the Complete Psychological Works of Sigmund Freud*, ed. and trans. James Strachey, vol. 14 (1914–1916) (London: The Hogarth Press, 1957), pp. 243–58.

'Screen memories' (1899), in Gali S. Reed and Howard B. Levine (eds.), *On Freud's 'Screen Memories'* (London: Karnac Books, 2015), pp. 1–25.

Friedländer, Saul, *Nazi Germany and the Jews: The Years of Persecution, 1933–1939* (Frome and London: Butler & Tanner, Ltd., 1998).

Frihammar, Mattias and Helaine Silverman, 'Heritage of death: emotion, memory and practice', in Mattias Frihammar and Helaine Silverman (eds.), *Heritage of Death: Landscapes of Emotion, Memory and Practice* (London and New York: Routledge, 2017), pp. 3–20.

Frostig, Karen, 'Activism and citizenship: performing memory and acts of memorialization in Austria', in Corey Dzenko and Theresa Avrila (eds.), *Contemporary Citizenship, Art, and Visual Culture: Making and Being Made* (New York and London: Routledge, 2018), pp. 145–57.

Galmozzi, Luciano, *Monumenti alla libertà. Antifascismo, resistenza e pace nei monumenti italiani dal 1945 al 1985* (Milan: La Pietra, 1986).

Garofalo, Francesco and Luca Veresane, *Adalberto Libera* (New York: Princeton Architectural Press, 2002).

Garton Ash, Timothy, 'Our new Guernica', *The Guardian*, 10 March 2005, available at www.guardian.co.uk/world/2005/mar/10/spain.comment.

Geschiedenis is meer dan herinneren (*History Is More Than Remembering*), authored by 151 Belgian historians and published in *De Standaard Online* on 25 January 2006, availablc at www.familickundc-brussel.bc/pdf/misc/geschiedenis_is_meer_dan_herinneren.pdf.

Geurst, Jeroen, *Cemeteries of the Great War by Sir Edwin Lutyens* (Rotterdam: 010 Publishers, 2010).

Gili, Mónica (ed.), *The Last House* (Barcelona: Editorial Gustavo Gili, 1999).

Gillis, John R., 'Introduction: memory and identity: the history of a relationship', in John R. Gillis (ed.), *Commemorations: The Politics of National Identity* (Princeton, NJ: Princeton University Press, 1994), pp. 3–27.

Godfrey, Mark, *Abstraction and the Holocaust* (New Haven, CT and London: Yale University Press, 2007).

Goebel, Stefan, *The Great War and Medieval Memory: War, Remembrance and Medievalism in Britain and Germany, 1914–1940* (Cambridge: Cambridge University Press, 2007).

Gold, Tanya, 'Smile for the Auschwitz selfie: why Holocaust memorials have failed', *New Statesman*, 13 March 2017, www.newstatesman.com/culture/2017/03/smile-auschwitz-selfie-why-holocaust-memorials-have-failed.

Goldsmith, Jill, 'Memory in the making', *The New York Times*, 8 September 2011, www.nytimes.com/2011/09/11/arts/design/slowly-building-a-memorial-of-the-shoah-in-milan.html?_r=1&ref=design.

Gravagnuolo, Benedetto, *Adolf Loos: Theory and Works*, Idea Books Architectural Series, US edn (New York: Rizzoli, 1982).

Griswold, Charles L. and Stephen S. Griswold, 'The Vietnam Veterans Memorial and the Washington Mall: philosophical thoughts on political iconography', *Critical Inquiry* 12.4 (Summer 1986), 688–719.

Grossman, Elizabeth G., 'Architecture for a public client: the monuments and chapels of the American Battle Monuments Commission', *Journal of the Society of Architectural Historians*, 42.3 (May 1984), 119–44.

Hagopian, Patrick, 'The commemorative landscape of the Vietnam War', in Joachim Wolschke-Bulmahn (ed.), *Places of Commemoration: Search for Identity and Landscape Design* (Washington, DC: Dumbarton Oaks Research Library and Collection, 2001), pp. 311–76.

Harrison, Robert Pogue, *The Dominion of the Dead* (Chicago, IL: University of Chicago Press, 2003).

Hartman, Hattie, 'Madrid memorial', *Architects Journal* (10 January 2008), pp. 40–2.

Hays, K. Michael, *Sanctuaries: The Last Works of John Hejduk* (New York: Whitney Museum of American Art, 2003).

Hein, George E., *Learning in the Museum* (London: Routledge, 2002).

Herf, Jeffrey, 'How and why did Holocaust memory come to the United States? A response to Peter Novick's challenge', in Jeffry Diefendorf and Theodore Zev Weiss (eds.), *Lessons and Legacies VI: New Currents in Holocaust Research* (Evanston, IL: Northwestern University Press, 2004), pp. 457–74.

Herscher, Andrew, 'In ruins: architecture, memory, countermemory', *Journal of the Society of Architectural Historians*, 73.4 (2014), 464–9.

Hertz, Robert, *Death and the Right Hand*, trans. Rodney and Claudia Needham (Aberdeen: Cohen & West, 1960). Originally published in French as 'Contribution à une étude sur la représentation collective de la mort', *L'Année sociologique (1896/1897–1924/1925) 10e Année* (1905–6), 48–137, and as 'La prééminence de la main droite: Étude sur la polarité religieuse', *Revue Philosophique de la France Et de l'Etranger*, 68 (1909), 553–80.

Hilderbrand, Grant, *Origins of Architectural Pleasure* (Berkeley, CA: University of California Press, 1999).

Hinz, Berthold, *Art in the Third Reich* (New York: Pantheon Books, 1979).

Hirsch, Marianne, *The Generation of Postmemory: Writing and Visual Culture after the Holocaust* (New York: Columbia University Press, 2012).

Hoffmann-Curtius, Kathrin, 'Memorials for the Dachau concentration camp', *Oxford Art Journal*, 21.2 (1998), 21–44.

Hoheisel, Horst and Andreas Knitz, 'Kunst der Erinnerung, Erinnerung der Kunst. Zermahlene Geschichte. Kunst als Umweg' (2015).

Homans, Peter, *Symbolic Loss: The Ambiguity of Mourning and Memory at Century's End* (Charlottesville, VA: University of Virginia Press, 2000).

Hornstein, Shelley, 'Invisible topographies: looking for the mémorial de la déportation in Paris', in Shelley Hornstein and Florence Jacobowitz (eds.), *Image and Remembrance: Representation and the Holocaust* (Bloomington, IN: Indiana University Press, 2003), pp. 305–24.

Losing Site: Architecture, Memory and Place, Ashgate Studies in Architecture (Farnham and Burlington, VT: Ashgate, 2011).

Horvatinčić, Sanja, 'Povijest Nemogućeg Spomenika: Podizanje spomenika žrtvama fašizma u Jajincima', *Anali Galerije Antuna Augustinčića*, nos 32–33/34–34, special issue: 'Simpozij problem spomenika: spomenik danas: zbornik radova' (2012–15), 261–82.

Horvatinčić, Sanja and Beti Žerovc (eds.), *Memorial Production in Socialist Yugoslavia 1945–1990* (Berlin: Archive Books, 2019).

Hoskins, Andrew, 'Memory of the multitude: the end of collective memory', in Andrew Hoskins (ed.), *Digital Memory Studies: Media Pasts in Transition* (London and New York: Routledge, 2017), pp. 85–109.

'The restless past: an introduction to digital memory and media', in Andrew Hoskins (ed.), *Digital Memory Studies: Media Pasts in Transition* (London and New York: Routledge, 2017), pp. 1–24.

Hutton, Patrick H., 'The art of memory reconceived: from rhetoric to psychoanalysis', *Journal of the History of Ideas*, 48.3 (1987), 371–92.

Huyssen, Andreas, *Twilight Memories: Marking Time in a Culture of Amnesia* (New York and London: Routledge, 1995).

'Monumental seduction', in Mieke Bal, Jonathan Crewe and Leo Spitzer (eds.), *Act of Memory: Cultural Recall in the Present* (Hanover, NH: Dartmouth College & University Press of New England, 1999), pp. 191 208.

Present Past: Urban Palimpsest and the Politics of Memory (Stanford, CA: Stanford University Press, 2003).

Irwin, Rachel and Velma Šarić, *Call for War Memorials Divides Bosnia – Little Consensus on Whether Monuments Commemorating Wartime Help or Hinder Reconciliation Process*, International Criminal Tribunal for the former Yugoslavia, TRI Issue 673, 6 December 2010, available at http://iwpr.net/report-news/calls-war-memorials-divide-bosnia.

Jackson, Kenneth T. and Camilo José Vergara, *Silent Cities: The Evolution of the American Cemetery* (New York: Princeton Architectural Press, 1989).

Jacobi, Fritz, Mordechai Omer and Jule Reuter (eds.), *Dani Karavan Retrospective* (Tubingen and Berlin: Ernst Wasmuth Verlag, 2008).

Jalland, Pat, *Death in War and Peace: A History of Loss & Grief in England, 1914–1970* (New York: Oxford University Press, 2010).

Jansen-Verbeke, Myriam and Wanda George, 'Memoryscapes of the Great War (1914–1918): a paradigm shift in tourism research on war heritage', *Via Tourism Review: International Journal, Multilingual and Interdisciplinary*, 2.8 (2015), available at http://viatourismreview.com/2015/11/varia-art4.

Janson, Alban and Florian Tiggers (eds.), *Fundamental Concepts of Architecture. The Vocabulary of Spatial Situations* (Basel: Birkhäuser, 2014).

Janson, Horst W., *The Rise and Fall of the Public Monument* (New Orleans, LA: The Graduate School, Tulane University, 1976).

Janssens, Ugo, *Historische Gids voor België: Een boeiende kennismaking met ons verleden* (Antwerp: Standaard, 2002).

Joffroy, Pascale, 'Le mémorial de la Shoah à Drancy, un bâtiment qui regarde', *D'Architectures*, 214 (2012), 86–91.

Johnson, Christopher D., *Memory, Metaphor, and Aby Warburg's Atlas of Images, Signale: Modern German Letters, Cultures, and Thought* (Ithaca, NY: Cornell University Press and Cornell University Library, 2012).

Jones, Jonathan, 'War memorials have failed – we have forgotten the chaos of fascism', *The Guardian*, 9 December 2016, www.theguardian.com/artanddesign/jonathanjonesblog/2016/dec/09/war-memorials-have-failed-peter-eisenman-holocaust.

Jones, Peter Blundell, *Gunnar Asplund* (London: Phaidon Press, 2006).

Judt, Tony, *Postwar: A History of Europe since 1945* (New York: Penguin Press, 2005).

Kamin, Blair, 'A first look at the national September 11 memorial: a tough work of abstract minimalism, softened by waterfalls and oak trees, seeks to meld remembrance and regeneration', *Chicago Tribune*, 14 August 2011, http://featuresblogs.chicagotribune.com/theskyline/2011/08/a-first-look-at-the-soon-to-open-national-september-11-memorial-a-tough-work-of-abstract-minimalism-.html

Kansteiner, Wulf, 'Genealogy of a category mistake: a critical intellectual history of the cultural trauma metaphor', *Rethinking History*, 8 (2004), 193–221.

In Pursuit of German Memory: History, Television, and Politics after Auschwitz (Athens, OH: Ohio University Press, 2006).

'The Holocaust in the 21st century. Digital anxiety, transnational cosmopolitanism, and never again genocide without memory', in Andrew Hoskins (ed.), *Digital Memory Studies: Media Pasts in Transition* (London and New York: Routledge, 2017), pp. 110–40.

Kevane, Bridget, 'A wall of indifference: Italy's Shoah memorial', *The Jewish Daily Forward*, 29 June 2011, http://forward.com/articles/139293/a-wall-of-indifference-italy-s-shoah-memorial.

Klein, Kerwin L., *From History to Theory* (Berkeley, CA: University of California Press, 2011).

Kollwitz, Hans (ed.), *The Diary and Letters of Kaethe Kollwitz*, trans. Richard and Clara Winston (Evanston, IL: Northwestern University Press, 1955).

Körner, Theodor, 'Friedrichs Totenlandschaft', in Kurt Eberlein (ed.), *Caspar David Friedrich: Bekenntnisse* (Bremen: Europäischer Hochschulverlag GmbH&Co KG, 2010), pp. 260–1.

Koselleck, Reinhart, 'War memorials: identity formations of the survivors', in *The Practice of Conceptual History: Timing, History, Spacing Concepts*, trans. Todd Samuel Presner and others (Stanford, CA: Stanford University Press, 2002), pp. 285–326.

Sediments of Time: On Possible Histories, trans. Sean Franzel and Stefan-Ludwig Hoffmann (Stanford, CA: Stanford University Press, 2018).

(ed.), *Zur politischen Ikonographie des gewaltsamen Todes. Ein deutsch-französischer Vergleich* (Basel: Schwabe, 1998).

Krauss, Rosalind, 'Notes on the index: seventies art in America', *October*, 3 (1977), 68–81.

'Structure in the expanded field', *October*, 8 (1979), 30–44.

Krier, Leon (ed.), *Albert Speer, Architecture 1932–1942* (Brussels: Archives d'architecture moderne, 1985).

Kurto, Nedžad, 'Memory of the dying city', in Azra Junuzović, *Sarajevo Roses: Towards Politics of Remembering* (Sarajevo: Armis Print, 2006), pp. 147–50.

LaCapra, Dominick, *Writing History, Writing Trauma* (Baltimore, MD: Johns Hopkins University Press, 2001).

Lacayo, Richard, 'Remains of the day: at the 9/11 museum, history is preserved in memories and debris', *Time*, 26 May 2014, 38–41.

Lagrou, Pieter, *The Legacy of Nazi Occupation. Patriotic Memory and National Recovery in Western Europe, 1945–1965* (Cambridge: Cambridge University Press, 2000).

Landsberg, Alison, *Prosthetic Memory: The Transformation of American Remembrance in the Age of Mass Culture* (New York: Columbia University Press, 2004).

Landsman, Mark, 'Property and the banality of memory', *Cabinet*, 10: Property (2003), 94–7.

Langford, Paul, T. O. McLoughlin and James T. Boulton (eds.), *The Writings and Speeches of Edmund Burke: Volume I: The Early Writings* (New York: Oxford University Press, 1997).

Laugier, Marc-Antoine, *Essai sur l'architecture* (Paris: Chez Duchesne, 1753).

Lefebvre, Henry, *The Production of Space* (Oxford: Blackwell Publishing, 1991).

Lepik, Andreas, 'Red Location Museum of Struggle', in Andreas Lepik (ed.), *Small Scale, Big Scale: New Architectures of Social Engagement* (New York: Museum of Modern Art, 2010), pp. 53–62.

Lésnikowski, Wojciech, *East European Modernism: Architecture in Czechoslovakia, Hungary, and Poland between the Wars 1919–1939*, 1st edn (London: Thames & Hudson Ltd, 1996).

Levine, Emily J., *Dreamland of Humanists* (Chicago, IL and London: University of Chicago Press, 2013).

Libeskind, Daniel, *Jewish Museum, Berlin* (Amsterdam: G + B Arts International, 1999).

'Trauma', in Shelley Hornstein and Florence Jacobowitz (eds.), *Image and Remembrance: Representation and the Holocaust* (Bloomington, IN: Indiana University Press, 2003), pp. 43–58.

Linenthal, Edward T., *Preserving Memory: The Struggle to Create America's Holocaust Museum* (New York: Penguin Group, 1997).

Lipstadt, Deborah E., *The American Press & the Coming of the Holocaust 1933–1945: Beyond Belief* (New York: The Free Press, 1986).

Lipstadt, Hélène, 'Learning from Lutyens: Thiepval in the age of the anti-monument', *Harvard Design Magazine* (1999), 65–70.

Loos, Adolf, 'Architecture' (1910), in *On Architecture*, selected and introduced by Adolf and Daniel Opel, trans. Michael Mitchell (Riverside, CA: Ariadne Press, 2002), pp. 73–85.

Lowenthal, David, *The Past Is the Foreign Country* (Cambridge: Cambridge University Press, 1985).

Lubell, Sam, 'Inside the fury: an interview with James Young', *Architectural Record*, 192.2 (2004), 24.

Lyotard, Jean-François, *Heidegger and 'the jews'*, trans. Andreas Michel and Mark S. Roberts (Minneapolis, MN: University of Minnesota Press, 1990).

Macdonald, Sharon, *Memorylands: Heritage and Identity in Europe Today* (London: Routledge, 2013).

(ed.), *A Companion to Museum Studies* (Oxford: Blackwell Publishing, 2011).

McLeod Bedford, Steven, *John Russell Pope: Architect of Empire*, 1st edn (New York: Rizzoli, 1998).

McNally, Richard J., *Remembering Trauma* (Cambridge, MA and London: The Belknap Press of Harvard University Press, 2003).

Maddrell, Avril, 'Mapping grief. a conceptual framework for understanding the spatial dimensions of bereavement, mourning and remembrance', *Journal of Social & Cultural Geography*, 17.2, 166–88.

Maier, Charles S., *The Unmasterable Past: History, Holocaust, and German National Identity* (Cambridge, MA: Harvard University Press, 1998).

Marcuse, Harold, *Legacies of Dachau: The Uses and Abuses of a Concentration Camp, 1933–2001* (Cambridge: Cambridge University Press, 2001).

'Holocaust memorials: the emergence of a genre', *American Historical Review*, 115.1 (February 2010), 53–89.

Marschall, Sabine, *Landscape of Memory: Commemorative Monuments, Memorials and Public Statuary in Post-Apartheid South Africa* (Leiden: Brill, 2010).

Marter, Joan, 'Postwar sculpture re/viewed' and 'The ascendancy of abstraction for public art: the Monument to the Unknown Political Prisoner competition', *Art Journal*, 53.4, special issue: 'Sculpture in postwar Europe and America, 1945–59' (1994), 20–2 and 28–36.

Melchior, Inge and Oane Visser, 'Voicing past and present uncertainties: the relocation of a Soviet World War II memorial and the politics of memory in Estonia', *Focaal-Journal of Global and Historical Anthropology*, 59 (2011), 33–50.

Meng, Michael, *Shattered Spaces: Encountering Jewish Ruins in Postwar Germany and Poland* (Cambridge, MA: Harvard University Press, 2011).

Michalski, Sergiusz, *Public Monuments: Art in Political Bondage 1870–1997* (London: Reaction Books Ltd, 1998).

Milton, Sybil, 'Perilous landscapes: concentration camp memorials between commemoration and amnesia', in Joachim Wolschke-Bulmahn (ed.), *Places of Commemoration: Search for Identity and Landscape Design* (Washington, DC: Dumbarton Oaks Research Library and Collection, 2001), pp. 257–68.

Miquel, Mathieu, 'March 11, 2004. The Madrid 3/11 bombings: was it really an attack by "Islamic Terrorists"?', *Global Research* (28 November 2009) available at www.globalresearch.ca.

Moneo, Rafael, 'Aldo Rossi: the idea of architecture and the Modena cemetery', trans. Angela Giral, in K. Michael Hays (ed.), *Oppositions Reader: Selected Readings from a Journal for Ideas and Criticism in Architecture, 1973–1984* (New York: Princeton Architectural Press, 1998), pp. 105–34.

Moore, Rowan, 'Ground Zero 9/11 memorial flows with mournful splendour', *The Guardian*, 15 August 2001, www.theguardian.com/artanddesign/2011/aug/15/ground-zero-memorial-september-9-11.

'Notre Dame de Lorette international memorial review: a different perspective', *The Guardian*, 2 November 2014, available at www.theguardian.com/artanddesign/2014/nov/02/notre-dame-de-lorette-international-memorial-review.

Moriarty, Catherine, '"Remnants of patriotism": the commemorative representation of the greatcoat after the first world war', *Oxford Art Journal*, 27.3 (2004), 291–309.

Mosse, George L., *Germans and Jews: The Right, the Left, and the Search for a "Third Force" in Pre-Nazi Germany* (New York: Howard Fertig, 1970).

Fallen Soldiers: Reshaping the Memory of the World Wars (New York and Oxford: Oxford University Press, 1990).

Mucci, Massimo, *La Risiera di San Sabba. Un'architettura per la memoria*, 6th edn (Gorizia: Libreria Editirice Goriziana, 2012).

Mumford, Lewis, *The Culture of Cities* (New York: Harcourt, Brace, and Company, 1938).

'Museum 21st October', *Architecture and Urbanism*, 33–34 (1965), 39.

Musil, Robert, 'Monuments' (1927), in *Posthumous Papers of a Living Author*, trans. Peter Wortsman (Hygiene, CO: Eridanos Press, 1987), pp. 64–8.

Neidhardt, Juraj, 'Monument of Marx and Engels on Marindvor', in Dušan Grabrijan and Juraj Neidhardt (eds.), *Arhitektura Bosne i put u Savremeno (Architecture of Bosnia and the Way to Modernity)*, trans. M. P. Moll and B. Vrčon (Ljubljana: Državna Založba Slovenije (Ciril Vidmar) under favor of the Government of the PR of Bosnia and Herzegovina and of the PR of Slovenia, 1957), p. 429.

'Spomenici (Monuments)', in Dušan Grabrijan and Juraj Neidhardt (eds.), *Arhitektura Bosne i put u Savremeno (Architecture of Bosnia and the Way to Modernity)*, trans. M. P. Moll and B. Vrčon (Ljubljana: Državna Založba Slovenije (Ciril Vidmar) under favor of the Government of the PR of Bosnia and Herzegovina and of the PR of Slovenia, 1957), pp. 430–41.

Nietzsche, Friedrich, 'Book three. Principles of a new evaluation. IV. the will to power as art', in Walter Kaufmann (ed.), *Friedrich Nietzsche: The Will to Power*, trans. Walter Kaufmann and R. J. Hollingdale (New York: Vintage Books, 1968), pp. 419–57.

Nora, Pierre, 'Between memory and history: les lieux de mémoire', *Representations*, 26 (1989), 7–24.

Norberg-Schultz, Christian, *Genius Loci: Towards a Phenomenology of Architecture* (New York: Rizzoli, 1991).

Novick, Peter, *The Holocaust in American Life* (Boston, MA and New York: A Mariner Book, Houghton Mifflin Company, 2000).

Olick, Jeffrey K., 'Collective memory', in *International Encyclopedia of the Social Sciences*, 2nd edn (Detroit, MI: MacMillan Reference USA, 2007), pp. 7–8.

The Politics of Regret: On Collective Memory and Historical Responsibility (New York and London: Routledge, 2007).

Pallasmaa, Juhani, 'The space of time', *Oz: Journal of the College of Architecture, Planning & Design, Kansas State University*, 20 (1998), 54–7.

Encounters, vol. 1: Architectural Essays, ed. Peter MacKeith (Helsinki: Rakkenustieto, 2012).

Paulsson, Gregor, Henry Russell Hitchcock, William Holford, Sigfried Giedion, Walter Gropius, Lucio Costa and Alfred Roth, 'In search of a new monumentality: a symposium', *The Architectural Review*, 104.621 (September 1948), 117–30.

Pérez-Gómez, Alberto, 'The architecture of Richard Henriquez: a praxis of personal memory', in Howard Shubert (ed.), *Richard Henriquez, Memory Theatre* (Montreal: Canadian Centre for Architecture, 1993), pp. 9–29.

Peterson, Anna, 'The production of a memorial place: materialising expressions of grief', in Avril Maddrell and James D. Sidaway (eds.), *Deathscapes: Spaces for*

Death, Dying, Mourning and Remembrance (Farnham: Ashgate Publishing, 2010), pp. 141–61.

Polgar, Michael, *Holocaust and Human Rights Education. Good Choices and Sociological Perspectives* (Bingley: Emerald Publishing Limited, 2018).

Potteiger, Matthew and Jamie Purinton, *Landscape Narratives: Design Practices for Telling Stories* (New York: John Wiley & Sons, 1998).

Potts, Alex, 'Louise Bourgeois: sculptural confrontations', *Oxford Art Journal*, 22.2 (1999), 37–53.

Prost, Philippe, 'Mémorial international de Notre-Dame-de-Lorette. Construction d'un mémorial aux soldats tombés dans le Nord-Pas de Calais au cours de la Première guerre mondiale' (September 2014).

Ragon, Michel, *The Space of Death: A Study of Funerary Architecture, Decoration, and Urbanism*, trans. Alan Sheridan (Charlottesville, VA: University of Virginia Press, 1983).

Rampley, Matthew, 'From symbol to allegory: Aby Warburg's theory of art', *The Art Bulletin*, 79.1 (1997), 41–55.

Rando, Therese A., *Treatment of Complicated Mourning* (Champaign, IL: Research Press, 1993).

Rectanus, Mark W., 'Globalization: incorporating the museum', in Sharon Macdonald (ed.), *A Companion to Museum Studies* (Oxford: Blackwell Publishing, 2011), pp. 802–37.

Reinares, Fernando, 'The Madrid bombings and global jihadism', International Institute for Counter-Terrorism, 17 April 2010, available at www.ict.org.il. Originally published in *Survival*, 52.2 (2010), 83–104.

Renshaw, Layla, 'The archeology and material culture of modern military death', in Sarah Tarlow and Liv Nilsson Stutz (eds.), *The Oxford Handbook of the Archeology of Death and Burial* (Oxford: Oxford University Press, 2013), pp. 763–80.

Riegl, Aloïs, 'The modern cult of monuments: its character and its origin', *Oppositions*, 25 (1982), 21–56.

Ritter, Katharina, Ekaterina Shapiro-Obermair, Dietmar Steiner and Alexandra Wachter (eds.), *Soviet Modernism 1955–1991: Unknown History* (Vienna: Park Books/Architekturzentrum Wien, 2012).

Rosenau, Helen (ed.), *Boullée & Visionary Architecture*, trans. Sheila de Vallée (London: Academy Editions; New York: Harmony Books, 1974).

Rosenfeld, Gavriel D., *Munich and Memory: Architecture, Monuments, and the Legacy of the Third Reich* (Berkeley, CA: University of California Press, 2000).

Building after Auschwitz: Jewish Architecture and the Memory of the Holocaust (New Haven, CT and London: Yale University Press, 2011).

Rossi, Aldo, 'L'azzurro del cielo', *Controspazio*, 10 (1972), 4–9.

'Cemetery of San Cataldo, Modena, 1971', in K. Michael Hays (ed.), *Architecture Theory Since 1969* (Cambridge, MA: MIT Press, 2000), pp. 68–72.

Rossi, Paolo, *Clavis Universalis: Arti Mnemoniche e logica combinatorial da Lullo a Leibniz* (Milan: Ricciardi, 1960).

Roth, Michael, *Memory, Trauma, and History: Essays on Living with the Past* (New York: Columbia University Press, 2011).

Rothberg, Michael, *Multidirectional Memory: Remembering the Holocaust in the Age of Decolonization* (Paolo Alto, CA: Stanford University Press, 2009).

Rothstein, Edward, 'Museum review: bearing witness beyond witnesses', *The New York Times*, 24 March 2011, www.nytimes.com/2011/03/24/arts/design/holocaust-museum-in-los-angeles-makes-hard-choices-review.html.

Rousso, Henry, *The Vichy Syndrome: History and Memory in France since 1944* (Cambridge, MA: Harvard University Press, 1991).

Rowland, Ingrid D. and Thomas Noble Howe (eds.), *Vitruvius: 'Ten Books on Architecture'* (Cambridge: Cambridge University Press, 2017).

Rowlands, Michael, 'Remembering to forget: sublimation as sacrifice in war memorials', in Adrian Forty and Susan Kuchler (eds.), *The Art of Forgetting* (Oxford: Berg, 2001), pp. 129–45.

Rukschcio, Burkhardt and Roland Schachel (eds.), *Adolf Loos: Leben und Werk* (Salzburg and Vienna: Residenz Verlag, 1982).

Saerens, Lieven, 'Van vergeten naar genegeerd: Dossin en Joodse herinnering', *Belgisch Tijdschrift voor Nieuwste Geschiedenis*, 42.2 (2012), 138–69.

Safdie, Moshe, *Yad Vashem: Moshe Safdie – the Architecture of Memory* (Baden: Lars Müller, 2006).

Samuel, Flora, *Le Corbusier and the Architectural Promenade* (Basel: Birkhäuser, 2010).

Samuel, Raphael, *Theatres of Memory, vol. 1: Past and Present in Contemporary Culture* (London: Verso, 1994).

Sánchez-Carretero, Cristina, Antonio Cea, Paloma Díaz-Mas, Pilar Martínez and Carmen Ortiz, 'On blurred borders and interdisciplinary research teams: the case of the "Archive of Mourning"', *Forum: Qualitative Social Research Sozialforschung*, 12.3 (2011), available at www.qualitative-research.net.

Sanchez-Carretero, Christina and Carmen Ortiz, 'Grassroots memorials as sites of heritage creation', in Helmut Anheier and Yudhishthir Raj Isar (eds.), *The Culture and Globalization Series [4]: Heritage, Memory & Identity* (London: Sage, 2011), pp. 106–13.

Santino, Jack, 'Not an unimportant failure: rituals of death and politics in Northern Ireland', in Michael McCaughan (ed.), *Displayed in Mortal Light* (Antrim: Antrim Arts Council, 1992), n.p.

Sassoon, Siegfried, 'On passing the new Menin Gate', in Tim Kendall (ed.), *The Oxford Handbook of British and Irish War Poetry* (New York: Oxford University Press, 2007), p. 551.

Sayare, Scott, 'At Holocaust Center, Hollande confronts past', *The New York Times*, 22 September 2012, www.nytimes.com/2012/09/22/world/europe/at-drancy-holocaust-center-hollande-confronts-grim-chapter-for-france.html.

Scheper-Hughes, Nancy and Margaret M. Lock, 'The mindful body: a prolegomenon to future work in medical anthropology', *Medical Anthropology Quarterly*, 1.1 (1987), 6–41.

Schneede, Uwe M., 'The avant-garde and the war: the visual arts between 1914 and 1918', in 1914/18 Retrospektiven, Paradoxien, Perspektiven 2014/18, Goethe-Institut, November 2013, available at www.goethe.de/ges/prj/nzv/par/en12354686.htm.

Schneider, Bernhard, *Daniel Libeskind, Jewish Museum Berlin: Between the Lines* (Munich and New York: Prestel, 1999).

Schram, Laurence, 'The transit camp for Jews in Mechelen: the antechamber of death', *Online Encyclopedia of Mass Violence*, 6 February 2008, www.massviolence.org.

Schumacher, Thomas L., *The Danteum: Architecture, Poetics, and Politics under Italian Fascism* (London: Triangle Architectural Publishing, 1993).

Schwartzenberg, Susan, 'Re-creating the past: notes on the neurology of memory', in Marc Treib (ed.), *Spatial Recall: Memory in Architecture and Landscape* (New York and London: Routledge, 2009), pp. 42–60.

Senie, Harriet F., 'Mourning in protest: spontaneous memorials and the sacralization of public space', *Harvard Design Magazine*, 9: Constructions of Memory (1999), 23–7.

Shanken, Andrew, 'Planning memory: living memorials in the United States during World War II', *The Art Bulletin*, 84.1 (2002), 130–47.

'The memory industry and its discontents: the death and life of a keyword', in Marc Treib (ed.), *Spatial Recall: Memory in Architecture and Landscape* (New York and London: Routledge, 2009), pp. 218–39.

'Towards a cultural geography of modern memorials', in Jill A. Franklin, T. A. Heslop and Christine Stevenson (eds.), *Architecture and Interpretation: Essays for Eric Fernie* (Rochester, NY: Boydell & Brewer, 2012), pp. 357–80.

Shapira, Harel, 'Reflecting absence: an interview with Michael Arad', *Public Books*, 20 August 2013, www.publicbooks.org/reflecting-absence-an-interviewwith-michael-arad/.

Shelby, Karen, *Flemish Nationalism and the Great War: The Politics of Memory, Visual Culture and Commemoration* (Basingstoke and New York: Palgrave Macmillan, 2014).

Sherman, Daniel J., *The Construction of Memory in Interwar France* (Chicago, IL and London: University of Chicago Press, 1999).

Skelton, Tim and Gerald Gliddon, *Lutyens and the Great War* (London: Frances Lincoln, 2008).

Smets, Bas, 'BBS292 Brussels: Memorial 22/3' (unpublished text, 2016).

Smith, William and Hiroshi Kaneko, 'Memorial in the Sky', available at http://matterbetter.com/media/competitioners/files/f9e000eb-7e0d-49ca-8838-7a7c5bbcbbe6.pdf.

Snyder, Timothy, *Bloodlands: Europe between Hitler and Stalin* (New York: Basic Books, 2011).

Sodaro, Amy, *Exhibiting Atrocity: Memorial Museums and the Politics of Past Violence* (New Brunswick, NJ: Rutgers University Press, 2018).

Solomon, Deborah, 'Art/architecture; from the rubble, ideas for rebirth', *The New York Times*, 30 September 2001, www.nytimes.com/2001/09/30/arts/art-architecture-from-the-rubble-ideas-for-rebirth.html.

Sommer, Richard M., 'Time incorporated: the romantic life of the modern monument', *Harvard Design Magazine*, 9: Constructions of Memory (1999), 38–44.

Sorkin, Michael, *Starting from Zero: Reconstructing Downtown New York* (London: Routledge, 2003).

Speer, Albert, *Inside the Third Reich: Memoirs by Albert Speer* (New York: Simon & Schuster, 1970).

Stern, Michael A., 'The national cemetery system: politics, place, and contemporary cemetery', in Joachim Wolschke-Bulmahn (ed.), *Places of Commemoration: Search for Identity and Landscape Design* (Washington, DC: Dumbarton Oaks Research Library and Collection, 2001), pp. 107–30.

Stevens, Quentin, 'Waarom het Holocaustmonument in Berlijn zo'n geliefd speelterrein is' ('Why the Holocaust memorial is such a popular playground'), *Oase*, 77: Into the Open (2008), 71–9.

'Nothing more than feelings: abstract memorials', *Architectural Theory Review*, 14. 2 (2009), 156–72.

Stevens, Quentin and Karen A. Franck, *Memorials as Spaces of Engagement: Design, Use and Meaning* (New York: Routledge, 2016).

Stevenson, Angus (ed.), *Oxford Dictionary of English*, 3rd edn (Oxford: Oxford University Press, 2010).

Stroobants, Eric, 'De Klok tikt voor Kazerne Dossin', *Gazet van Antwerpen*, 8 June 2012, www.gva.be/regio-mechelen/mechelen/de-klok-tikt-voor-kazerne-dossin.aspx.

Sturken, Marita, 'Monuments: historical overview', in Michael Kelly (ed.), *Encyclopedia of Aesthetics*, vol. 3 (New York: Oxford University Press, 1998), pp. 272–8.

Sultan, Terrie, 'Redefining the terms of engagement: the art of Louise Bourgeois', in Charlotta Kotik, Terrie Sultan and Christian Leigh (eds.), *Louise Bourgeois: The Locus of Memory, Works 1982–1993* (New York: Harry N. Abrams, 1994), pp. 28 50.

Tanner, Laura E., *Lost Bodies: Inhabiting the Borders of Life and Death* (Ithaca, NY: Cornell University Press, 2006).

Terdiman, Richard, *Present Past: Modernity and Memory Crisis* (Ithaca, NY: Cornell University Press, 1933).

Thompson, Henrietta, 'Fitting tribute: Blakstad Haffner Architects unveil latest piece in Utøya's rebuilding', *Wallpaper*, 22 August 2016, www.wallpaper.com/architecture/blakstad-haffner-architects-remembers-utoya-massacre-with-new-memorial-and-learning-centre-hegnhuset.

Tilley, Charles, *A Phenomenology of Landscape: Places, Paths and Monuments* (London: Berg, 1993).

Tollebeek, Jo et al. (eds.), *België, een parcours van herinnering: II. Plaatsen van tweedracht, crisis en nostalgie* (Amsterdam: Bert Bakker, 2008).

Tournikiotis, Panayotic, *Adolf Loos* (New York: Princeton Architectural Press, 2002).

Treib, Marc, 'The landscape of loved ones', in Joachim Wolschke-Bulmahn (ed.), *Places of Commemoration: Search for Identity and Landscape Design* (Washington, DC: Dumbarton Oaks Research Library and Collection, 2001), pp. 81–105.

Uchowicz, Katarzyna, 'Reading Muranów: memory of a place / memory of an architect. Commentary on the post-war work of Bohdan Lachert', *RIHA Journal*, 0108, special issue (31 December 2014), available at www.riha-journal.org/articles/2014/2014-oct-dec/special-issue-contemporary-art-and-memory-part-1/uchowicz-muranow-en.

Usher, Shaun (ed.), *More Letters of Note: Correspondence Deserving of a Wider Audience* (London: Canongate Books Ltd., 2015).

Van Alstein, Maarten, *The Great War Remembered: Commemoration and Peace in Flanders Fields* (Brussels: Flemish Peace Institute, 2011).

From Ypres to Brussels? Europe, Peace, and the Commemoration of WWI (Brussels: Flemish Peace Institute, 2014), available at http://eu.boell.org/sites/default/files/uploads/2014/06/from_ypres_to_brussels.pdf.

Van der Kolk, Bessel, *The Body Keeps the Score: Brain, Mind, and Body in the Healing of Trauma* (New York: Viking Penguin Group, 2014).

Van der Laarse, Rob, 'Beyond Auschwitz? Europe's terrorscapes in the age of postmemory', in Marc Silberman and Florence Vatan (eds.), *Memory and Postwar Memorials: Confronting the Violence of the Past* (New York: Palgrave Macmillan, 2013), pp. 71–92.

Van Gennep, Arnold, *The Rites of Passage*, trans. Monika B. Vizedom and Gabrielle L. Caffe (London: Routledge, 2004). Originally published in 1909.

Van Hensbergen, Gijs, *Guernica: The Biography of a Twentieth-Century Icon* (New York and London: Bloomsbury, 2005).

Van Reeth, Bob, 'Bouwen aan een eervolle plaats van herinnering', *de Nieuwe Maan*, May 2012, pp. 14–15, www.mechelen.be.

'Ik heb schaamte in stenen willen bouwen', Campuskrant (magazine of University of Leuven), 2 (2012), 8.

Versluys, Kristiaan, *Out of the Blue: September 11 and the Novel* (New York: Columbia University Press, 2009).

Vidler, Anthony, *The Architectural Uncanny: Essays in the Modern Unhomely* (Cambridge, MA: MIT Press, 1992).

Virilio, Paul, *Art and Fear*, trans. Julie Rose (London: Continuum, 2003).

Von Buttlar, Adrian, *Leo van Klenze: Leben, Werk, Vision* (Munich: C. H. Beck, 1999).

Vuković, Vladimir, 'Writing about cities: literary works of Bogdan Bogdanović about cities and urbanism', *SAJ*, 3.1 (2011), 1–14.

Vulliamy, Ed, *The War Is Dead, Long Live the War: Bosnia: The Reckoning* (London: The Bodley Head, 2012).

Wachtel, Nathan, 'Memory and history: introduction', *History and Anthropology* 12 (1986), 207–24.

Wainwright, Oliver, '"We had to tell this dark story"... how Utøya is remembering the massacre', *The Guardian*, 5 October 2016, www.theguardian.com/artanddesign/2016/oct/05/utoya-massacre-memorial-norway-architects.

Watkins, Nicholas, 'Mirror, mirror on the wall: ambiguous place attachment and the Vietnam Veterans Memorial', in Janice M. Bissell (ed.), *Proceedings of the Thirty-Eighth Annual Conference of the Environmental Design Research Association* (Oklahoma City, OK: EDRA 38-2007: Building Sustainable Communities, 2007), pp. 46–50.

Watkins, Nicholas, Frances Cole and Sue Weidemann, 'The war memorial as healing environment: the psychological effect of the Vietnam Veterans Memorial on Vietnam War combat veterans' posttraumatic stress disorder symptoms', *Environment and Behavior*, 42.3 (2010), 351–75.

Weill, Nicolas, 'Drancy, mémoires à vif', *Le Monde*, 13 September 2012, available at www.lemonde.fr/culture/article/2012/09/13/drancy-memoires-a-vif_1759966_3246.html.

Whittington, Karl, 'Caspar David Friedrich's medieval burials', *Nineteenth-Century Art Worldwide*, 11.1 (2012), available at www.19thc-artworldwide.org/index.php/spring12/whittington-on-caspar-david-friedrichs-medieval-burials.

Wiedmer, Caroline, *The Claims of Memory: Representations of the Holocaust in Contemporary Germany and France* (Ithaca, NY and London: Cornell University Press, 1999).

Wieviorka, Annette, *The Era of the Witness*, trans. from the French by Jared Stark (Ithaca, NY: Cornell University Press, 2011).

Williams, Paul, *Memorial Museums: The Global Rush to Commemorate Atrocities* (Oxford and New York: Berg, 2007).

Willey, David, 'Italy memorial to fascist hero Graziani sparks row', BBC News, 15 August, 2012, www.bbc.co.uk/news/world-europe-19267099.

Wilson, Colin St. John, *Architectural Reflections: Studies in Philosophy and Practice of Architecture* (Oxford: Butterworth-Heinemann, 1992).

Winkler, Klaus-Jürgen and Herman van Bergeijk, *Das Märzgefallenen-Denkmal* (Weimar: Bauhaus-Universität Weimar, 2004).

Winnicott, D. W., 'Transitional objects and transitional phenomena' (1951), in D. W. Winnicott, *Playing and Reality* (London and New York: Routledge, 2005), pp. 1–35.

Winstone, Martin, *The Holocaust Sites of Europe: An Historical Guide* (London and New York: I.B. Tauris, 2010).

Winter, Jay, *Sites of Memory, Sites of Mourning: The Great War in European Cultural History* (Cambridge: Cambridge University Press, 1995).

'Remembrance and redemption: a social interpretation of war monuments', *Harvard Design Magazine*, 9, special issue: 'Constructions of Memory' (1999), 71–7.

Remembering War: The Great War between Memory and History in the Twentieth Century (New Haven, CT and London: Yale University Press, 2006).

'Sites of memory and the shadow of war', in Astrid Erll, Ansgar Nünning and Sara B. Young (eds.), *Cultural Memory Studies: An International and Interdisciplinary Handbook* (Berlin and New York: De Gruyter, 2008), pp. 61–73.

'Thinking about silence', in Efrat Ben-Ze'ev, Ruth Ginio and Jay Winter (eds.), *Shadows of War: A Social History of Silence in the Twentieth Century* (Cambridge: Cambridge University Press, 2010), pp. 1–30.

War beyond Words: Languages of Remembrance from the Great War to the Present (Cambridge: Cambridge University Press, 2017).

Wodiczko, Krzysztof, *Critical Vehicles: Writings, Projects, Interviews* (Cambridge, MA: MIT Press, 1999).

Wolschke-Bulmahn, Joachim, 'The landscape design of the Bergen-Belsen concentration camp memorial', in Joachim Wolschke-Bulmahn (ed.), *Places of Commemoration: Search for Identity and Landscape Design* (Washington, DC: Dumbarton Oaks Research Library and Collection, 2001), pp. 269–300.

Woods, Lebbeus, *Einstein Tomb*, Pamphlet Architecture 6 (New York: Princeton Architectural Press, 1980).

War and Architecture, Pamphlet Architecture 15 (New York: Princeton Architectural Press, 1993).

Yacobi, Haim, (ed.), *Constructing the Sense of Place: Architecture and Zionist Discourse* (Aldershot: Ashgate Publishing, 2004).

Yates, Frances A., *The Art of Memory* (London: Routledge & Kegan Paul, 1992). Originally published in 1966.

Yehuda, Rachel et al., 'Holocaust exposure induced intergenerational effects on FKBP5 methylation', *Biological Psychiatry: A Journal of Psychiatric Neuroscience and Therapeutics* 80.5 (1 September 2016), 372–80.

Yilmaz, Ahenk, 'Memorialization on war-broken ground: Gallipoli war cemeteries and memorials designed by Sir John James Burnet', *Journal of the Society of Architectural Historians*, 73.3 (September 2014), 328–46.

Young, James E., *The Texture of Memory: Holocaust Memorials and Meaning* (New Haven, CT: Yale University Press, 1993).

At Memory's Edge: After-Images of the Holocaust in Contemporary Art and Architecture (New Haven, CT and London: Yale University Press, 2000).

'Memory/Monument', in Robert S. Nelson and Richard Shiff (eds.), *Critical Terms for Art History*, 2nd edn (Chicago, IL and London: University of Chicago Press, 2003), pp. 234–47.

'Memory, counter-memory, and the end of the monument', in Shelley Hornstein and Florence Jacobowitz (eds.), *Image and Remembrance: Representation and the Holocaust* (Bloomington, IN: Indiana University Press, 2003), pp. 59–78.

'The stages of memory at Ground Zero', in Oren Baruch Stier and J. Shawn Landres (eds.), *Religion, Violence, Memory, and Place* (Bloomington, IN: Indiana University Press, 2006), pp. 214–35.

'Utøya and Norway's July 22 memorial process: the memory of political terror', in James E. Young, *The Stages of Memory: Reflections on Memorial Art, Loss, and the Spaces Between* (Amherst, MA: Boston University of Massachusetts Press, 2016), pp. 185–210.

Zabalbeascoa, Anatxu, *Igualada Cemetery: Enric Miralles and Carme Pinos (Architecture in Detail)* (London: Phaidon Press, 1996).

Zachwatowicz, Jerzy, 'The international memorial at Auschwitz', *Poland* (January 1965), 11–13.

Zeiger, Mimi, 'John Hejduk's The House of the Suicide structures get new life in Prague', *Architects Newspaper*, 19 January 2016, https://archpaper.com/2016/01/hejduks-house-suicide-structures-get-new-life-prague.

Index

Lightning Source UK Ltd.
Milton Keynes UK
UKHW030749290922
409643UK00006B/685

9 781108 707824